Adobe Animate 2022 for Creative Professionals

Second Edition

Implement professional techniques and create vivid animated and interactive content with Animate

Joseph Labrecque

BIRMINGHAM—MUMBAI

Adobe Animate 2022 for Creative Professionals
Second Edition

Copyright © 2022 Packt Publishing

Group Product Manager: Rohit Rajkumar
Publishing Product Manager: Ashitosh Gupta
Senior Editor: Keagan Carneiro
Content Development Editor: Aamir Ahmed
Technical Editor: Shubham Sharma
Copy Editor: Safis Editing
Project Coordinator: Rashika BA
Proofreader: Safis Editing
Indexer: Pratik Shirodkar
Production Designer: Nilesh Mohite

First published: February 2021
Second edition: January 2022
Production reference: 1011221

Published by Packt Publishing Ltd.
Livery Place
35 Livery Street
Birmingham
B3 2PB, UK.

ISBN 978-1-80323-279-9

www.packt.com

*This book is dedicated to everyone who has helped me along the way.
I don't express my thanks enough and hope you all know in some way how
grateful I am.*

– Joseph Labrecque

Contributors

About the author

Joseph Labrecque is a creative developer, designer, and educator with nearly two decades of experience creating expressive web, desktop, and mobile solutions. He joined the **University of Colorado Boulder** College of Media, Communication, and Information as an instructor of technology for the Department of Advertising, Public Relations, and Media Design in Autumn 2019. His teaching focuses on creative software, digital workflows, user interaction, and design principles and concepts. Before joining the faculty at CU Boulder, he was associated with the University of Denver as adjunct faculty and as a senior interactive software engineer, user interface developer, and digital media designer.

Labrecque has authored a number of books and video course publications on design and development technologies, tools, and concepts through publishers including Packt, LinkedIn Learning (Lynda.com), and Adobe. He has spoken at large design and technology conferences such as Adobe MAX and for a variety of smaller creative communities. He is also the founder of Fractured Vision Media, LLC, a digital media production studio and distribution vehicle for a variety of creative works.

Joseph is an Adobe Education Leader, Adobe Community Professional, and member of Adobe Partners by Design. He holds a bachelor's degree in communication from Worcester State University, and a master's degree in digital media studies from the University of Denver.

I want to thank my wife, Leslie… and our daughters, Paige and Lily. Also, Poe. Good kitty.

About the reviewers

Matthijs Clasener was schooled as a multimedia designer. He now is a well-experienced educator at the Grafisch Lyceum Rotterdam, in the Netherlands.

He teaches media and design and is highly interested in animation. He takes the lead in the animation curriculum at his vocational career school, and Adobe Animate is of course one of the topics under 2D animation.

His lessons are characterized by interaction with students, gamification, and attempts at humor.

Matthijs is an Adobe Education Leader and is well known for his contributions to educational (online) events.

Johnathan Kuehl spotted a rare opportunity to use Animate (known as Flash at the time) to combine his graphic design, web, and animation skills all into one — which inspired him to start BlooVooDoo Studio back in the early 2000s.

Since then, Johnathan has developed creative solutions to unique problems for a variety of clients in all different types of industries. He has created engaging illustrated, animated, and interactive material for television, video games, advertisements, e-learning, apps, and more.

Johnathan is amazed every day at Animate's capability to bring a wide range of diverse content to life, and he looks forward to where the software will go in the future!

Table of Contents

Preface

Section 1 – Getting up to Speed

1

A Brief Introduction to Adobe Animate

Technical Requirements	4
Understanding Adobe Animate	4
A Bit of History	4
Familiar uses of Adobe Animate	8

Exploring the New Features of Animate	9
Modern Rigging with Warped Objects	9
Layer Parenting Enhancements	13
Last Frame Options for Graphic Symbol Looping	13
Paint Fills Only Option when Drawing	15

Fill on Active Layer with the Paint Bucket Tool	16
Color Effect Tweening for HTML5 Canvas Documents	17
Asset Panel Updates	18

Keeping Up to Date with Animate Releases	19
Adobe Creative Cloud Desktop	19
Adobe MAX	21

Summary	22

2

Exploring Platform-Specific Considerations

Technical Requirements	24
Exploring Animate Document Types	24
Flash Platform Runtimes	25
Branching Out to the Native Web	26
Open to Custom Platforms	27

Understanding ActionScript 3.0 Documents	28
Adobe Flash Player	29
The SWF File Format	30
The ActionScript Programming Language	31

Understanding HTML5 Canvas Documents   32

HTML and JavaScript   33
The Canvas Element   34
The CreateJS Libraries   35

Exploring the Adobe Integrated Runtime   36

Adobe AIR   36
Adobe AIR and ActionScript 3.0   37

Adobe AIR and HARMAN   37
AIR for Desktop   38
AIR for iOS   39
AIR for Android   40

Experimenting with Animate Beta Platforms   41

WebGL glTF – Standard and Extended   42
VR Panorama and VR 360   42

Summary   43

3

Settling into the User Interface

Technical Requirements   46
Exploring the Animate interface   46

Important User Interface Elements   46
Choosing Your Start Settings   53
Changing Your Start Settings   54

Managing Workspaces and Panels   56

Using the Default Workspaces   57
Customizing the Workspaces   57
Saving a Custom Workspace   60
Managing Workspaces   60

Customizing the Tools and Timeline Panels   62

Customizing the Tools Panel   62
Exploring the Timeline Tools   64
Customizing the Timeline Tools   65

Managing Animate Preferences 66

Customizing Preferences   66
Keyboard Shortcuts   68
Managing Your Preferences   70

Summary   72

4

Publishing and Exporting Creative Content

Technical Requirements   74
Publishing versus Exporting   74

Publishing your Projects   76
Exporting your Content   78

Differences between Document Types when Publishing   79

Publishing ActionScript 3.0 Documents   79

Publishing HTML5 Canvas Documents   81
Publishing AIR Document Types   86
Publishing Beta Document Types   88

Options for Exporting your Content   89

Exporting Video Files   89
Exporting Animated GIFs   91

Exporting Image File Sequences   94
Export Options from the Library Panel   95

Sharing Content as Animate
Asset Packages   96

Social Share and Quick Publish 101
Social Share   102
Quick Publish   102

Summary   103

Section 2 – Animating with Diverse Techniques

5

Creating and Manipulating Media Content

Technical Requirements   108
Working with Shapes   108
Understanding the Shape Tools   108

Creating a Shape for Animation 111
Animating with Shape Tweens   113
Exploring Shape Tween Properties   116
Manipulating Shape Properties
across Tweens   118

Working with Symbols   123
Creating Symbols   123
Exploring Symbol Types   129

Animating with Classic Tweens   135
Using Classic Motion Guides   139
Exploring Classic Tween Properties   141

Summary   143

6

Interactive Motion Graphics for the Web

Technical Requirements   146
Designing a Document for the
Native Web   146
Creating a New Document for Digital
Advertising   146
Importing External Content   149
Creating Text Objects   155

Animating with Motion Tweens 158
Building Symbols for use in Motion
Tweens   159

Including Additional Library Items   165
Adjusting the Timeline   166
Animating with Motion Guides   168
Exploring Motion Tween Properties   170

Adding Interactivity with
JavaScript   173
Writing Code with the Actions Panel   173

Summary   176

7

Character Design through Layer Parenting

Technical Requirements	178	Animating using Layer Parenting	191
Working with Advanced Layers Mode	178	Exploring Additional Character Animation Features	194
Assessing Layer Mode Benefits and Gotchas	178	Making use of Graphic Symbols	194
Switching Between Layer Modes	181	Importing Audio for Stream Sync	196
		Configuring our Graphic Symbol Frames	198
Animating a Character with Layer Parenting	182	Assigning Visemes and Automating Lip Syncing	200
Preparing Assets for Layer Parenting	183	Summary	205
Establishing a Layer Hierarchy	188		

8

Animating Poses with IK Armatures

Technical Requirements	208	Animating an IK Armature	225
Building an Armature using Inverse Kinematics	208	Creating Additional Poses	225
		Managing Armature Poses	230
Understanding Inverse Kinematics vs. Forward Kinematics	208	Sharing a Completed IK Rig	232
Using the Bone Tool to Rig Symbol Instances	211	Saving a Rig for Reuse	232
Refining the Rig Properties	215	Importing a Rig within the Assets Panel	235
Using Bone Tool to Rig Shapes	222	Summary	238

9

Manipulating Warped Objects through Advanced Rigging

Technical Requirements	240	Animating Warped Object Meshes	250
Warped Objects and the Asset Warp Tool	240	Animating Warped Objects using Armatures	253
Creating Distortion Meshes using Pins	244	Creating Armatures using Warped Objects	255

Animating with Modern Rigging Techniques 263

Summary 268

10

Working with the Camera and Layer Depth

Technical Requirements 270
Understanding the Camera 270
Examining the Starter Project 271
Activating and Manipulating the Camera 273

Understanding and Manipulating Layer Depth 276
Activating the Layer Depth Panel 276
Modifying Layer Depth 279

Animating the Camera 284
Setting Camera Keyframes 284
Adding Motion and Easing to the Camera 289

Applying Layer Effects and Filters 293
Adding Effects to the Camera 294
Adding Filters to a Layer 295

Summary 296

Section 3 – Exploring Additional Platforms

11

Developing Web-Based Games

Technical Requirements 300
Understanding the Game Concept 300
Starter Document Overview 300
Exploring the Timeline and Stage 302
Exploring the Project Library 306

Preparing the Game Timeline, Stage, and Library 307
Labeling the Timeline 308
Creating Dynamic Text and Clickable Overlays 310

Adding Linkage IDs within the Library 318

Programming the Game with JavaScript 320
Creating Global Variables 321
Programming the Start Screen 322
Programming Player Actions 325
Programming Enemy Behavior 327
Programming the Game Loop 329
Programming the End Screen 332

Finishing the Game Project 333
Summary 335

12

Producing Virtual Reality Content for WebGL

Technical Requirements	338
Overview of Virtual Reality Documents	338
Managing Scenes for Virtual Reality	340
Capturing Photographs for Virtual Reality	342
Adding Textures to Virtual Reality Scenes	346
Adding Additional Content	349
Importing Transparent 3D Renders	349

Animating with the Asset Warp Tool	351
Animating the Spectre Warped Object	354
Writing Code for Virtual Reality Interactions	356
Moving from Scene to Scene	357
Interacting with Animated Objects	361
Refining Perspective within the VR View Panel	363
Summary	366

13

Building Apps for Desktop and Mobile

Technical Requirements	368
Working with the Adobe Integrated Runtime	368
Installing an AIR SDK in Animate	368
Configuring an AIR for Desktop Project	373
Testing Your AIR Project	377
Building a User Interface	380
Working with Button Symbols	381

Using Components within an AIR Project	384
Exploring Advanced Movie Clip Symbol Settings	387
Programming an AIR Application	390
Establishing a Document Class	390
Writing ActionScript Code	393
Converting an AIR Application for Mobile Devices	400
Summary	401

14

Extending Adobe Animate

Technical Requirements	404

Creating Custom In-App Tutorials	404

Writing JSFL Scripts   411   Understanding the Animate
                                                                    Custom Platform SDK   420

                                                                    Summary   428

Index

Other Books You May Enjoy

Preface

Adobe Animate is a platform-agnostic asset creation, motion design, animation, and interactivity software packed full of time-tested tools and workflows. Using this software, you can target multiple platforms to produce motion design content, character animations, interactive displays, games, desktop and mobile applications, and anything else you might think of. Perhaps the greatest strength of Animate is in the diversity of its toolset, along with the unique workflows that allow developers to use it for design and for designers to use it for development. Animate is a true creative powerhouse for hybrid creative work unlike any other.

Given Animate's previous incarnation as Flash Professional, a fair amount of what the software can produce is web-based, but the past few years have really opened things up in order to target all manner of diverse platforms. We can target the native web through the HTML canvas element or via WebGL, generate rich animated content for broadcast via television and film, develop games and applications for Apple iOS, Google Android, Microsoft Windows, and Apple macOS, and even generate content for virtual reality. By the end of this book, you'll be able to produce a variety of media assets, motion design materials, animated artifacts, and interactive content pieces—all while targeting a wide set of compelling platforms.

This book will not teach you everything there is to know about Animate—as no book could possibly do that. It isn't an introductory book either as there are many such works available elsewhere. The intent of this book is to help you gain mastery of Animate through the diversity of its various workflows and platforms built upon a solid foundation of its history alongside present capabilities. I hope you enjoy the contents of these pages and take the concepts within to further the creative legacy of this wonderful software!

Who this book is for

This book is perfect for web, graphic, and motion design professionals with elementary experience in animation who want to take their existing skills to the next level. Building upon an initial understanding of fundamental animation concepts will help you to get the most out of this book and produce results that extend beyond the basic expectations.

What this book covers

Chapter 1, A Brief Introduction to Adobe Animate, provides background and context around the history and capabilities of the software. We'll also take a deep dive into all the new features available in Animate 2022.

Chapter 2, Exploring Platform-Specific Considerations, covers the various target platforms that are natively supported by Animate by exploring the underlying aspects of each platform and when to use one over another, and we'll even see how to convert between document types.

Chapter 3, Settling into the User Interface, explores the Animate interface in depth, alongside tips and tricks to get the most out of working with the software. You'll discover how to customize the entire workspace to your liking to achieve a more customized workflow.

Chapter 4, Publishing and Exporting Creative Content, explores ways of getting your content outside of Animate in a form that can be consumed by users or reused in additional ways within other software and systems.

Chapter 5, Creating and Manipulating Media Content, covers the fundamentals of Animate workflows, including both the creation of content with various vector shape tools and the use of different tweening mechanisms within the software. In addition to shape data, we also examine the use of symbols and instances within Animate and see how to apply motion to both simple shape and symbol instances, along with the application of easing presets.

Chapter 6, Interactive Motion Graphics for the Web, explores traditional motion graphics workflows for the web through the creation of an animated advertisement using both imported bitmap graphics and vector content native to Animate.

Chapter 7, Character Design through Layer Parenting, explores the Advanced Layers mode and the ability to rig character animations across layers using layer parenting mechanisms. We'll also see how to create automated lip-sync animations through the power of Adobe Sensei!

Chapter 8, Animating Poses with IK Armatures, explores a more refined and controlled way of rigging an armature through the use of the Bone tool and IK armatures with full joint constraints and the management of poses across the timeline. We'll also see how to share completed rigs and related assets through the use of Animate Asset files and the new Assets panel.

Chapter 9, Manipulating Warped Objects through Advanced Rigging, expands on rigging concepts explored in the previous two chapters with the introduction of the Asset Warp tool, mesh deformations, and rigging with a variety of bone types through the use of warped objects.

Chapter 10, Working with the Camera and Layer Depth, dives into the camera as a means to animate an entire scene that is otherwise fairly static and even taps into layer depth manipulation and the use of layer effects and filters.

Chapter 11, Developing Web-Based Games, explores the construction of a playable web-based game targeting HTML5 Canvas using CreateJS JavaScript libraries as we build out the logic for our entire game bit by bit across the timeline and through the use of global scripts.

Chapter 12, Producing Virtual Reality Content for WebGL, explores the virtual reality and WebGL glTF document types within Animate through the assembly of fully interactive virtual reality environments using scenes, textures, and additional imported assets.

Chapter 13, Building Apps for Desktop and Mobile, focuses on the AIR document type, through which we will build a small utility application for browsing photographs using ActionScript 3.0 as a programming language and the Adobe AIR SDK as a development platform for desktop and mobile platforms.

Chapter 14, Extending Adobe Animate, examines a set of options available to extend Adobe Animate through the creation and execution of custom in-app tutorials, the use of the JavaScript API to automate actions, and an overview of the Custom Platform Support Development Kit.

To get the most out of this book

You will need Adobe Animate 2022 or a later version installed on a compatible macOS or Windows computer in order to most effectively follow along with this book. A full Adobe Creative Cloud subscription is the most beneficial way of doing this, as you'll get access to the Adobe Fonts service we use in certain projects and will have additional access to useful software such as Photoshop, Fresco, and Dimension or Substance 3D Stager to create content for use within your Animate projects. For the web-based projects in this book, an up-to-date web browser is highly recommended as well.

Software covered in the book	OS requirements
Adobe Animate 2022	Windows or macOS
Web browser	Windows or macOS

Also refer to the Animate System Requirements page for specific hardware and software specifications: `https://helpx.adobe.com/animate/system-requirements.html`.

If you are using the digital version of this book, we advise you to type the code yourself or access the code via the GitHub repository (link available in the next section). Doing so will help you avoid any potential errors related to the copying and pasting of code.

Download the example projects, media assets, and code files

You can download the example files for this book from GitHub at `https://github.com/PacktPublishing/Adobe-Animate-2022-for-Creative-Professionals-Second-Edition`. In case there's an update to these assets, it will be updated on the existing GitHub repository.

We also have other code bundles from our rich catalog of books and videos available at `https://github.com/PacktPublishing/`. Check them out!

Code in Action

Code in Action videos for this book can be viewed at `https://bit.ly/3cmGUzC`.

Download the color images

We also provide a PDF file that has color images of the screenshots/diagrams used in this book. You can download it here: `https://static.packt-cdn.com/downloads/9781803232799_ColorImages.pdf`.

Conventions used

There are a number of text conventions used throughout this book.

`Code in text`: Indicates code words in text, database table names, folder names, filenames, file extensions, pathnames, dummy URLs, user input, and Twitter handles. Here is an example: "Locate the `PondSign.png` image files within your filesystem and drag each into the appropriate scene."

A block of code is set as follows:

```
private function photoSelected(e:Event):void {
    var selectedPhoto:File = photos[e.target.selectedIndex];
    PhotoViewer.source = selectedPhoto.url;
}
```

Bold: Indicates a new term, an important word, or words that you see onscreen. For example, words in menus or dialog boxes appear in the text like this. Here is an example: "Select **More Settings** from the **Properties** panel."

> **Tips or important notes**
> Appear like this.

Get in touch

Feedback from our readers is always welcome.

General feedback: If you have questions about any aspect of this book, mention the book title in the subject of your message and email us at customercare@packtpub.com.

Errata: Although we have taken every care to ensure the accuracy of our content, mistakes do happen. If you have found a mistake in this book, we would be grateful if you would report this to us. Please visit www.packtpub.com/support/errata, selecting your book, clicking on the Errata Submission Form link, and entering the details.

Piracy: If you come across any illegal copies of our works in any form on the Internet, we would be grateful if you would provide us with the location address or website name. Please contact us at copyright@packt.com with a link to the material.

If you are interested in becoming an author: If there is a topic that you have expertise in and you are interested in either writing or contributing to a book, please visit authors.packtpub.com.

Share Your Thoughts

Once you've read *Adobe Animate 2022 for Creative Professionals Second Edition*, we'd love to hear your thoughts! Scan the QR code below to go straight to the Amazon review page for this book and share your feedback.

https://packt.link/r/1-803-23279-X

Your review is important to us and the tech community and will help us make sure we're delivering excellent quality content.

Section 1 – Getting up to Speed

Welcome to *Adobe Animate 2022 for Creative Professionals*! This book is divided into three sections, each containing a set of chapters that focus on a variety of fundamental topics. This first section of the book includes all the foundational and background content you must understand before tackling the more advanced chapters. You'll be introduced to a number of must-know concepts and related background information that will be steadily built upon as we proceed through the remainder of the book.

This section comprises the following chapters:

- *Chapter 1, A Brief Introduction to Adobe Animate*
- *Chapter 2, Exploring Platform-Specific Considerations*
- *Chapter 3, Settling into the User Interface*
- *Chapter 4, Publishing and Exporting Creative Content*

1

A Brief Introduction to Adobe Animate

This chapter provides background information on **Animate**, discusses what it is used for in the industry, and explores some of its new features for 2022 and how to put them to use. When new features are released, the software release notes usually just aren't enough to give an in-depth description of how to use them – so, we'll explore each of the new features in-depth so that you can start using them right away. These include the new bone creation and rigging capabilities of the **Asset Warp** tool and Warped Objects, the last frame options for **Graphic Symbol** instance looping, and a set of convenient features for the **Paint Bucket**, **Classic Brush**, and **Fluid Brush** tools. We'll also cover some resources for keeping up-to-date with all things Animate. You'll come away from this chapter with a refreshed understanding of Animate as a creative platform for designers, animators, and developers.

After reading this chapter, you'll come away with the following skills:

- Understand the history of Animate and what the software can be used for.

- Learn which features have been added to the software, what their purpose is, and how to put them to use.

- Know where to look for new releases and how to stay abreast of new resources for Animate, as well as its related software and the industry generally.

Technical Requirements

You will need the following software and hardware to complete this chapter:

- Adobe Animate 2022 (version 22.0.2 or above)

- Refer to the Animate System Requirements page for hardware specifications, please refer to the Adobe *Animate system requirements* page:

  `https://helpx.adobe.com/animate/system-requirements.html`

Understanding Adobe Animate

Animate has a lengthy history that is full of growth, accolades, disappointments, crushing defeats, pivots, and at least one notable resurrection. To cover the entire history of this software would take a book in itself, so we'll only touch on the relevant points here. However, it is important to know that beginning a new project in Adobe Animate is now a unique experience to its users, and without certain decisions being made by Adobe and the passion of the Animate community, this might not have been possible today.

A Bit of History

Animate began its journey as a simple vector graphics drawing program called **SmartSketch**, which was intended for use on stylus-based devices developed by a company called **FutureWave**. It soon gained such popularity that it was made available on both **Windows** and **macOS** with added motion capabilities and given the name **FutureSplash Animator**. The rising popularity of the **World Wide Web** during this period led to the software pivoting to target this young medium through the use of a browser-based runtime.

This was the beginning of both the authoring software that we still use today and what eventually became the **Flash Player** browser runtime. The idea behind this pairing was that you could author your content using FutureSplash Animator and play back the content through a web browser using an *installed extension* – often referred to as a **plugin**. The capabilities of web browsers at the time were such that **HTML** was a simple markup language for semantic text declaration and hyperlinks. Technologies such as **CSS** and **JavaScript** didn't even exist yet – even image files were barely supported! If you wanted a rich media experience on the web, you had to rely on browser plugins.

Macromedia acquired FutureWave (and FutureSplash Animator) in 1996 and rebranded the software as **Flash** – sort of a combination of the two names! They made huge investments in both the authoring software and web browser plugin, renaming the extension to Flash Player. Macromedia was also responsible for the **ActionScript** programming language and the expansion of the Flash platform across a number of areas, which included both web and server implementations, and it even took small steps into mobile.

From FutureWave to Macromedia and now to Adobe, Animate has changed a lot over the years!

Figure 1.1 – Over 25 years of Adobe Animate

In 2005, **Adobe Systems** acquired Macromedia and all of their properties (including Flash!) and have been holders of this technology ever since. In the years under Adobe, Animate has seen great strides, but also some missed opportunities over the years.

On the one hand, the Flash Platform was greatly expanded upon under a number of proprietary and open source initiatives – ActionScript 3.0 was released, and **MXML/Flex** was made much more accessible to many developers. We even had Flash Platform technologies integrated into nearly every piece of creative software Adobe distributes – for example, directly within the workspace panels of software such as **Photoshop** and **Illustrator**.

On the other hand, the push for Flash Player on mobile was so bungled that the platform could never recover from the fallout.

While Adobe did release a number of versions of Flash Player for **Android** and **RIM/ BlackBerry** devices, they were never able to get the runtime on **Apple** devices such as the **iPhone** and **iPad**. Adobe eventually gave up on Flash Player on mobile altogether and decided to refocus their efforts on **Adobe Integrated Runtime** (**AIR**) – which allowed **iOS**, Android, and even Windows and macOS applications and games to be developed with Flash technologies. However, Adobe did continue to focus on Flash Player for desktop browsers and took a renewed interest in 3D and gaming technologies in the form of **Stage3D**.

Adobe made huge efforts with Flash Player at one point, developing Stage3D, concurrency, and other options designed to create a blazing-fast experience for the user that appealed to game developers.

> **Important Note**
>
> If you'd like to learn more about mobile Flash Player and AIR for Android, have a look at *Flash Development for Android Cookbook* by Joseph Labrecque, also from Packt:
>
> https://www.packtpub.com/product/flash-development-for-android-cookbook/9781849691420

During this time, **Flash Professional** (the authoring software) was neglected quite a bit. The focus on mobile and developers left creative software such as Flash Professional with fewer resources, and once Adobe lost the war for mobile, the association of Flash Player with Flash Professional was one that even they had trouble justifying. Many expected Adobe to abandon the software entirely. But while Adobe was focused on developers during these years, animators were still making heavy use of Flash Professional to produce content for television, web, and film projects.

> **Tip**
> If you are curious about the television series that have used Animate, have a look at the following resource at `https://en.wikipedia.org/wiki/List_of_Flash_animated_television_series`.

In late 2015, following a year or two of visible increases in both the creative feature set of the software and the inclusion of new target platforms such as **HTML5 Canvas**, Adobe announced that the next version of Flash Professional would be re-branded as Animate:

Figure 1.2 – Adobe Animate being announced

The name change was primarily a way to let the world know that the software was no longer bound to a single platform (Flash) and that creative motion was going to be a big focus moving forward. Since that time, Animate has only gotten better, and it continues to be used by creatives and developers alike to target multiple platforms without restriction.

> **Note**
>
> The year 2021 marked 25 years of Animate – encompassing all of its identities over the years. From FutureSplash Animator to Macromedia Flash, then to Adobe Flash Professional, and all the way to the present with Adobe Animate – 2021 was a well-deserved milestone!

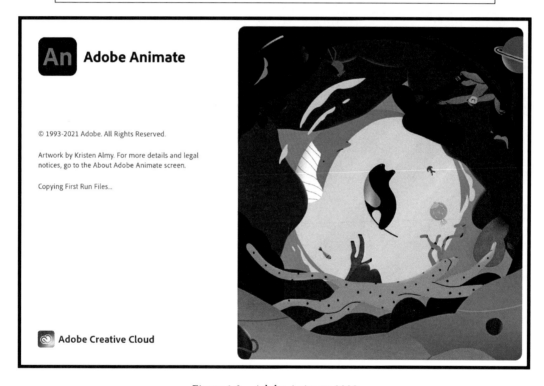

Figure 1.3 – Adobe Animate 2022

Animate 2022 is the latest release, and the major Animate features that have shipped over the past year will be detailed within this chapter.

Familiar uses of Adobe Animate

With over 25 years of history behind it, Animate has been used in all sorts of projects. In recent years, as the focus of the application has moved from a purely Flash-based experience to one that is much more platform-agnostic and increasingly expansive, the creative possibilities have expanded as well. This is a great time for new users to learn the software and for those who may have used older versions of Animate to revisit it and see what is now possible.

Animation and motion design remain two of the biggest uses for Animate. People all over the world are exposed to content created in Animate every day, and it's likely they do not even realize it! This content is hosted on the web, streamed through subscription services, and can be viewed on a wide assortment of television channels.

Of course, many digital advertisements across web and mobile settings are also created with Animate. The software even has a number of presets that conform to such ad standards – making it easy to get going with this platform.

However, something that makes Animate unique is its ability to create dynamic and interactive content. Non-interactive animated features such as *Star Wars: Galaxy of Adventures* and *My Little Pony: Friendship is Magic* are all great, but Animate can produce rich, interactive content as well.

Dumb Ways to Die and *Angry Birds* are two well-known examples of interactive content created with the software. Animate – and Flash before it – has a long history of producing games and interactive applications. They have frequently been hosted on the web, utilizing Flash Player and HTML5 Canvas. But they have also been launched on Android and iOS – packaged natively for these platforms using AIR. In fact, **YouTube** originally got its start and saw such immense popularity thanks to Flash Player and owes much of its early success to what was made possible by these technologies.

So, Animate is unique and powerful, with its ability to combine both design and development capabilities seamlessly within the same environment.

In this section, we explored the history of Animate and gained an understanding of the ways in which it has changed identities over the decades. We also had a look at some common uses for the software. Coming up, we'll take a comprehensive look at the new features that were introduced between Animate 2021 and Animate 2022.

Exploring the New Features of Animate

With nearly every new Animate release, users receive access to new features and improved workflows. Since the previous major release, which was Animate 2021 in October 2020, there have been important features added to the software that both new and seasoned users should know about. We'll go over each of these features now, but we'll work with many of them more thoroughly in subsequent chapters of this book!

> **Note**
> Those of you who are coming to Adobe Animate for the first time should approach this section as a glimpse toward the sort of improvements and additions that are made during each release cycle. Those of you who are more seasoned users of Animate can use this section for a comprehensive rundown of changes to expect in this version of the software.

Modern Rigging with Warped Objects

While Animate has included the Asset Warp tool and warped objects for a couple of years now, this feature's initial set of capabilities was only a stepping stone to something much greater. With the release of Animate 2022 (version 22.0.2), the capabilities of this feature have been greatly expanded to include the rigging of warped objects through bones and joints, as well as a modernized rigging system.

When you select the Asset Warp tool from the toolbar, you can now set a number of new tool properties in addition to the previous options:

Figure 1.4 – The Asset Warp tool properties

As you can see in the preceding figure, the Warp Options have been expanded! Let's go over these options briefly:

- **Mesh**: Selecting this universal checkbox when using the Asset Warp tool allows you to view a mesh overlay over any warped object or to hide it to better see the artwork.

- **Create Bones**: We now have the option of *creating bones* within a warped object. Creating a branching set of bones will establish an *armature*. Toggling this option off will allow the creation of *pins*, as per the existing workflows in Animate.

- **Bone Type**: When the **Create Bones** toggle is enabled, you can choose between creating hard or soft bones. Each armature can have a mix of both bone types and they can be converted from one to another.

- **Propagate Changes**: If you have established keyframes in your timeline that are tied to the properties of a warped object, this will propagate any changes you make to various pins and bones across existing keyframes.

These are all tool-level properties. Once either pins or bones are established as part of a warped object, a number of properties can be tweaked that belong to each individual joint or handle.

> **Note**
>
> This feature was not included in the first version of Animate 2022 that was released but it was originally intended to be. It was released in a follow-up version (22.0.2). If you do not see these options in your installed version of Animate 2022 then check for an update!

In the following figure, you can see how pins now appear within a warped object and the various properties associated with them:

Figure 1.5 – Pins and Warped Object Properties

The **Mesh** Density Slider allows for finer control over the mesh deformation and how it impacts the underlying artwork. Just as we have been able to do in previous versions of Animate, we can set an individual pin's **Handle Mode** radio buttons to either **Open** or **Fixed**, depending on our needs. An open handle allows for a greater degree of freedom when making a transformation, while a fixed handle allows less movement but also allows for rotation around the pin. The other options shown in Figure 1.5 pertain only to bones.

In the next figure, you can see how the new bones appear within a warped object and the various properties associated with them:

Figure 1.6 – Bones and Warped Object Properties

Since this is also a warped object, we still get access to the same **Mesh Density Slider** control. Additionally, we can set any joint as a *Freeze Joint*, which pins it in place on the stage as immovable. The **Handle Mode** radio buttons function in a similar way to before, with the option of either open or fixed. However, it is not possible to perform rotations in this instance, as rotation is handled differently in the case of bones.

We have the option of using the **Bone Type** radio buttons to specify the bone type as either Hard or Soft, and an armature can contain a mixture of both types. Soft bones are great for things like ropes, tentacles, and that sort of thing – whereas hard bones are intended to work as more rigid structures. Note that there is also a **Rotation Angle** field that takes a numerical value that can be manipulated for each bone, and you might prefer to work in that fashion instead of through the onscreen overlays.

Even though the two previous figures showed the use of pins and bones separately, you can actually combine them both and include multiple armatures within the same warped object – it is an incredibly flexible system.

We'll examine these new capabilities in much greater detail in *Chapter 9, Manipulating Warped Objects Through Advanced Rigging.*

Layer Parenting Enhancements

Layer parenting itself is not new, but this release of Animate includes extended capabilities for this feature. When making use of layer parenting workflows, we now have the ability to scale, skew, and flip parent objects and have these properties propagate to their children.

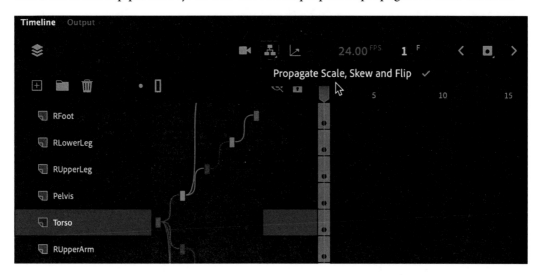

Figure 1.7 – The Propagate Scale, Skew and Flip feature is activated by default

This feature can be toggled by holding the cursor down over the Layer Parenting toggle above the timeline and either checking or unchecking the option. You can also temporarily enable this functionality by holding the accent key (`) while performing these transformations.

Last Frame Options for Graphic Symbol Looping

Adobe has been slowly adding extra options for controlling graphic symbol instance playback through the use of keyframes. Since graphic symbols cannot be manipulated with code in any way, this is the ideal mechanism for providing such instances with specific behavioral instructions. With the new release of Animate, we now have the ability to define a *last frame* option along with the previously available *first frame* option, allowing us to specify a frame span as a looped region within any graphic symbol instance.

To further explain the usefulness of this property, consider the following figure:

Figure 1.8 – Deciding on a segment of the graphic symbol timeline to loop

If we wanted to have this animated character loop in the main timeline from frames 51 to 103, we'd need to add a lot of keyframes in the parent timeline to make it happen.

With the new *last frame* property, we can set all these options using only a single keyframe through either the **Object** tab of the **Properties** panel or even the integrated **Frame Picker** panel:

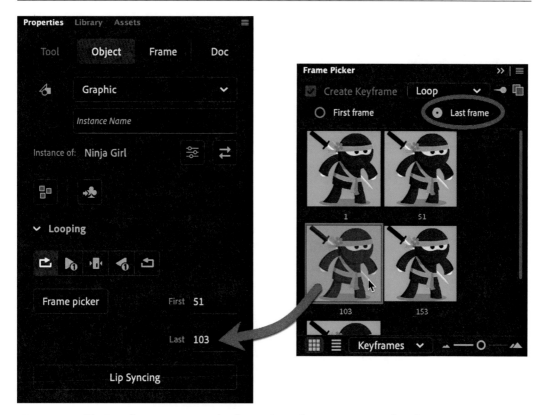

Figure 1.9 – The Last frame option can be chosen from the Properties panel or the Frame Picker panel

Setting both a first and last frame value and setting the behavior to loop effectively creates a looping region of the internal graphic symbol timeline that is all controlled from a single keyframe.

Paint Fills Only Option when Drawing

Throughout its history, Animate has had a number of brush modes to choose from when using certain tools (such as the Classic Brush tool, or the newer Fluid Brush tool). These brush modes include *Paint Normal*, *Paint Behind*, *Paint Selection*, and *Paint Inside*. Depending on the brush mode that is selected, the brush will apply to certain portions of the artwork and avoid others.

A new brush mode, **Paint Fills Only**, has now been added alongside the existing options. This has now been added to the brush modes dropdown in the **Classic Brush** and **Fluid Brush** properties:

Figure 1.10 – The Paint Fills Only brush mode

This new brush mode is designed to speed up shading workflows by affecting only existing fills on the active layer.

Fill on Active Layer with the Paint Bucket Tool

The *active layer* in an Animate timeline is the layer that is currently selected. A new option exists when using the Paint Bucket tool that will apply the Paint Bucket to the active layer only.

This can be activated from the **Paint Bucket** Options section of the **Tool** properties in the **Properties** panel if the Paint Bucket tool is selected:

Figure 1.11 – The new Fill on Active Layer option for the Paint Bucket tool

With this option selected, the Paint Bucket will only be applied to content within the active layer.

Color Effect Tweening for HTML5 Canvas Documents

Before this release of Animate, when a *Color Effect* was applied to a tweened symbol instance within an HTML5 Canvas document, upon publication, the appearance would be frozen at the first frame of the tween. In other words, color effects could not be animated at all using this document type.

However, now any color effect applied to a symbol instance can be tweened with the confidence that the animation will continue to exist – even within the published version of the HTML5 Canvas project:

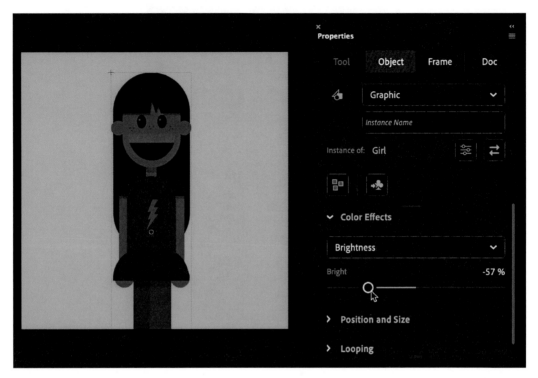

Figure 1.12 – Color effects can now be tweened in HTML5 Canvas documents

When published, any color effects in HTML5 Canvas documents are now properly tweenable.

Asset Panel Updates

Adobe has made the workflow for using assets from within the **Assets** panel a simpler process by automatically increasing the timeline frame span when an animated asset is placed on the stage for the first time. This removes the step that was previously required for the user to make many of the assets actually animated.

To make use of this feature, you simply need to drag animated content from the **Assets** panel to the stage:

Figure 1.13 – Automated timeline frame span expansion

The existing frame span is automatically expanded based on the chosen asset's internal timeline length.

In this section, we took a comprehensive look at all the new features introduced in Animate over the past year. Next, we'll learn how to keep up-to-date with new versions of the software and any related industry activity.

Keeping Up to Date with Animate Releases

As we have seen, Animate receives a significant number of new features between major versions! It's always a good idea to be aware of the changes introduced in any software – this helps you reap the benefits of new functionality and stay up to date on things like compatibility with other software. Aside from the software itself, it's also beneficial to understand how people are using the software and general thoughts around intersections will stay in touch with others in the industry.

Adobe Creative Cloud Desktop

Just like any other Adobe **Creative Cloud Desktop** application, Animate is managed through the **Creative Cloud Desktop** application. You can download the desktop application from `https://www.adobe.com/creativecloud/desktop-app.html` – this works if you need to install it for the first time or if you need to perform a forced update.

The Creative Cloud Desktop application will alert you whenever a new version of Animate has been released:

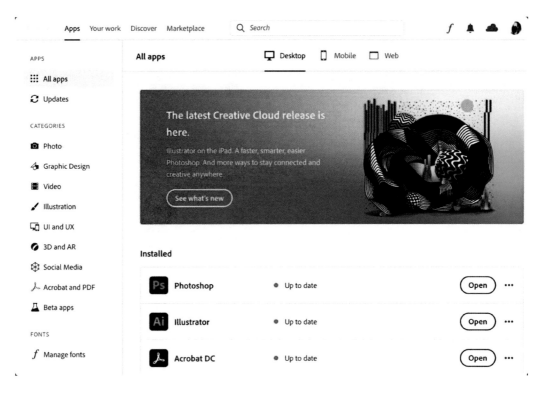

Figure 1.14 – Adobe Creative Cloud for desktop

If you have the application installed, you can easily see whether Animate is up-to-date by viewing your installed applications.

Any applications that are up to date will indicate this, and any that have an available update will display that information as well:

Figure 1.15 – Animate is up to date!

This is a great mechanism for staying on top of new updates across all Creative Cloud software.

To manually check for updates, click the **Updates** tab along the side and locate the **More Actions** button on the upper right-hand side of the screen. Clicking this button allows you to either select **Enable Auto Update** or select **Check for Updates**. With the automatic update option disabled, you'll need to manually update Animate when a new version is released.

Adobe MAX

Generally, new versions of Animate (and most Adobe Creative Cloud software) are released at the annual creativity conference called **Adobe MAX**. You can learn more about Adobe MAX at `http://max.adobe.com/` and even register to attend if it is the right time of year. Adobe MAX normally takes place in the autumn and runs for about 3 days.

It is a great place to learn more about Animate and other creative software while being inspired by industry experts:

Figure 1.16 – The Adobe MAX creativity conference logo

Animate 2021 was released at Adobe MAX 2020 and Animate 2022 was released during Adobe MAX 2021. You can see how important this conference is to Adobe and its release strategy!

In this section, we discovered how to keep Animate updated and also how to explore any news and related ongoings in the wider Adobe community.

Summary

This was only the first chapter, but we have already gone over a lot of content! You should now have a good understanding of the history of Adobe Animate and know about its current capabilities. You will also have an excellent understanding of all the new features that have been released since the previous major version of the software. These features include being able to use bones within warped objects, the functionality to implement a graphic symbol instance loop with the last frame option, and new options for the Paint Bucket tool and various other brush tools. We also covered some good places to look to ensure your installation of Animate remains up to date and that you stay abreast of any changes to the software.

In the next chapter, we'll explore the various target platforms supported by Animate. Get ready to learn about HTML5 Canvas, ActionScript 3.0, AIR for desktop, WebGL glTF, and more!

2

Exploring Platform-Specific Considerations

We will now spend some time exploring the various target platforms that are natively supported by Adobe Animate. To be successful with Animate, you must understand the underlying technologies involved in each platform and when to use one over another, as they each have their strengths and weaknesses. This understanding enables sound decisions when selecting a target document type upon starting a new Animate project.

We'll begin with an overview of the major platforms supported natively as publish targets within Animate. Following this, we can then explore the variety of document types that support and target different aspects of these platforms for a greater understanding of why you might use certain document types over others.

After reading this chapter, you will be able to do the following:

- Understand the set of platforms native to Adobe Animate.
- Explore best practices around the ActionScript 3.0, HTML5 Canvas, and AIR document types.
- Employ recommendations around beta document types, including both **Virtual Reality** (**VR**) and WebGL (standard and extended).

Technical Requirements

You will need the following software and hardware to complete this chapter:

- Adobe Animate 2022 (version 22.0 or above).

- Refer to the Animate System Requirements page for hardware specifications: `https://helpx.adobe.com/animate/system-requirements.html`.

The code in action video for this chapter can be found here: `https://bit.ly/3nnCM8X`

Exploring Animate Document Types

While Flash Professional was, for years, focused entirely on the Flash Platform, Adobe Animate seeks to define itself as a platform-agnostic software application. This basically means that any target platform is welcome to be part of the publish pipeline – even those not traditionally associated with the software.

Even though Animate seeks to play well with any platform that wants in on the game, it does support a number of important platforms natively:

Figure 2.1 – Publish targets native to Animate

Today, Animate comes prepackaged with a number of target platforms for common usage. These include ActionScript 3.0, AIR for Desktop, AIR for iOS, AIR for Android, HTML5 Canvas, VR 360, VR Panorama, and WebGL glTF (in both standard and extended flavors). Some of these target platforms are still Flash-based, but most newer platforms have been added as to target native web technologies, such as the HTML canvas element with JavaScript, and include specifications such as WebGL and glTF to achieve some pretty neat stuff!

You can see all the available document types by choosing **File | New** from the application menu or by choosing **Create New** or **More Presets** from the **Home** screen and then choosing the **Advanced** category of the **New Document** dialog.

Figure 2.2 – New Document dialog – Advanced presets

The **Advanced** category of presets allows you to create a new document based upon a specific publishing platform, while the other category presets tend to only allow the choice of ActionScript 3.0 or HTML5 Canvas.

> **Tip**
>
> Within the **New Document** dialog, document types are listed under **Platforms** and **Beta Platforms**. You may need to scroll down to see them all. Any third-party platforms that have been enabled will show up even farther down the stack.

We'll next proceed through an overview of the major platforms available in Animate today. These are all based upon the Flash Platform runtimes, native web technologies, and a set of beta platforms that extend these technologies.

Flash Platform Runtimes

As we detailed in the previous chapter, Animate was once only able to author content for **Flash Platform** technologies. You could create content to publish as a `.swf` file to be executed using Adobe **Flash Player** in the web browser. For a long time, that was pretty much it! Of course, Flash content was absolutely huge during that time and Flash Platform designers and developers had no problem with this popularity.

The Flash Platform covers two main runtimes: the web-based Flash Player and the **Adobe Integrated Runtime (AIR)**.

Figure 2.3 – The Adobe Flash runtimes – Flash Player and AIR

Both publish targets are based upon ActionScript 3.0, but in Animate terminology, the ActionScript 3.0 document type publishes a .swf file for use with Flash Player or other external mechanisms.

With all major web browsers – and even Adobe – no longer supporting Flash Player in the browser, we've come to a very interesting point in time. Even with web browsers no longer supporting Flash Platform content, the .swf format and other files published in various forms using the platform are still usable for many purposes. These purposes include the format's role as a motion graphics interchange format for other software, such as Adobe After Effects, as packaged **projector** content, and most importantly, as an application development platform in Adobe AIR with the ability to target macOS, Windows, iOS, Android, and more!

Branching Out to the Native Web

In 2011, Adobe began an experiment with converting documents created with Flash Professional to **HTML5**. The project was codenamed **Wallaby** and only existed for a few years until other technologies and superior workflows took its place. Wallaby required an existing .fla file for conversion and only included about 50% of the capabilities of a Flash .swf file.

This was followed in 2012 by **Toolkit for CreateJS**, an extension that would allow Flash Professional users to export to HTML5 directly from the software without having to produce an intermediate .fla file. The problem with this mechanism was that it was an optional extension that users would need to install, and it was still not tightly coupled with the authoring environment in the way that users would expect, and so was limited when compared to producing Flash content. Toolkit for CreateJS ran as an extension and appeared as a panel within the interface – very different from the normal publishing process.

Eventually, with the maturity of the **CreateJS** libraries, coupled with a more platform-agnostic approach to publishing within the software, Flash Professional made CreateJS a native document type within the software through the use of the HTML5 Canvas document type.

Since that time, Adobe and the CreateJS team have expanded capabilities and integrations to the point where HTML5 Canvas is one of the primary document types within Animate. For interactive, web-based content, HTML5 Canvas is the go-to document type.

In addition, Animate can publish to the native web beyond the use of CreateJS through the use of the **WebGL** standard alongside additional WebGL and VR JavaScript runtime engines. We'll explore some basic information around these additional native web-based target platforms in a bit!

Open to Custom Platforms

We mentioned previously that Adobe Animate is a **platform-agnostic** software application. This is a pretty major change in the software since, for most of its existence, Flash Professional produced content that ran exclusively within Flash Player.

We've explained a bit about expanding to additional platforms with CreateJS and related standards such as WebGL, but Animate actually goes even further by opening up the entire publishing **API** for anyone to incorporate their publish target platform of choice into the software.

Animate

The Animate Custom Platform SDK lets you extend Animate to support custom platforms. In addition, the Unity reference import plugin allows you to import animations orchestrated in Animate to...

(View downloads)

Figure 2.4 – Animate Custom Platform SDK

Using the **Custom Platform Support Development Kit** (**CPSDK**), anyone can create an extension that allows Animate users to target a platform of their own choosing. The CPSDK extends the power of Animate to new platforms, such as PixiAnimate and **LottieFiles**. Support for these additional platforms is maintained and implemented by third-party developers engaged with those platforms. They generally supply Animate with either new document types or export and publish options. We'll look more deeply into different examples of extending Animate in *Chapter 14*, *Extending Adobe Animate*.

> **Note**
>
> Animate can be extended in various ways. It includes a **JavaScript API** (**JSAPI**) to automate actions in the user interface and the CPSDK to extend the power of Animate to new platforms.

In this section, we had a brief introduction to the three main target platform types supported by Adobe Animate: Flash/ActionScript-based targets, HTML/JavaScript-based targets, and custom platforms. Coming up, we'll have a look at the particulars around using ActionScript 3.0 documents.

Understanding ActionScript 3.0 Documents

It makes sense to first explore what was at one time the single target platform supported by Animate for most of its existence: Flash Player and the `.swf` file format. Since Flash Player is a runtime, it exists to execute a packaged set of assets and data in order to run a program. The `.swf` file format is basically a compressed little bundle of creative assets and code that Animate can publish for this purpose.

> **Note**
>
> ActionScript 3.0 used to be used to produce all sorts of rich, interactive content. With the deprecation of Flash Player in the web browser, however, the role of `.swf` has become more focused.

There is a bit of confusion around the naming of this document type within Animate, as you won't find a document type that targets "Flash Player" or "SWF" but rather "ActionScript 3.0" instead.

Figure 2.5 – The ActionScript 3.0 document type

Newcomers are often confused by this terminology and expect that, if creating an ActionScript 3.0 document, they will be writing code. While you can absolutely write full applications using this document type, it isn't necessary to do so.

ActionScript 3.0 documents are ideal for working in Animate when exporting to video or even for integration with After Effects and other compositing software. ActionScript 3.0 is the document most often chosen for creative, non-interactive content today. If you want to create interactive content for the web or other platforms, Animate can do those things too! You'll want to use other document types, such as HTML5 Canvas or AIR, for these purposes.

Okay, let's dig deeper through an overview of the technologies behind ActionScript 3.0 documents in Animate by exploring Adobe Flash Player, the SWF file format, and the ActionScript programming language.

Adobe Flash Player

There are a couple of different versions of Flash Player to know about. There is, of course, the once-ubiquitous web browser plugin that was finally deprecated on December 31, 2020, after years of being a staple web technology and even being built into major browsers such as Google Chrome and Microsoft Internet Explorer due to its status as a de facto standard.

Adobe announced that Flash Player in the web browser would be deprecated way back in 2017 and we should assume from now on that no user will be able to run such content through the browser plugin.

The reasoning behind this decision was stated that native web standards such as **HTML5**, **WebGL**, and **WebAssembly** had reached a point of maturity that they could now be relied upon to serve the same (or similar) needs that Flash Player in the browser had fulfilled in years past, thus making Flash Player redundant.

> **Important Note**
>
> For more insight into the thinking behind this, I suggest you have a look at the Adobe Flash Player EOL General Information Page at `https://www.adobe.com/products/flashplayer/end-of-life.html`.

The web browser is only part of the story, though. There are also standalone and debug versions of the Flash Player runtime, which can operate outside of the browser environment. A good example of this is the Flash Player that is built into Animate itself. Whenever a **Test Movie** action is performed from an ActionScript 3.0 project, Animate opens a `.swf` file produced from your project within this version of Flash Player. It's very convenient to be able to test your animated content directly within the authoring software in this way.

The SWF File Format

As mentioned previously, when publishing an ActionScript 3.0 document in Animate, a `.swf` file is produced. The `.swf` file extension is so named due to Macromedia wanting to extend its **Shockwave** branding that was being used by another software product, **Director**, to produce content that would run on the web.

When Macromedia acquired **FutureSplash Animator** and renamed it *Flash*, they also named the files it produced **Shockwave Flash** – SWF!

Figure 2.6 – ActionScript 3.0 produces an SWF file

What made this file format so desirable for use on the web was that it could contain all sorts of media: vectors, bitmaps, sound, video, data, and program code. It did all of this in a very efficient way, as these files were known for being small in size and as such, quite suitable for transfer over the web.

In 2008, Adobe published portions of the .swf file format as part of their **Open Screen Project** initiative, but since much of the technology is either licensed or strictly proprietary, anyone wanting to build an open source version of Flash Player to interpret .swf files will have a difficult time replicating all functionality.

With the decline of Flash Player and the eventual removal of the runtime from web browsers, it has become increasingly difficult to play .swf files as originally intended. Thankfully, the .swf file format can also be used as a transport format, and other applications such as Adobe After Effects can use this as part of an animator's compositing pipeline.

The ActionScript Programming Language

ActionScript is the programming language native to Flash Player and the .swf file format. There are three versions of the language: **ActionScript 1.0** and **ActionScript 2.0** are very similar to one another and are executed by the same **virtual machine** (**VM**) within Flash Player, while **ActionScript 3.0** is a completely new language that runs in its own dedicated VM.

Similar to JavaScript, ActionScript is based upon **ECMAScript**, and while both languages do share many features, ActionScript 3.0 is based upon **ECMAScript 4**, which was ultimately abandoned which explains the various differences between ActionScript and JavaScript as they exist today.

A simple example of an ActionScript class is the following:

```
package com.josephlabrecque.example {
    public class Example {
        public function Example() {
            // constructor code
        }
    }
}
```

Even with this small example, you can see how organized the language structure and syntax are. Each *class* exists within a *package* and requires a constructor function. The language also supports object-oriented concepts such as interfaces and instantiation.

Even with Flash Player in the web browser being a thing of the past, ActionScript is still an excellent language, fun to write, and feature-rich. In the present day, we can effectively write applications and games for desktop and mobile using ActionScript and target these platforms with AIR technologies. We'll read more about AIR in a little bit.

Additionally, ActionScript is used when writing code for native web platforms through the integrations available in open source frameworks such as **Apache Royale**: `https://royale.apache.org/`. ActionScript is by no means a dead language!

Tip

ActionScript documentation can be found on Adobe's website: `https://help.adobe.com/en_US/as3/learn/`.

In this section, we explored the technologies involved when using the ActionScript 3.0 document type. Coming up, we'll perform a similar examination of the document type known as HTML5 Canvas.

Understanding HTML5 Canvas Documents

If you want to target the native web using Animate, the most popular option is to use the **HTML5 Canvas** document type. This is a native document type that is deeply integrated within Animate and produces animated and interactive content that will run in any modern web browser on desktop or mobile.

The HTML5 Canvas document type includes nearly all the capabilities and features that are available in older formats such as Flash, without the need for a separate plugin, extension, or runtime.

Figure 2.7 – The HTML5 Canvas document type

This is a native document type that is deeply integrated within Animate and produces animated and interactive content that will run in any modern web browser on desktop or mobile.

> **Note**
>
> HTML5 Canvas does not support the **Scenes** feature in Adobe Animate. Just about every other document type does though – including the native web (beta) WebGL and VR document types.

In our explorations of the HTML5 Canvas document type, we'll begin with a look at how Animate leverages both HTML and JavaScript to produce published content, followed by an overview of the canvas element, specifically. We'll round things off with a quick look at what makes all these technologies work together, the CreateJS libraries.

HTML and JavaScript

When publishing an HTML5 Canvas document, Animate will produce a bundle of files that includes HTML, JavaScript, and additional assets depending upon the project. The two main files that will always result when publishing this document type include a .html file and a .js file.

The HTML will act as a container document, while the JavaScript controls what happens within.

Figure 2.8 – HTML5 Canvas produces HTML and JavaScript

If using bitmap assets or sound files, they will also be included in the output within the folders you specify in the document's **Publish Settings**.

> **Note**
>
> **CSS** can also be used in HTML5 Canvas documents through the use of **HTML5 components**. To access these components, choose **Window | Components** from the application menu when using a document targeting HTML5 Canvas.

The CreateJS libraries themselves can be loaded via a **Content Delivery Network (CDN)** or can be exported along with your files (it's completely up to you). If you want to view your published files, it is best to transfer them from your local drive to a real web server. Browser security restrictions being what they are, they will likely not allow your canvas-based content to execute properly unless served from a web server.

> **Tip**
> When testing your HTML5 Canvas content via the **Test Movie** command within Animate, the software actually spins up a small, local web server to get around any potential browser security restrictions. It's very convenient!

The Canvas Element

The HTML5 Canvas document type is so named because it makes heavy use of the `<canvas/>` element of HTML in order to provide a dynamic, interactive canvas for content playback and rendering. It basically defines a rectangular "stage" area in which all of our media resides as part of a larger HTML document.

A canvas element in HTML is established in the following manner using HTML markup language:

```
<canvas width="1280" height="720"></canvas>
```

Here, we are only specifying a width and height for our element. You may want to also provide an ID in order to target this element specifically.

> **Tip**
> To learn more about the HTML canvas element, refer to the documentation on Mozilla Developer Network: `https://developer.mozilla.org/en-US/docs/Web/HTML/Element/canvas`.

To interact with and make adjustments to the canvas element and content rendered within, JavaScript is used. Have a look at the following example:

```
<script>
    const canvas = document.querySelector('canvas');
    const ctx = canvas.getContext('2d');
    ctx.fillStyle = 'darkred';
    ctx.fillRect(440, 160, 400, 400);
</script>
```

Here, we are defining our JavaScript code within an HTML `<script/>` tag. We initially set a constant to act as a reference to our canvas element and then set the context to operate in 2D. Following that, we are able to then draw content within this element through the use of the various canvas functions. In this simple example, we draw a red square and center it within the canvas element.

Animate, of course, does all this heavy lifting for us when working in HTML5 Canvas. There is no reason to manually create and manage HTML elements or specific canvas element instructions – we only provide these examples here for context.

> **Note**
>
> If you use components within an HTML5 Canvas project, they will be published within a special overlay that sits directly over the canvas element. Such projects will make use of both the canvas element and an additional set of elements representing the chosen components.

The CreateJS Libraries

While HTML and JavaScript establish the basic foundation of an HTML5 Canvas project, the real heavy-lifter for this target platform is CreateJS. This JavaScript library is actually a suite of libraries that includes the following:

- **EaselJS**: This library makes working with the HTML canvas element a more pleasant experience for those used to developing content using Flash technologies via the abstraction of the underlying APIs.

- **TweenJS**: We make use of this library to allow tweening and motion through the HTML canvas element and underlying native JavaScript APIs.

- **SoundJS**: Again, this library makes working with underlying web-native media APIs a more pleasant experience with a focus on audio management and playback for the web.

- **PreloadJS**: This allows the simplified management of both assets and data when working with other CreateJS libraries.

Together, these individual libraries form the CreateJS suite of tools. They can be used outside of Animate as well, but given that these libraries were designed specifically to emulate the Flash display list, they are a perfect match for Adobe Animate.

In this section, we saw how the canvas element of HTML combined with the CreateJS JavaScript library is used to form HTML5 Canvas documents in Animate. Coming up, we'll look at another important document type, Adobe AIR.

Exploring the Adobe Integrated Runtime

Adobe AIR was a major component of what used to be called the Flash Platform. It was one of two runtimes for the platform – and while AIR is certainly more powerful than its sister runtime, Flash Player, it is perhaps even more misunderstood. People generally understand web browsers and their capabilities and uses, but an installable package that runs similar to a native application on desktop and mobile such as AIR is somehow more difficult for the average person to get a handle on.

There is a lot to cover when it comes to AIR. We'll begin our overview with a look at a general explanation of what AIR is and its relationship to other technologies, such as the ActionScript language. An explanation of the relationship between the two AIR **Software Development Kit (SDK)** providers will follow as we go over recent partnerships between Adobe and HARMAN. To wrap things up, we'll explore the supported AIR document types within Animate: **AIR for Desktop**, **AIR for iOS**, and **AIR for Android**.

Adobe AIR

AIR itself is built upon Flash technology and in most cases, a `.swf` file is even produced that is packaged as part of the bundle.

Figure 2.9 – The AIR for Desktop document type

For platforms such as iOS that do not support `.swf`, the entire code base is actually translated into a native iOS application.

The main thing about AIR is that it runs entirely divorced from the web browser environment, while Flash Player was tied to the browser directly. This allows AIR to be much more powerful due to reduced security restrictions and tight integration with the underlying operating system. It uses the same language as Flash Player for writing interaction – ActionScript 3.0 – and so was easy to adopt by the millions of Flash developers when it was first introduced.

Adobe AIR and ActionScript 3.0

Just as with ActionScript 3.0 document types within Animate, AIR makes use of ActionScript 3.0 as its primary programming language. Unlike targeting the output format as a limited `.swf`, though, AIR is a natively installable package and because of this can have deep hooks within the operating system itself.

A great example of this is the **Extended Desktop** profile, which can be assigned within the **AIR Settings** dialog.

Figure 2.10 – The AIR publish settings allow deep integrations

When **Extended Desktop** has been chosen, AIR is then able to tap into the native processes of the operating system and communicate with any available process in order to really extend the capabilities of the runtime. This makes AIR far more powerful than anything targeting Flash Player or the web browser as it runs on the operating system itself and not through a security-restricted web browser prison.

> **Note**
>
> Initial versions of AIR actually supported developers in writing applications using either ActionScript or JavaScript. As the runtime developed further, the focus was placed on the ActionScript workflows, and eventually, JavaScript was dropped completely.

Adobe AIR and HARMAN

With Adobe having halted all development on Flash Player in preparation for the December 31, 2020 deprecation event, they began looking for a partner to continue work on AIR, since it is still heavily used in the creation of applications and games and is completely unrelated to web browsers and the restrictions around that platform.

In May 2019, the decision was made to partner more closely with **HARMAN**, a division of **Samsung**, which was heavily experienced in Flash Platform technologies. HARMAN would begin by focusing on an AIR solution targeting Android's upcoming 64-bit requirement and eventually expand to other platforms and systems supported by Adobe's version of the runtime.

Why was this decision made? With the end-of-life announcement of its sister runtime, Flash Player, Adobe had to decide whether they would continue supporting AIR or look to partners in the effort to maintain and grow the technology. In 2019, Adobe transitioned the development and support of AIR over to HARMAN due to their long history as a partner in the development and implementation of this technology for specific, bespoke implementations.

To read the announcement around this transition, have a look at *The Future of Adobe AIR* at `https://blog.adobe.com/en/publish/2019/05/30/the-future-of-adobe-air.html`.

HARMAN also released a statement about this new partnership on the same day as Adobe, in which they described the partnership and transition from their perspective. They explained, similar to the message from Adobe, their long partnership together on the AIR SDK and runtimes. The agreement between the two entities allows HARMAN to take on the support and maintenance of both the AIR runtime and the SDK. They also restated their commitment to ensuring the future growth and support of the technologies across various platforms.

Read more about the partnership from HARMAN's perspective in their FAQ: `https://airsdk.harman.com/faq`.

Since we are now well past 2020, the partnership between Adobe and HARMAN has solidified and it is recommended that a new version of the AIR SDK is acquired from HARMAN and configured within Animate. We'll examine how this is done in *Chapter 13, Building Apps for Desktop and Mobile*.

The Animate team has repeatedly stated that Adobe remains committed to supporting AIR within Animate as part of this partnership, though you can also make use of the AIR SDK as a completely standalone SDK as well!

AIR for Desktop

An often-overlooked target for Adobe AIR is major operating systems through AIR for Desktop. Developers were able to target both **Windows** and **macOS** long before AIR became available for mobile systems. Originally, the only way to package and distribute applications built with AIR was through the use of a `.air` file. The `.air` format was special because it was completely cross-platform, but because of this, you needed to have the AIR runtime installed separately in order to install and run any AIR program. This was, of course, different from native applications.

As time went on, and the separate AIR runtime became more of a hindrance to users, additional packaging and installation options became available.

Figure 2.11– AIR for Desktop produces an AIR package or application installer

Today, when developing AIR applications, you can still produce `.air` files that run on both Windows and macOS, but you can also produce operating system-specific installers that actually have a number of advantages over the `.air` approach. The first of which is that the user does not need to have an AIR runtime installed separately. The second is that a native installer allows even deeper integrations within the host operating system.

AIR for iOS

If you want to target Apple iOS or iPadOS, you can choose the AIR for iOS document type when creating a new project. This will always produce a native iOS package in the form of a `.ipa` file.

Figure 2.12 – AIR for iOS produces an IPA

There are also many settings specific to Apple's platforms that can be configured within the **AIR for iOS Settings** dialog, but you cannot produce anything other than a .ipa package.

Note

AIR for iOS never had the ability to produce .air files supported by desktop and Android because of Apple's policies against such things within their mobile systems. Adobe got around this by translating all of the assets and code produced in Animate to native iOS code, which is why the package type is so inflexible.

AIR for Android

Choosing the **AIR for Android** document type will allow a developer to target mobile devices and tablets running **Google Android**. The workflow is very similar to working with AIR for iOS, with platform-specific settings available as in the **AIR for iOS Settings** dialog.

When targeting Android, you will produce a .apk file – the native format for Android applications.

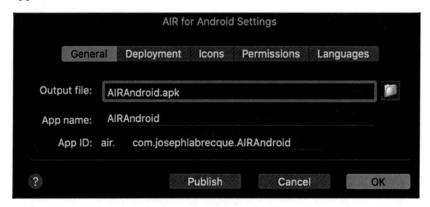

Figure 2.13 – AIR for Android produces an APK

While we have no choice in the output file produced when targeting Android today, the AIR runtime was once also available for this platform in a way similar to how it functions on desktop operating systems. The AIR runtime for Android has since been deprecated and AIR applications must be packaged to .apk, similar to the situation with iOS.

> **Note**
>
> There is now a 64-bit requirement when publishing to Android. Because apps published through **Google Play** will need to support 64-bit architectures, you must use an AIR SDK capable of this. Be sure to use an SDK from HARMAN since the older AIR SDKs from Adobe only produce 32-bit apps.

Because AIR can publish for iOS and Android, platforms related to these two core targets are available as well.

Figure 2.14 – Android TV profile selection in the publish settings

AIR for iOS and AIR for Android can also publish for Apple TV and Android TV, respectively.

In this section, we took a deep look at what Adobe AIR is and how it can be used to build installable applications and games for popular platforms such as macOS, Windows, iOS, and Android. Coming up, we'll take a look at the final set of document types available through a fresh install of Animate, the **WebGL glTF** and **VR** beta platforms.

Experimenting with Animate Beta Platforms

In recent versions of Animate, Adobe has included a number of new document types that are intended for different use cases. This includes a set of four document types currently marked specifically as **beta**. They include **WebGL glTF (Standard)**, **WebGL glTF (Extended)**, **VR Panorama**, and **VR 360**. These can only be accessed through the **Advanced** category of the **New Document** dialog.

Since these document types are still in beta development, we won't spend as much time on them as we have the previously covered document types in Animate, but they are certainly exciting and worth our attention, so we'll give each a quick overview before moving on.

WebGL glTF – Standard and Extended

The two WebGL glTF document types in Animate allow the creation of web-based content as part of a GPU-accelerated experience. WebGL is a cross-platform web standard focused on low-level 3D graphics and the term **glTF** (**GL Transmission Format**) is an API-neutral runtime asset delivery format Animate uses alongside WebGL.

Figure 2.15 – The WebGL glTF Standard document type

The *standard* document type does not allow any interactivity, as the WebGL glTF standard does not allow it. This is an example of why you may want to use the *extended* document type, though it does break with the established standard to achieve this.

> **Note**
> The extended document type is only meant to run using Adobe's WebGL glTF runtime, while the standard document type can be played within any standard WebGL glTF playback – **Babylon.js** and **Three.js** are examples of this.

VR Panorama and VR 360

These document types include a number of features specific to VR, including the ability to use a 360-degree or panoramic photograph as a texture and a special **VR View** panel that allows more precise placement of interactive and animated assets within the environment.

Figure 2.16 – The VR Panorama document type

You can design your environment by marking certain layers in your timeline as textures, which, upon publication, get wrapped to the inside of either a cylinder or sphere – creating the illusion of being within the virtual space. Both of these target formats are for pretty specific use cases, including museum walkthroughs, real estate, or more creative efforts such as experiments, environmental design, or even the creation of simple games.

Like other web-based documents, the VR betas publish to native web technologies and so you would use JavaScript as the coding language.

> **Tip**
> No matter what document type you choose, you can always convert from one target platform to another by choosing **File | Convert To** from the application menu. This will convert all assets and animation but any code will need to be rewritten as it is specific to each platform.

In this section, we looked a bit into what makes up the various beta platforms under development at Adobe. We'll read more about these platforms in later chapters, of course - with a special focus on using VR through WebGL within *Chapter 12, Producing Virtual Reality Content for WebGL*!

Summary

With this chapter behind us, you should now have a good overall picture of just how vast and varied the supported native document types within Animate are, and this doesn't even begin to touch upon the array of export formats available! We had a look at some history behind the different major platforms Animate supports and then explored many of the considerations and practices around each specific document type involved in these overall target platforms. We will continue to build upon the foundational knowledge established here in later chapters.

In the next chapter, we'll jump directly into Animate to examine the interface and overall layout of the software, with a comprehensive look at how to customize the toolbar, timeline, workspaces, and overall preferences of the application.

3

Settling into the User Interface

In this chapter, we'll start by exploring Animate with an overview of the general workspace and explore how to get the most out of working with the software through customization. While Animate does come bundled with a number of workspaces targeting common workflows, it's also possible to create your own custom setup. You'll see how to choose which tools appear in the **Tools** panel and which ones are hidden away, in order to keep your go-to tools immediately present and accessible. We'll also look into customizing the timeline controls for more rapid animating and keyframe management. Finally, we'll have a look at the mechanisms that are in place for managing and preserving your finely tuned preferences. Animate boasts a very customizable experience across all aspects of the program!

After reading this chapter, you will be able to do the following:

- Achieve a working recognition of the general **user interface (UI)**.
- Understand how to manage and customize the workspace to your liking.
- Learn how to manipulate the available tools and timeline options.
- Gain the ability to manage, export, and import Animate preferences.

Technical Requirements

You will need the following software and hardware in order to complete this chapter:

- Adobe Animate 2022 (version 22.0 or above).

- Refer to the Animate system requirements page for hardware specifications: `https://helpx.adobe.com/animate/system-requirements.html`.

Exploring the Animate interface

While Adobe does perform an interface refresh every 5 years or so on most of its creative software, many of the various panels and tools within Animate should be easily recognizable to those who have only had experience with Adobe Flash Professional or even Macromedia Flash. Animate has long been admired for the general workflows within the application and it would be a shame to break a good experience!

> **Note**
>
> Of course, that is not to say that the Animate UI hasn't changed and improved over the years. In fact, the 2020 version of Animate saw a complete interface refresh that was tweaked and improved upon for Animate 2021 and somewhat for Animate 2022 as well.

We'll now look over some of the more persistent interface elements that are part of any Animate workspace, no matter what type of project you are working on.

Important User Interface Elements

While it is absolutely true that the Animate interface can be customized to create hundreds of variants depending upon specific user preferences and workflows, there are certain elements of the general interface that remain so important as to be included in just about any imaginable configuration.

We'll now take some time to identify and provide some helpful information regarding these primary elements.

The Document Panel

The largest visual portion of the Animate interface is the **Document** panel, which includes both the **Stage** and **Pasteboard**:

Figure 3.1 – Document panel with Stage and Pasteboard

Each document in Animate opens within the **Document** panel and multiple documents can be open simultaneously, through a system of tabs that display the document name above this panel.

Each document has both a **Stage** and a **Pasteboard** surrounding it. The **Stage** is effectively a viewable area through which any visual elements are displayed as you work on your project, and when published. This is the only portion that will be visible to the viewer once a document has been published or exported.

The **Pasteboard** is simply the area around the **Stage**. While objects on the **Pasteboard** are visible as you author your content, once published, viewers are not able to see anything on the **Pasteboard** unless these elements are animated across the **Stage**.

> **Tip**
> You can show or hide content on the **Pasteboard** when working in Animate
> by toggling the **Clip content outside the stage** button at the top right of the
> **Document** panel. It's just to the left of the document-level zoom percentage.

The Timeline Panel

Just as important as the **Document** panel is the **Timeline** panel, which contains your
layers, frames, keyframes, tweens, and a full set of tools to manage these items along with
project playback controls, as illustrated in the following screenshot:

Figure 3.2 – The Animate Timeline

The **Timeline** is where you control all of the layers within your project. They behave
similarly to other Adobe creative applications, such as Photoshop, in that the content of
layers at the top of the layer stack will obscure content within the layers beneath. Layers
can be created and managed from tools within this panel.

Each **layer** has a number of frames that span the timeline. These **frames** can be basic frames
to extend the content of that layer across time, **keyframes**, which designate some sort of
change in properties, and various types of **tweens** to create motion across these frames.

Finally, we have a set of frame management, tween creation, and playback tools available
here as well. We'll see later on in this chapter how to customize these tools.

The Tools Panel

When it comes to asset creation and manipulation within Animate, the **Tools** panel
contains a set of varied selection, drawing, manipulation, and specialized creative tools for
you to choose from, as illustrated in the following screenshot:

Figure 3.3 – The Tools panel

By default, certain tools are exposed, and certain others are hidden, requiring you to edit your **Tools** panel. Other tools are grouped among one another, requiring a long press to expose the full array. This can all be managed through the included customization dialog, which provides complete control over your entire set of tools.

The various tools are grouped into distinct sections, by default. There exists a visible separator between each section. It is also possible to widen the **Toolbar** so that there are multiple columns instead of just one as the default. Simply hover over the right edge and drag the **Toolbar** toward the **Stage** to widen it.

Selection tools include the **Selection, Subselection, Free Transform**, and **Lasso** tools:

- The following section includes various brush and shape tools, including the **Fluid Brush, Classic Brush, Eraser, Rectangle, Oval, PolyStar**, and **Line** tools.

- Next, we have a mix of variable tools, including the **Pen**, **Text**, **Paint Bucket**, **Ink Bottle**, and **Asset Warp** tools.

- Below that are the **Hand** and **Zoom** tools, which control the panning and zooming of your **Stage** within an open document.

The **Tools** panel also includes a set of **Fill** and **Stroke** selection tools, followed by an options area that can change to elevate certain tool properties, as illustrated in the following screenshot:

Figure 3.4 – Fill, stroke, and tool options shown with a wide Toolbar

This area is dependent upon the selected tool and changes depending upon which tool is currently chosen.

> **Note**
> Certain tools are only available with certain document types. For instance, the **3D Transform** tool is only available with ActionScript 3.0 document types and is not available with any other type. It will appear grayed out in other document types, letting you know that it is unable to be used.

We'll see how to customize the tools that are visible as part of the **Tools** panel later in this chapter.

The Properties Panel

The **Properties** panel is essentially an ever-changing hub through which you can adjust the various attributes of anything you could possibly want within your project:

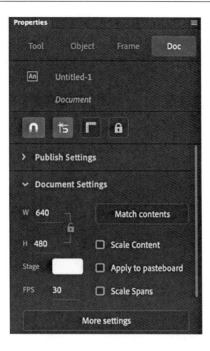

Figure 3.5 – The Properties panel

In older versions of Animate, it was a bit tricky to get to the set of properties you wanted at any given time, but no more! Now, a tabbed interface allows easy switching between the **Tool**, **Object**, **Frame**, and **Doc** (**Document**) properties, if available. Here's some further information about these properties:

- **Tool** properties include options for the currently selected tool in the **Tools** panel.

- **Object** properties appear once you've selected any object on the **Stage**. They often include properties for **position** and **scale**, but otherwise vary depending upon the type of object selected.

- **Frame** properties allow you to adjust both frame- and tween-specific attributes. These can include such things as binding a sound file to a frame span or modifying the specific easing options of a tween.

- Finally, **Document** properties involve everything to do with general document settings, including **width**, **height**, **background color**, and **frames-per-second** (**FPS**). This section will also include all your **Publish settings**.

The **Properties** panel cannot be customized much, though the content will constantly adapt to your current needs in light of the available options. One thing you can do is expand and collapse each properties section or even rearrange the section stacking order.

The Library and Assets Panels

Another set of important panels are the **Library** and **Assets** panels. Both of these panels are used to manage various objects within your Animate projects, but their purpose and use are entirely different.

While the **Library** panel has been around for quite some time, the **Assets** panel is entirely new:

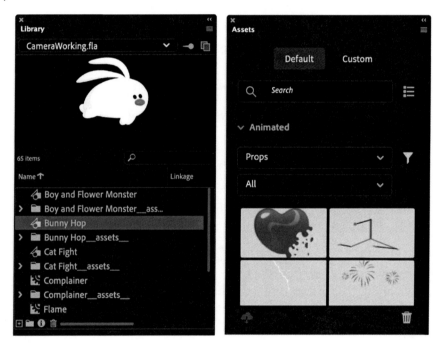

Figure 3.6 – The Library and Assets panels

The **Library** panel is used to manage bitmap images, audio files, symbols, and other complex object types within your Animate document. It is important to note that this panel represents the project library and that each Animate document has its own library distinct from other documents. Therefore, objects in the **Library** panel are only accessible for the document they are associated with.

The **Assets** panel, on the other hand, exists apart from any particular Animate document in particular. It contains a shared set of assets that can be accessed across any document that you might be using and is in no way tied to a project, but rather is bound to the Animate software itself. Once you select and make use of any objects available in the **Assets** panel, those objects will then appear within that document's **Library** panel as well.

We will now move on to exploring the Animate start settings and how to manage them after your first run.

Choosing Your Start Settings

Apart from the general, persistent interface settings and panels previously outlined, how the Adobe Animate interface appears for you will largely depend upon a single choice made when you first run the application from a fresh install. A dialog appears before anything else and asks a simple question, **New to Animate?**:

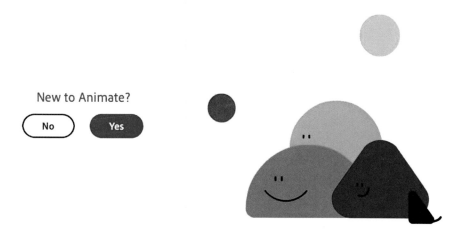

Figure 3.7 – The New to Animate? decision dialog

Answering **Yes** on this screen will create a default workspace within Animate that is simplified and caters to new users. Answering **No** will present a more traditional experience within the software.

You will either be taken to the **Basic** workspace with **Beginner Preferences** enabled or to the **Essentials** workspace with **Expert Preferences** enabled, as indicated in the following screenshot:

A "**Yes**" Choice   A "**No**" Choice

Figure 3.8 – The result of your choice

There are notable differences in the interface layout and preferences depending upon your choice. For instance, the **Basic** workspace includes far fewer panels and the overall UI elements are given a **Comfortable** appearance, where the various icons, panel sections, and other elements are given a bit more space between them all. In addition, the **Assets** panel is given prominent placement and the **Timeline** view is set to **Preview in Context**, displaying each frame as a visual preview.

The **Essentials** workspace includes many more panels; in fact, it includes an entire column of additional panels along the right-hand side of the interface. The **Properties** panel is given prominence here, and the **Assets** panel is hidden away. The UI elements are given a tighter, more **Compact** feel, with the icons and panel sections being given less space between them all. The **Timeline** view is also set to the much more traditional **Standard** setting, displaying keyframes rather than frame preview thumbnails.

Changing Your Start Settings

Okay—so, what if your choice of start settings was misguided, or you simply want to switch? Don't panic! It's not that difficult to switch between the results you've been given. Again, Animate is highly customizable.

The first course of action will be to change your preferences settings. From the application menu, choose **Animate | Preferences** on macOS and **Edit | Preferences** on Windows. This will reveal a submenu that includes the choices of **Beginner Preferences** or **Expert Preferences**. To follow along with this book and other references more closely, I suggest you switch to **Expert Preferences**:

Figure 3.9 – Switching preferences

Once you switch your preferences settings in this way, much of the Animate interface should conform to those settings and you are likely very close to getting Animate in proper shape. There are two additional items to check though, just to be sure.

The first additional item to check is your **Workspace** setting. In the upper right-hand area of the Animate interface is the **Workspace switcher**. The icon looks a bit like an application window:

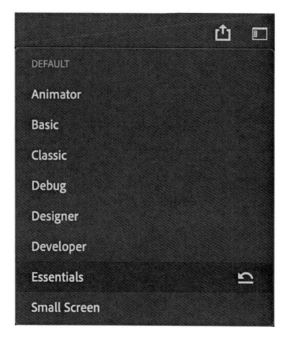

Figure 3.10 – Switching the workspace

Clicking on this icon reveals the available workspaces you can choose.

> **Tip**
> When working alongside this book, I recommend that you choose the
> **Essentials** workspace if it hasn't already been chosen.

The second additional item to look for is the **Timeline view** setting. In the upper right-hand corner of the **Timeline** panel is a small icon that looks like three lines stacked atop one another:

Figure 3.11 – Fixing the Timeline view

All panels in Animate include this icon, and clicking it reveals additional options for that specific panel along with a number of standard options, such as the ability to close the panel. You will want to make sure that **Standard** is chosen here, not **Preview** or **Preview in Context**. Additional options, such as a frame height of **Short**, **Medium**, or **Tall**, are left to your discretion.

In this section, we had an overview of the set of important, persistent panels in Animate and talked about their specific functions. We then went on to explain the Animate start settings and the differences between the choices you are presented with. We concluded with information regarding how to adjust these settings following your initial choice. Coming up, we'll examine ways in which you can switch workspace settings and even create and manage your own custom workspaces.

Managing Workspaces and Panels

As we've seen, the Animate interface consists of a series of panels, arranged in specific configurations. These configurations are called **Workspaces**, and you can easily switch between them by using the workspace switcher. You can even configure and save your own custom workspaces!

We'll now see how to access and switch between workspaces in Animate, and also how to build your own.

Using the Default Workspaces

Animate comes with a number of preconfigured workspaces to choose from. As we saw earlier, depending upon your initial choices when first running Animate with a fresh installation, you will either be using the **Essentials** or the **Basic** workspaces.

You will find these default workspaces and more by activating the workspace switcher in the upper right-hand corner of the interface. Again, the icon looks like a tiny application window.

You initially have a choice between eight different workspaces:

- **Animator**: Emphasizes the **Timeline** panel along with the **Library** panel.
- **Basic**: This is a minimal configuration intended for new users.
- **Classic**: Rearranges the panels so that the **Timeline** panel is above the **Stage**, in the manner of Macromedia Flash.
- **Debug**: A specific configuration used when debugging ActionScript code.
- **Designer**: Focused on an expanded **Tools** panel and various layout panels.
- **Developer**: For those who use the programming features of Animate.
- **Essentials**: This is what was once the default configuration for everyone and is quite balanced and accessible.
- **Small Screen**: Intended for those running Animate on low-resolution displays.

In addition to this set of initial workspaces, we can add as many custom workspace configurations as we want. Let's see how to do this next.

Customizing the Workspaces

You can customize any workspace to your exact specifications through two primary methods. The first is to add and remove panels entirely from the interface, and the second is to arrange, place, and group the visible panels in certain ways that are beneficial to your work.

Any open panels can be closed by clicking the **Close** button in the corner of floating panels (looks like a small **x**), or by clicking the panel options button and choosing **Close**.

To open panels that have been closed and add them to the interface, look at the application menu and choose **Window**, as shown in the following screenshot:

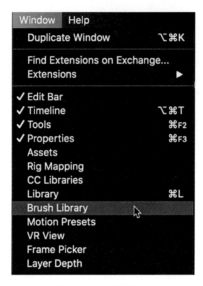

Figure 3.12 – Showing and hiding active panels

This action will display a list of all available panels, and clicking upon any panel without a checkmark next to it will open it up, adding it to the interface.

> **Tip**
> Choosing a panel from the **Window** menu with a checkmark next to it will actually close the panel, removing it from the existing interface configuration.

Once you have the panels that you want to include in your workspace open and available, you can then group them with other panels, move them to other areas of the interface, and even change their state from collapsed to fully open, floating, or docked—it's entirely up to you.

When open, each panel's contents are immediately accessible, but with a collapsed panel you must first click a panel icon to access the contents within, as indicated in the following screenshot:

Figure 3.13 – Expanded vs. Collapsed panel group

All panels can be docked and grouped in various ways:

- To dock panels to other areas of the interface, click and drag the panel name to tear off the panel (or simply reposition a floating panel) to another area until a blue line appears in order to dock the panel at that location when the mouse is released.

- To group panels together, click and drag the panel name to tear off the panel (or simply reposition a floating panel) to another panel or panel group until a blue outline appears in order to group the panels when the mouse is released.

- To collapse a panel or panel group into its icon state, click on the small double-arrow icon at the top right of that panel or panel group.

- To expand a collapsed panel or panel group, click on the small double-arrow icon at the top right of that panel or panel group.

- To temporarily show the contents of a collapsed panel or panel group, simply click on the icon.

How you manage the variety of panels in any workspace is completely up to you. Of course, when you find a configuration you like, you can go ahead and save it for later use.

Saving a Custom Workspace

Saving a custom panel configuration as your own custom workspace couldn't be simpler. Follow these steps to create your own reusable workspace:

1. After your customizations are complete, open the workspace switcher and note that there is a **New Workspace** section at the top of the overlay:

Figure 3.14 – Saving your custom workspace

2. Provide the new workspace with a meaningful name and click the **Save Workspace** button immediately to the right of the name input field.

3. The workspace is now saved! To verify this, open the workspace switcher once more and look at the very bottom of the overlay:

Figure 3.15 – Your saved custom workspace

Your saved workspace will appear under the **SAVED** section of the workspace switcher, and you can now freely switch between that and other workspaces as required.

Managing Workspaces

Depending upon whether you are using one of the default workspaces or one that you created yourself, the management options will differ. No matter which kind of workspace is currently in use, if you've made any changes to the layout of your panels, you will see a small button with an arched arrow pointing backward next to the workspace name.

If you click this button, it will reset both the default and custom workspaces to their original state:

Figure 3.16 – Resetting a workspace

A dialog will appear asking if you are sure that you'd like to reset the workspace. Click **Yes** to reset the workspace.

When it comes to custom workspaces, you also have an option to remove the workspace entirely through the **Delete Workspace** button, which appears as a little trash can icon alongside any custom workspace while that workspace is in use. This cannot be undone, so be certain that this is what you want!

To delete a custom workspace, click the trash can button that appears alongside the **Reset** button:

Figure 3.17 – Deleting a custom workspace

This will cause another confirmation dialog to appear, but this time it asks if you want to delete the custom workspace. Clicking **Yes** will make it so.

In this section, we explored the workspace switcher and saw how to create and manage our own custom workspaces. Coming up, we'll explore the new capabilities of both the **Tools** panel and the **Timeline** panel toolset and see how to customize each to our individual liking.

Customizing the Tools and Timeline Panels

Both the **Tools** and **Timeline** panel customizations are relatively new to Animate but are absolutely required, with more tools and features being added in these areas. You can now keep your most frequently used tools in both the **Tools** and **Timeline** panels ready for immediate access instead of being hidden or grouped beneath other tools. It's completely under your control!

Customizing the Tools Panel

As of the time of writing, the Animate **Tools** panel consists of 37 individual tools— a lot to fit on one tiny panel! As a result of this, older versions of Animate would have many of these tools grouped together, making them difficult to locate. In newer versions of Animate, we can now hide any tools that we do not often use and can make individual decisions regarding whether to group tools together:

1. To edit your **Tools** panel, look at the bottom area of the panel and locate the **Edit Toolbar...** button. It appears as a small set of three dots:

Figure 3.18 – Activating the tools editor

2. Clicking the **Edit Toolbar...** button will reveal the **Drag and drop tools** editor, allowing you to make changes to the tools available within the **Tools** panel, how they are grouped, their order, and where tool separations occur:

Figure 3.19 – The Drag and drop tools editor

3. To customize your tools, simply drag them from the editor to the **Tools** panel or from the **Tools** panel to the editor. You can change groupings, rearrange locations, and add or remove separators to cluster tools in the way that makes the most sense to you.

4. To close the editor when you are finished customizing your tools, hit the *Esc* key on your keyboard, or simply click anywhere outside of it.

> **Note**
> Certain tools will not be available for all target documents. Tools that are unavailable in the currently open document will appear disabled in the **Tools** panel and have a small, yellow warning indicator in the lower-left corner when viewing the **Drag and drop tools** editor.

If you want to create additional, smaller toolbars in your workspace, you can drag a separator from the **Tools** panel and that cluster of tools will now appear as a floating mini toolbar:

Figure 3.20 – Floating toolbar orientations

Hovering over the end of the toolbar will activate its rotation feature, allowing it to be presented either vertically or horizontally.

With these customization options available to us, we can craft the ideal **Tools** panel for our particular needs and preferences, or even create small toolbars for specific use cases.

Exploring the Timeline Tools

The **Timeline** panel also has a set of tools. These, however, relate directly to the function of the timeline itself and include tools for managing frames, keyframes, tweens, and viewing options, along with general playback and navigation controls:

Figure 3.21 – The Timeline tools

Just about all of these tools can be modified and removed through the use of the **Customize Timeline** editor.

Customizing the Timeline Tools

To customize the tools within the **Timeline** panel, you will need to access the Customize timeline editor:

1. In the **Timeline** panel, locate the panel options button in the upper-right corner (the three horizontal lines). Clicking this will expose the available options for this panel:

Figure 3.22 – The Customize Timeline Tools option

2. With the options menu exposed, locate and choose the option labeled **Customize Timeline Tools**. This will open the **Customize timeline** editor.

3. Now that the editor is open, you have a number of different actions you can take in order to customize which tools appear in the **Timeline** panel and even how they appear:

Figure 3.23 – The Customize timeline editor

By default, frame and tween options are grouped together within an **Insert Frames** group and an **Insert Tweens** group. When customizing the tools here, you can separate these groups out into individual buttons and include only those you specifically need. You can also disable any other controls that you do not normally use as well or add in extra controls such as the **Remove Frames** button, which is not regularly part of the **Timeline** tools.

Clicking each tool or tool group will cause the **Timeline** tools to adapt to your choices. Click away from the editor or hit the *Esc* key to dismiss the editor. Clicking the **Reset** button in the upper-right corner of the editor will reset the **Timeline** tools to their default configuration.

> Tip
>
> From this same panel options menu that we accessed during the last task, you can also choose to place the **Timeline** tools along the top or bottom of the **Timeline** panel by selecting the appropriate option.

In this section, we explored the **Tools** panel and the **Timeline** panel, seeing how to customize and manage the tools across both. Coming up, we'll have a look at how to manage our Animate preferences, explore keyboard shortcuts, and see how to export and save our individual preference settings through the use of an **Animate preferences** file.

Managing Animate Preferences

The preferences in Animate range from general settings, to how your code appears, to various drawing and text options. All of this is under your control through the **Preferences** dialog.

Customizing Preferences

To access the Animate **Preferences** dialog, go to the application menu and choose one of the following options:

- **Animate | Preferences | Edit Preferences…** on macOS
- **Edit | Preferences | Edit Preferences…** on Windows:

Figure 3.24 – Accessing Animate preferences

You'll be taken to the **Preferences** dialog and be able to customize your preferences according to the category:

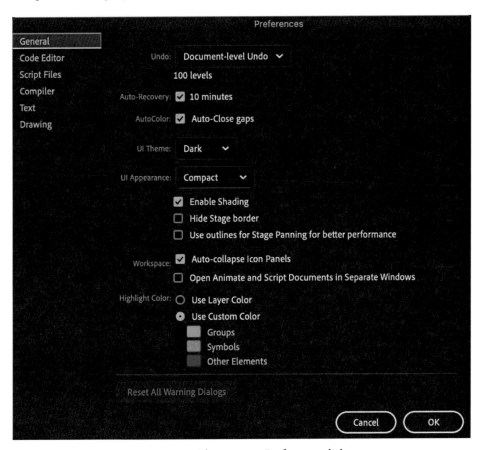

Figure 3.25 – The Animate Preferences dialog

The various tabs along the side allow you to customize preferences for all sorts of things across the application:

- **General**: This is the most important area. Here, you can adjust the Animate user interface from dark to light and hide or show the **Stage** border, in addition to many other common settings.

- **Code Editor**: This area controls preferences for the **Actions** panel and coding preferences, including font family and font size.

- **Script Files**: You will likely not need to modify this. It is minimal and mostly has to do with the encoding of code files.

- **Compiler**: Again, no longer very important and you can likely leave this be. It has more to do with the **Flex software development kit (SDK)** and settings pertaining to that.

- **Text**: If you want to change the general font options, this is where you can do so.

- **Drawing**: This is actually more useful than most other tabs for most Animate users. It has to do with how vector paths are established while being drawn.

Clicking **OK** will commit your choices.

Keyboard Shortcuts

Keyboard shortcuts are a more advanced way of interacting with any software in a manner that is often much quicker than using a mouse or stylus. Many long-time Animate users use these shortcuts to perform common tasks, such as inserting keyframes or converting objects to symbols. You also have access to more common shortcuts, such as copy or paste.

Of course, you can also customize your keyboard shortcuts! To display the **Keyboard Shortcuts** dialog, choose one of the following options:

- **Animate | Keyboard Shortcuts…** on macOS
- **Edit | Keyboard Shortcuts…** on Windows:

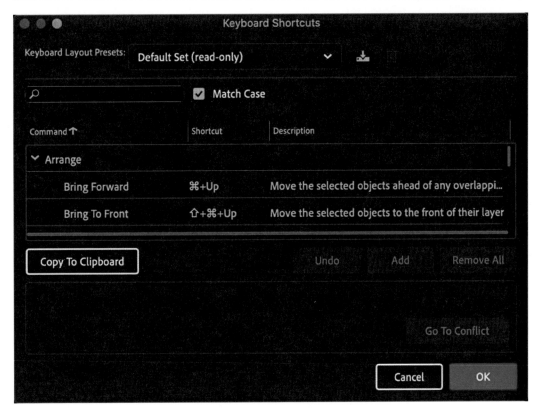

Figure 3.26 – Managing keyboard shortcuts

You can customize or add as many shortcuts as you like through this dialog. In fact, not every function in Animate has a keyboard shortcut attributed to it, so if you have a workflow you'd like to speed up, adding a custom keyboard shortcut is a great way to accomplish this.

> **Tip**
> I would recommend keeping commonly used shortcuts in place and not changing them since many tutorials and guides will reference the default shortcuts. If an action does not have a shortcut assigned, however… it is fair game.

Managing Your Preferences

In more recent versions of Animate, you can export and import your preferences. This exported package can optionally include your custom workspaces and keyboard shortcuts.

To export your preferences, go to the application menu and choose one of the following options:

- **Animate | Preferences | Export Preferences...** on macOS
- **Edit | Preferences | Export Preferences...** on Windows:

Figure 3.27 – Export preferences

The **Export Preference** dialog will allow you to choose what you would like bundled into the export file, including **Workspace**, **Keyboard Shortcuts**, and **Application Settings**. You can even choose specific workspaces and shortcut definitions to include if you do not want to package them all.

Clicking on the **Export** button will prompt you for a filename and location to save your preferences:

Figure 3.28 – Preferences are stored within an Animate Preferences (.anp) file

The resulting file is of the .anp type – an **Animate Preferences** file. You can use this file as a backup or for distribution to others.

To import a .anp file, open the **Preferences** menu once more and this time choose **Import Preferences...** from the submenu. You can browse for a .anp file and even choose which aspects of it to import, as indicated in the following screenshot:

Figure 3.29 – The Import Preference dialog

Clicking **Import** will result in your choices being imported from the chosen .anp file.

> **Note**
>
> A .anp file is also necessary when creating an **In-App Tutorial** for Animate. Now you know how to generate one! We'll see how to create such a tutorial in *Chapter 14, Extending Adobe Animate*.

In this section, we looked at Animate preferences and discovered how to manage these preferences alongside keyboard shortcuts, as well as how to export these same preferences for backup or distribution.

Summary

With this chapter concluded, you should now have a good general understanding of the Animate interface and which portions of that interface are most essential to working with the software. We also took some time to understand how to customize the workspace itself, along with the various tools and timeline controls that are available. Finally, we had a look at the various preferences available to us and how to preserve them for later use.

In the next chapter, we'll explore the various methods of getting content out of Animate to be used across different platforms through both the publish and export processes.

4
Publishing and Exporting Creative Content

In the previous chapter, we had a look at some of the more important features of the overall Adobe Animate **user interface** (**UI**). We'll now look specifically at creating content within Animate in a form that can be accessed or reused in additional ways. We will explain the differences between publishing to a specific target platform and exporting to various file types, and we'll see why you'd want to choose one workflow over the other in certain cases. We'll also have a look at the new **Assets** panel and how to package assets for distribution and reuse through this mechanism. To close off the chapter, we'll examine the quick share and publish workflow.

After reading this chapter, you'll come away with the following skills:

- Understand the differences between publishing and exporting content from your projects.

- Gain awareness as to which platforms you should target for various use cases and the differences in publish settings between them.

- Understand the options available through various export formats and settings.

- Become familiar with the **Assets** panel and mechanisms for sharing assets with others using this workflow.

- Utilize the quick share and publish workflow to get your content out into the world.

Technical Requirements

You will need the following software and hardware to complete this chapter:

- **Adobe Animate 2022** (version 22.0 or above).

- Refer to the Adobe *Animate system requirements* page for hardware specifications: https://helpx.adobe.com/animate/system-requirements.html.

Publishing versus Exporting

In this section, we are going to compare what it means to *publish* a document versus what it means to *export* a document. When dealing with any Animate document, there are going to be a number of choices you can make depending on what type of files you want to generate from your project.

Let's consider what it means to *publish* your document first. Often, new users to Animate think that by choosing a certain document type, this choice will lock them into producing only a specific type of content. This is actually only the case when considering the publish workflow.

Every document in Animate publishes to a specific target platform, such as the following:

- **ActionScript 3.0** publishes to **SWF** for playback using **Adobe Flash Player**.

- **HTML5 Canvas** publishes to **HTML** and **JavaScript** for the native web.

- **WebGL glTF (Standard)** publishes a set of files that can be played back in any standard **glTF** player.

However, we are not restricted to the publishing format as the only way of generating content from Animate.

We'll now consider what it means to *export* your content. Consider an ActionScript 3.0 document. Yes, it publishes for Flash Player, and that may initially seem useless. If you consider the choices for exporting in place of publishing, though, the possibilities really open up. For example, you can export the following from a single ActionScript 3.0 project:

- **HD video** files in just about any format you wish

- Animated **GIF** files

- Still images and image sequences in the form of **PNG**, **JPG**, and even **SVG**

- **SWF** files, to be imported into other applications that read the format, such as **Adobe After Effects**

- **Sprite sheets** and **texture atlases**

Exporting your content allows you all the power and flexibility of your chosen document type without being locked into a specific platform!

In addition, the publish workflow will allow the generation of even more asset types, such as **SWC** files, **Projector** files, **SWF Archive** files, **OAM** bundles, and more! All of this, from a simple ActionScript 3.0 document! It is vitally important to understand both the publish and export workflows for every document type.

In this chapter, we'll be working with a simple set of example project files that engage various major document types available to Animate. You can find them as part of this book's chapter files available at `https://github.com/PacktPublishing/Adobe-Animate-2022-for-Creative-Professionals-Second-Edition`.

Locate the file named `ActionScript3.fla` and open it to view the project:

Figure 4.1 – A simple Animate project

It is a simple animation displaying the Adobe Animate logo scaling up across a color-shifting background. Of course, you can design your own projects as well if you would prefer to use your own creations.

We'll next learn specifically about the publish and export workflows and how they differ from one another.

Publishing your Projects

The full **Publish Settings** dialog can be accessed with two different methods. In the **Properties** panel, when working with the **Doc** tab selected, you will find a **Publish Settings** section, and here, clicking the **More settings** button will open the dialog:

Figure 4.2 – Document Publish Settings dialog

You can also open the **Publish Settings** dialog by choosing **File | Publish Settings…** from the application menu.

The **Publish Settings** dialog itself will differ in its appearance and available options depending on the document type you are working with. In the following figure, you can see the vast differences between this dialog when working with an ActionScript 3.0 document versus working with a document targeting HTML5 Canvas:

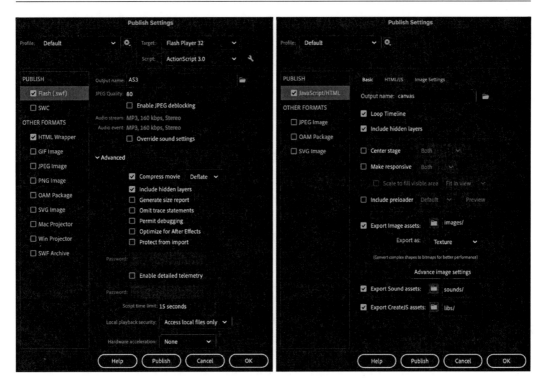

Figure 4.3 – Variations in the Publish Settings dialog by document type

In either case, the dialog will appear. From within this dialog, you can tweak a great variety of settings that determine how your project will publish. We'll learn more about these platform-specific settings later in this chapter. Clicking the **Publish** button from within the dialog will publish your project in accordance with these settings. The folder that your project is published to can be set within **Publish Settings** and will default to publish in the same location as the document (`.fla`) itself.

> **Tip**
> You can also publish directly, bypassing the **Publish Settings** dialog altogether, by choosing **File** | **Publish** from the application menu.

In addition to the publish workflow, we can also choose to export our content to a variety of different formats. We'll have a look at this next.

Exporting your Content

While *publishing* your content is intrinsically bound to your chosen document type, *exporting* content is completely different. These differences are not well understood by many Animate users and the differences are often overlooked.

There are actually a number of places in Animate through which you can invoke various export options. We'll cover them all in this chapter, but the most direct way to export content is from the Animate application menu.

Go to the application menu and choose **File | Export** – a submenu will appear, containing a variety of export options:

Figure 4.4 – Document export options

These export options are available to us regardless of the document type. They are not bound in any way to the publish options or restrictions inherent to a certain platform:

- **Export Image…**: This brings up a dialog with many different options for exporting PNG, JPG, and GIF file types to export a single image file based on the current **playhead** position in the **timeline**.

- **Export Image (Legacy)…**: This is an older – and much simpler – image export mechanism. You have minimal options when exporting to various image formats, but this dialog allows SVG export, as well as PNG, JPG, and GIF.

- **Export Movie…**: Using this option, you can export full image sequences (PNG, JPG, GIF, or SVG) that can then be brought into other applications. It will export one still image in the sequence for every frame in the document Timeline and number them accordingly. You can also export an SWF directly from this dialog, even when not using an ActionScript 3.0 document type!

- **Export Video/Media…**: This option will render your project into any video format supported by **Adobe Media Encoder**. We'll look at this option more closely in a bit.

- **Export Animated GIF…**: This option will open the same dialog as the **Export Image…** option; however, the settings will all be configured to produce an animated GIF file and not a still image.

- **Export Scene as asset**: This option allows you to export your entire project scene as an Animate **asset** (.ana) file for backup or distribution to others. A .ana file can be imported into the **Assets** panel and used across projects in Animate.

We'll explore many of these options in the latter part of this chapter.

In this section, we gave an overview of what it means to *publish* from Animate compared to what it means to *export* content from Animate. Coming up, we'll look specifically at the publish workflow and how the settings differ across the target platforms specified by the Animate document type.

Differences between Document Types when Publishing

In *Chapter 2, Exploring Platform-Specific Considerations*, we had a look at the variety of platforms that are tied to each document type in Animate. We'll now build upon that introduction to explore the various **publish settings** for these document types. The settings available for each document type vary quite a bit, with the ActionScript-based documents having the most settings due to their longevity and the beta documents having the least for the same reason.

We'll now look at the various native document types within Animate, focusing on particular associated settings when publishing your content.

Publishing ActionScript 3.0 Documents

By default, ActionScript 3.0 documents will publish both a .swf file and a .html file to act as a container document. Of course, due to Flash Player being completely banned from web browsers, this isn't all that useful!

With the **Publish Settings** dialog open, you'll immediately be struck with just how many settings there are for this publish workflow. You can view these settings in the following screenshot:

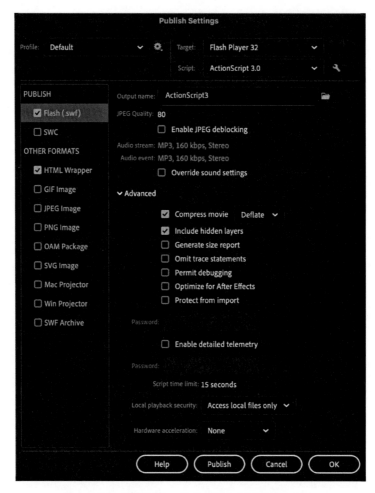

Figure 4.5 – Publishing ActionScript 3.0 documents

Along the side are the **PUBLISH** settings, for publishing your Flash content along with SWC, and also the **OTHER FORMATS**.

> **Note**
>
> **Shockwave Component (SWC)** is a format that was popular during the heyday of Flash Player, as it could be used to bundle assets and code together in a way that more code-based applications (such as **Flex Builder**) could interpret and make use of. It isn't so useful anymore.

These **OTHER FORMATS** include the aforementioned HTML wrapper, along with a number of image export types. There are two formats here that are especially noteworthy: Projector and SWF Archive.

Projector files can be published for either **macOS** or **Windows** and are basically a compiled executable program that contains your project alongside a special version of Flash Player that can be used to run your content on the desktop. The neat thing about this format is that there is no need to perform any sort of installation – it just runs!

SWF Archive is a mechanism that renders each individual layer of your project as a separate .swf file, then bundles the entire set as a .zip archive. This is a good mechanism for getting your project into additional applications such as After Effects for per-layer compositing workflows.

> **Tip**
> You can also import an entire .fla file directly into After Effects to achieve the same result. A new composition will be created with each layer from Animate translated to a layer in After Effects.

These are the overall settings to keep in mind when publishing ActionScript 3.0 document types. Let's turn our attention to HTML5 Canvas documents next.

Publishing HTML5 Canvas Documents

While HTML5 Canvas is a much more recent document type than ActionScript 3.0, it includes an impressive amount of publish settings due to its importance within the Animate software, especially since a .swf file can no longer be used within web browsers. Since HTML5 Canvas is a completely native web technology, it can step in and take over for Flash Player in many circumstances.

Just as with ActionScript 3.0, you'll find a variety of choices along the left-hand side of the **Publish Settings** dialog under **PUBLISH** and **OTHER FORMATS**. **PUBLISH**, in this case, includes only a single target – **JavaScript/HTML**. Here, you will find all the major publish settings for HTML5 Canvas documents.

These **JavaScript/HTML** settings are divided into three tabs, the first of which is the **Basic** tab:

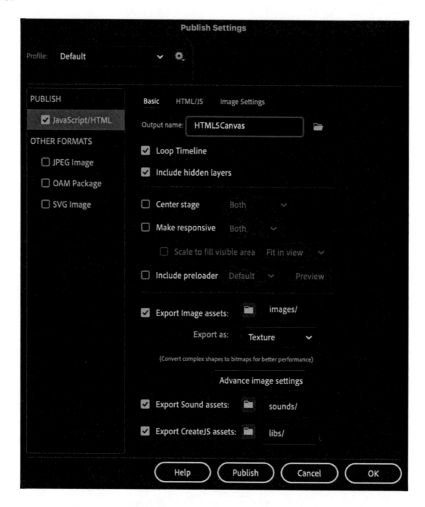

Figure 4.6 – Publishing HTML5 Canvas, Basic tab settings

Here, we find the most general settings to do with publishing HTML5 Canvas documents. Notable settings include the following:

- **Output name**: This is where you can name your published files and specify an output folder through the file browser.

- **Loop Timeline**: Checking this box allows the timeline playback to loop continually. Uncheck this box to have the playhead stop once playback ends.

- **Include hidden layers**: This determines whether to publish layers that have been hidden in the timeline or not.

- **Center stage**: By default, the published content appears in the upper left of the browser viewport. You can override this presentation and center your published content horizontally, vertically, or both.

- **Make responsive**: Enabling this option will scale your content down if it doesn't completely fit within the containing element. Additionally, you can also allow it to scale up to fill the containing element.

- **Include preloader**: Choose an animated GIF to serve as a preloading animation if your published file size is very heavy. You can, of course, create this animated GIF using Animate!

- **Asset locations**: Here is where you name each of the subfolders to which Animate will publish any audio files and the local **CreateJS** library files.

The second tab is centered around more advanced settings around how HTML and JavaScript are handled as part of the publish process:

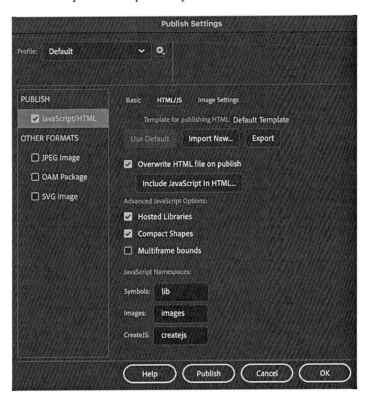

Figure 4.7 – Publishing HTML5 Canvas HTML/JS tab settings

The **HTML/JS** tab includes a number of more advanced settings when considering how your content is published. Settings of the greatest importance in this area include the following:

- **HTML template**: There is a default HTML template that includes a number of tokens to represent properties such as stage color, width, height, and so on. You can export this template, modify it to include additional elements, or perform more advanced actions through the code present in the template, and bring it back into Animate so that it is used when publishing your content. This is often used when creating digital ads that require specific structures and attributes. A small example of how these tokens appear in a `.html` file is shown here:

```
<canvas id="$CANVAS_ID" width="$WT" height="$HT"
style="position: absolute; display: $CANVAS_DISP;
background-color:$BG;"></canvas>
```

- **Overwrite HTML file on publish**: By default, Animate will overwrite the generated `.html` file each time you publish. Unchecking this option allows you to manipulate the `.html` that is exported without worrying that it will be overwritten with subsequent publish activity.

- **JavaScript inclusion**: Here, you can choose to include your JavaScript directly within the published `.html` file instead of in a separate `.js` file.

- **Hosted Libraries**: This checkbox determines whether the CreateJS JavaScript libraries are hosted on CreateJS servers or outputted to local files.

- **Compact Shapes**: This option will attempt to optimize shape data on publishing.

- **Mutiframe bounds**: When obtaining measurements and calculations against the width and height of certain objects, you must include data for multiframe bounds. This is especially useful for game development.

- **JavaScript Namespaces**: There are default namespaces already applied here to avoid code collision, but you can redefine these namespaces here if you need to.

The third and final tab (**Image Settings**) has to do entirely with how images are published as part of the HTML5 Canvas publish pipeline:

Figure 4.8 – Publishing HTML5 Canvas Image tab settings

These settings determine the handling of image files, including how they are exported, which image file type to use (along with specific encoding settings), and which portions of your content to render as part of this output:

- **Image export folder**: Similar to the audio folder location setting in the **Basic** tab, this allows you to determine the folder where published image files are located.

- **Export as**: You can choose from **Texture**, **Spritesheet**, or **Image Assets** from the dropdown. Your choice will determine which setting regarding image data can be further specified:

- **Texture**: This will convert all of your shape assets into bitmap textures for better performance. When this option is selected, you will be able to choose the image quality, resolution, and maximum size. These options determine how the image is encoded. You can even specify which symbols to include in this process.

- **Spritesheet**: This will combine all bitmap images into a sprite sheet, the settings of which you can define once selected. These settings include the file format itself and any associated settings such as quality, maximum size, and even the background color.

- **Image Assets**: This will simply publish all assets individually, with the choice to have Animate optimize image dimensions or not.

When publishing HTML5 Canvas documents it is obvious with so many settings available that this is considered one of the major publish options as part of Adobe Animate.

Publishing AIR Document Types

Whether dealing with AIR for desktop, AIR for iOS, or AIR for Android, there are a great number of publish settings to consider, and they differ a bit between each target platform. Additionally, whenever you're exploring the publish settings for any AIR document, you'll actually have two sets of publish settings to deal with.

The first group of settings is accessed and handled in exactly the same way as with an ActionScript 3.0 document:

Figure 4.9 – Publishing AIR

There are only two differences here as opposed to an ActionScript 3.0 document. The first is that your only options under **PUBLISH** are **Flash (.swf)** and **SWC**. This is due to the fact that AIR requires an SWF file to be generated first, in order to compile and package the AIR bundle. The second difference is that we are targeting AIR and not Flash Player, which leads directly into the second group of settings in a completely different dialog.

The second and perhaps most important group of AIR settings is accessed by clicking the small wrench icon directly to the right of the **Target** dropdown in the **Publish Settings** dialog. This reveals the **AIR Settings** dialog with an additional set of settings specific to your AIR project:

Figure 4.10 – AIR Settings

There are a lot of settings here, and they are grouped within the following tabs:

- **General**: These settings determine things such as what type of bundle is produced upon publication, the name and ID of the app produced, and various settings around window styles, profiles, and extra files you can define and package within the application.

- **Signature**: This includes settings around your code-signing certificates. The requirements for this vary by the target platform.

- **Icons**: This is where you define the application icons that show up once the app has been installed. The icon requirements vary by platform.

- **Advanced**: Here, you can define a varied set of options, which include file associations, initial window settings, the installation location, and more.

- **Languages**: The various languages your app can support are defined here.

We will have a deeper look at other aspects of the AIR settings when we build a small application in *Chapter 13, Building Apps for Desktop and Mobile*.

With the AIR settings out of the way, we'll finally have a peek at the various settings available in the WebGL glTF and **Virtual Reality** (**VR**) document types.

Publishing Beta Document Types

Since the various beta document types are still under development, these settings could change rather quickly. At this time, though, they are all nearly identical.

Choosing **Publish Settings** for the VR document types reveals a **Publish Settings** dialog similar to what we've seen for other platforms, while the **WebGL glTF** settings dialog appears a bit differently, as shown in the following figure:

Virtual Reality (VR)   **WebGL glTF**

Figure 4.11 – Publishing beta VR and WebGL glTF documents

Regardless of which document type you are working with, all four employ WebGL within the HTML `<canvas>` element and so they all have the same settings, aside from differences in the appearance of the dialog itself.

The particular settings are as follows:

- **Output name**: This is where you can name your published files and specify an output folder through the file browser.

- **Loop timeline**: Checking this box allows the timeline playback to loop continually. Uncheck this box to have the playhead stop once playback ends.

- **Include hidden layers**: Determines whether to publish layers that have been hidden in the timeline or not.

- **Use JavaScript hosted libraries**: This checkbox determines whether the JavaScript engine that makes these beta document types possible is hosted on Adobe's servers or whether they are output to local files.

Again, these settings are quite minimal when compared to ActionScript 3.0, HTML5 Canvas, or AIR, but that is to be expected with a set of new document types still in development.

> **Note**
> Animate also has the capability to support third-party publish and export workflows through the use of extensions. We'll have a look at some of these possibilities in *Chapter 14, Extending Adobe Animate*.

In this section, we had a look at the **Publish Settings** dialog across the native document types that ship with Adobe Animate. Coming up, we'll see how to *export* our content, bypassing the *publish* mechanisms in various ways.

Options for Exporting your Content

While publishing is completely dependent upon the Animate document type that's been chosen for a project, exporting is completely free from such restraints and can be undertaken regardless of the document type and publish platform. For instance, whether you're using ActionScript 3.0 or HTML5 Canvas documents, you can always export to an image sequence, animated GIF file, or HD video file through Adobe Media Encoder.

Let's have a look at some of these export options and see how they differ from the more restricted publish workflows.

Exporting Video Files

If your project is non-interactive, a video file is often the best format for producing it in a distributable format. Video, of course, is an incredibly popular format for sharing creative content, and it can be generated from any document type, making it quite versatile.

From the application menu, choose **File | Export | Export Video/Media…**, and the **Export Media** dialog will appear, as shown in the following screenshot:

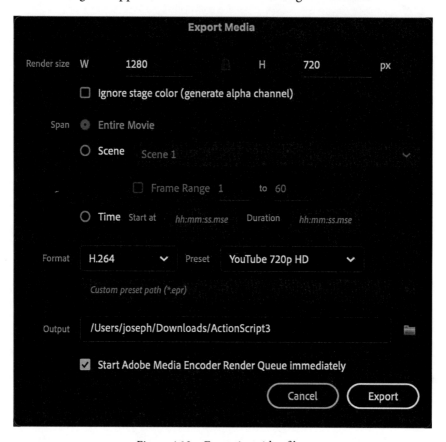

Figure 4.12 – Exporting video files

The **Export Media** dialog is dense with options. One of the nicer additions over the past few versions of Animate is the inclusion of the ability to define what portion of your timeline you'd like to render to video, in addition to being able to select the video format and preset directly within the dialog itself.

The options presented here include the following:

- **Render size**: This will default to the width and height defined in your document settings, but it can be increased or decreased here to modify the overall resolution of the output video.

- **Span**: Your entire project timeline will be used by default, but you can override this to only include certain scenes, frame ranges, or time selections.

- **Format/Preset**: These settings are drawn directly from Media Encoder and allow the selection of the video format and a format preset without even messing with Media Encoder directly.

- **Output**: This is where you can name your rendered video file and specify an output folder through the file browser.

You can also select whether you want to start the render queue immediately or not through a checkbox. Animate leverages Adobe Media Encoder to process video exports in a similar fashion to **Premiere Pro** and After Effects. Once you hit **Export**, Media Encoder will appear and process your video if that option has been selected, in accordance with the settings you have chosen. Media Encoder may take some time to open since it is a separate application from Animate – so be patient.

> Tip
>
> If the process doesn't kick off immediately after clicking **Export**, it may help to manually open Adobe Media Encoder first, then proceed to click **Export** after it is active.

Again, video is a tremendously popular option for producing content from Adobe Animate.

Exporting Animated GIFs

Perhaps just as popular as video among certain social networks and online platforms is the animated .gif file. The **Graphics Interchange Format** (**GIF**) file is one of the oldest available for internet playback and was supported in web browsers even before the existence of Flash Player. Traditionally, these files have been used as small, animated elements as part of a web page design, but in recent years, they've been used purely as content for use in social networks and online platforms.

From the application menu, choose **File | Export | Export Animated GIF...**, and the **Export Image** dialog will appear:

Figure 4.13 – Exporting animated GIF files

Unlike when exporting still images, this dialog will be tuned specifically for the export of animated `.gif` files. You will be presented with a preview of your resulting animation, underneath which are statistics such as file size and format properties. Along the opposite side are the settings you can tune to modify aspects of the resulting file.

> **Note**
>
> If you are using the stage background as a background color for your `.gif` image, it may appear incorrectly here. You can simply add in a background shape the same color as the background color of the stage to get around this anomaly.

The various settings are grouped into four categories:

- **Preset**: You'll want to leave the preset selection dropdown alone, but feel free to tweak other aspects of your GIF settings, including the number of colors and dither settings. To render the stage color as transparent pixels, enable the **Transparency** checkbox.

- **Image Size**: This allows you to adjust aspects of the width and height of your output. Depending upon the estimated file size, you may need to scale the resolution down somewhat.

- **Color Table**: A `.gif` file can have, at most, 256 colors. This table allows you to selectively add and remove colors.

- **Animation**: Here is something you'll want to check. You can set the output to loop forever or just once and stop. You also have access to a set of playback controls here to help preview the animation.

Clicking the **Preview…** button will generate a preview of your resulting GIF file and display it within a web browser.

Here is an example of what is shown during an animated GIF preview:

- **Format**: GIF

- **Dimensions**: 1280w x 720h

- **Size**: 392.7K

- **Settings**: Selective, 128 Colors, 100% Diffusion Dither, 60 frames, Transparency off, No Transparency Dither, Non-Interlaced, 0% Web Snap

Directly below that in the preview, you will find some example HTML tags that demonstrate how to incorporate the file into your documents:

```
<html>
<head>
<title>HTML5Canvas</title>
<meta http-equiv="Content-Type" content="text/html;
charset=iso-8859-1">
</head>
<body bgcolor="#FFFFFF" leftmargin="0" topmargin="0"
marginwidth="0" marginheight="0">
```

```
<img src="HTML5Canvas.gif" width="1280" height="720" alt="">
</body>
</html>
```

The entire preview process generates a single web view that includes an output of the image file encoding information, followed by an example of how to utilize the exported animated .gif file within a .html document. It couldn't get any easier.

> **Note**
>
> Be very careful to keep an eye on the file size of your exported .gif files. It is very easy to produce a GIF that is far larger than an equivalent video file!

To actually save your animated GIF, choose **Save**, and then you will be prompted for a name and location with which to save the exported file.

Now that we've covered the process required to generate an animated GIF file, let's have a look at additional image-based output choices.

Exporting Image File Sequences

Image file sequences are a series of .png, .jpg, or .svg files, which are generated frame by frame from your animation.

Choose **Export | Export Movie…** from the application menu and then choose an image sequence format and click **Save** to make an export dialog appear:

Figure 4.14 – Exporting image sequences

The dialog settings will vary depending upon the selected image sequence format.

> **Note**
>
> You can also export single image files instead of full sequences through the export menu by choosing **Export | Export Image…** or **Export | Export Image (Legacy)…** for .png, .jpg, .gif, or .svg file generation with the legacy choice. A single still image will be generated from the current playhead location on the timeline.

An image sequence is a useful way of getting your content into software that may not support formats such as SWF, as just about anything can handle a sequence of images. However, we can actually export a .swf file through this same export menu!

Export Options from the Library Panel

There is one more spot within Animate that allows the direct export of your content into a variety of formats, though this option works with individual assets and not the entire document.

If you open the **Library** panel and right-click on any symbol, a menu will appear:

Figure 4.15 – Exporting from the Library panel

This menu will include a set of additional export options that will export the selected object. You'll find a number of export options here that we've covered elsewhere, in addition to the additional options of exporting a symbol to a sprite sheet or texture atlas. Both of these options will open a dialog where you can tweak the settings to your needs.

In this section, we had a look at the variety of export options available across Animate document types. Coming up, we'll look specifically at how to export Animate content for use within Animate!

Sharing Content as Animate Asset Packages

A new method of getting content out of Animate is the ability to export Animate **asset** (.ana) files. These files can contain packaged objects, motions, bones, and audio for personal backup or distribution among other Animate users. This differs a bit from the other export options we've seen since the intended platform of use is Animate itself!

While Animate has had a **Library** panel for most of its existence, it is only used on a per-document basis to contain assets such as bitmap images, sound files, and internal symbols. Once that document is closed, you'd need to open it back up again to transfer any assets between documents for reuse.

> **Tip**
> If the **Assets** panel is not visible within your chosen workspace, you can enable it by selecting **Windows | Assets** from the application menu.

The new **Assets** panel works differently from the **Library** panel in that it contains a persistent set of assets that exist apart from any single document. When you first use the panel, it is prepopulated with a library of material from Adobe – but the real power of this panel comes into play once you create your own custom collection of assets and include them in the panel. Managing important assets in this way allows quick access to them – no matter what document you might be working in at any one time.

Assets are organized into main categories that include **Animated**, **Static**, and **Sound clips**:

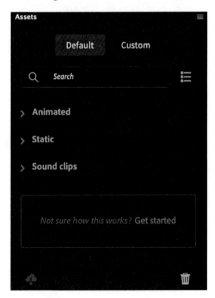

Figure 4.16 – The Assets panel

You can search the panel for keywords and tags or expand a number of subcategories to find what you need.

Upon the initial installation, Animate includes a small number of default assets within the **Assets** panel. Adobe makes additional assets available through a download mechanism located at the bottom of the panel. It appears as a small cloud with a downward-facing arrow. If additional assets are available for download, this icon becomes brightly colored and you can then click on it to download additional assets from Adobe's servers.

> **Note**
>
> You might expect an Animate authoring file to hold the `.ana` extension, however, the extension for an authoring file is actually `.fla`! The reason for this is due to Animate formerly being known as **Flash Professional**.

The most direct way of exporting Animate Asset files is from the **Library** panel:

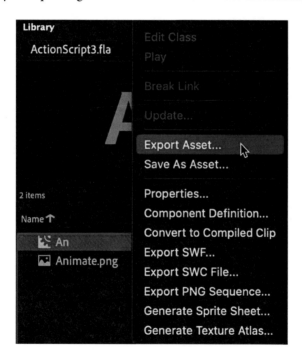

Figure 4.17 – Sharing a single asset

If you right-click on a symbol in the **Library** panel, you are given two menu options regarding asset files. Choosing **Export Asset…** will create a `.ana` file on your filesystem. Selecting **Save As Asset…** will not produce a `.ana` file but rather add the asset directly into your **Assets** panel without an intermediary import process.

Another mechanism for exporting assets can be found in the application menu by choosing **File | Export | Export Scene as asset**, as shown in the following screenshot:

Figure 4.18 – Sharing a scene as an asset

This option allows you to export a full scene from the main timeline as a single Animate asset. This method produces the exact same type of assets as the library method since the main timeline is basically a giant **Movie Clip** symbol anyway – it is only accessed differently.

When choosing to export an Animate asset file from either the Library panel or through the **File | Export | Export Scene as asset** menu, you are presented with the **Export Asset** dialog, as shown in the following screenshot:

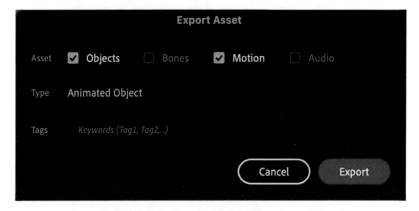

Figure 4.19 – Export Asset dialog options

From here, you can choose from the available assets to include in your file, depending on whether these types of assets exist in the selected symbol. A system of checkboxes allows you to include the following:

- **Objects**: Visual assets within your chosen symbol
- **Bones**: Any IK rigging you've designed within the symbol

- **Motion**: Any animation created with your provided assets
- **Audio**: Sound files that have been included in your symbol

You are also provided with the opportunity to tag the asset with keywords, which can then be searched through when using the **Assets** panel.

Once you click **Export**, your assets will be bundled into a .ana file on your local machine, ready to be imported or distributed:

Figure 4.20 – Animate asset file

There are a handful of uses for these Animate asset files. They can be preserved as a backup, distributed to other members of your team (or even strangers on the internet), or can be immediately imported back into Animate for use through the **Assets** panel:

1. To perform an import using a generated .ana file, open the **Assets** panel. If it isn't already open, you can access it from the application menu by choosing **Window | Assets**.

2. With the **Assets** panel open, look to the bottom left within the panel and click the **Import Assets** button (which looks like a big plus sign). Alternatively, open the panel options menu at the upper right and choose **Import** from the options that appear.

    You will then be taken to a file browser to locate your .ana file.

3. Select the file to include and click **Open** to complete the import process.

Once the .ana file has been imported, you can locate it within the **Custom** tab of the **Assets** panel:

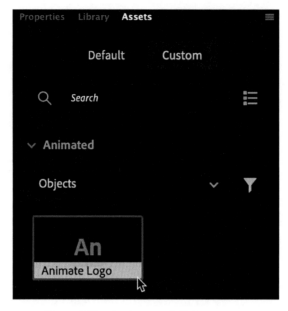

Figure 4.21 – An imported Animate asset

You can filter and search custom assets just as is possible with the default assets.

Tip

It is also possible to delete assets from the **Assets** panel that you no longer need. Right-click on the asset you want to remove and choose **Delete** from the right-click menu that appears. Note that you can also rename assets in this way!

In this section, we explored a new mechanism for exporting useful assets from Animate using the new Animate asset export and import features. Coming up, we'll look at how to quickly publish and export content using the **Quick Share and Publish** menu.

Social Share and Quick Publish

The **social share** and **quick publish** options allow us to produce content directly to some of the most common formats – regardless of the traditional differences between exporting and sharing your Animate content. Both are accessed from the **Quick Share and Publish** menu in the upper right of the Animate UI – left of both the workspace switcher and the **Play Movie** button:

Figure 4.22 – Quick Share and Publish appears as a box with an upward arrow emerging from it

When you click this button, you gain access to the **Social share** (**One click social media share**) and **Publish** (**Export in multiple formats**) options:

Figure 4.23 – Social share and Publish options

Choosing either option will open a secondary menu of choices. Let's take a look at these options.

Social Share

Choosing **Social share** will bring you to the next step in that process, which presents the choice of sharing directly to **Twitter** or **YouTube**, with more social channels coming soon:

Figure 4.24 – Social share options

Selecting either of these two options will necessitate an authentication task that allows Animate to publish directly to the selected platform on your behalf. You only need to provide permissions once for each social network.

Once authenticated, Animate generates the media in a format suitable for either channel and allows the inclusion of a small message (with hashtags, of course!) before posting. After the content is successfully posted to the chosen social channel, Animate lets you know through a small confirmation dialog – at that point, the media is live.

Quick Publish

Choosing **Publish** leads to some alternative choices that depend on your document target platform.

For instance, if you're using HTML5 Canvas, you'll get the option to publish an MP4 video file, an animated GIF file, or a set of files compatible with HTML/JavaScript:

Figure 4.25 – Quick Publish options for HTML5 Canvas

However, if working from an ActionScript 3.0 document type, you'll be presented with only options for video and animated GIF files – since a .swf file is no longer appropriate for public distribution.

Just as with the channel selection for social sharing, the quick publish options will likely change over time – especially as more targets are added to Animate.

In this section, we gave an overview of the **Quick Share** and **Publish** options that are available within Adobe Animate.

Summary

In this chapter, we explored a wide variety of *publish* options depending on the chosen document type, and also the *export* options available to us, regardless of document type and target platform. It is so important to understand the differences between these two ways of getting content outside of Animate!

When executing the publish workflow across different document types, we now have a better familiarity with the options available to each, and also how these settings can differ drastically between target platforms. Regarding export workflows, we've seen how varied these can be and the wide array of file formats that can be chosen – regardless of the initial document type. We also had a look at the various export options when generating Animate asset files, and we saw how to access and use the quick share features.

In the next chapter, we'll explore how to create and manipulate assets within Animate to design engaging animated content.

Section 2 – Animating with Diverse Techniques

With the foundational content out of the way, we will now begin to really explore some of the techniques used to animate content within the software. We'll start out fairly traditional but will soon move into more advanced topics, such as animating a figure with forward and inverse kinematics, animating with warped objects, the use of the camera to animate entire scenes, and how to enrich our animated camera movements with layer depth settings.

This section comprises the following chapters:

- *Chapter 5, Creating and Manipulating Media Content*
- *Chapter 6, Interactive Motion Graphics for the Web*
- *Chapter 7, Character Design through Layer Parenting*
- *Chapter 8, Animating Poses with IK Armatures*
- *Chapter 9, Manipulating Warped Objects through Advanced Rigging*
- *Chapter 10, Working with the Camera and Layer Depth*

5

Creating and Manipulating Media Content

In the previous chapter, we looked at the many ways of getting content outside of Animate for distribution or further work, but what about actually creating content?

This chapter covers many of the creative capabilities of the software, starting with a refresher regarding how to create shapes and add motion to them. We will follow up with the use of symbols and explore the various types of symbols available to us in Animate. We will learn why and when to use certain symbol types in different circumstances, and how to create motion with them. Importantly, we will explore the various easing profiles available within the software that allow us to refine our motion more naturally.

After reading this chapter, you'll be able to do the following in Animate:

- Design and animate vector content using shape tweens.
- Create symbols and animate them using classic tweens.
- Apply natural easing profiles to your animated content.
- Explore the properties of symbol instances and various applied tweens.

Technical Requirements

You will need the following software and hardware in order to complete this chapter:

- Adobe Animate 2022 (version 22.0 or above).

- Refer to the Animate system requirements page for hardware specifications: `https://helpx.adobe.com/animate/system-requirements.html`.

Working with Shapes

In this section, we are going to begin by looking at some of the shape creation tools within Animate and learn how to establish vector-based shape objects to apply motion to them in the upcoming sections.

While Animate can certainly make use of imported content, such as bitmap images, sound files, and other types of external media, the creation and manipulation of native vector shape objects is a workflow that Animate excels at. With a full range of tools that support the creation of vector shapes and a dedicated tweening engine to consider, there is no doubt that shapes are key to the Animate experience.

We'll now have a look at some of the important topics associated with the creation and manipulation of shapes within an Animate project. We'll examine the set of tools that allow us to create shape objects and learn how to set different tool property values that directly influence aspects of the resulting shapes.

Understanding the Shape Tools

There may be more shape tools than any other type of tool within the Animate toolbar. Since the software is used by artists and creators of all types, there has to be a set of tools for both freeform drawing and precise form generation.

You can view the full set of shape tools available in the following screenshot:

Figure 5.1 – Animate shape tools

These tools are arranged and listed in no particular order, and will differ depending on the current workspace that has been chosen:

- **Fluid Brush**: This is a GPU-accelerated brush that is built on the same technology as **Adobe Fresco** brushes. It allows you to draw smooth lines with a more fluid approach to painting and drawing. This brush produces a fill.

- **Classic Brush**: An older brush within Animate, this brush will produce a fill when used and contains a limited number of controls.

- **Paint Brush**: This tool produces strokes by default but can be toggled to produce fills instead. It works by mapping vector art across the paths that are generated.

- **Pencil**: Another older tool with a limited number of options, this one produces a stroke in the same way that Classic Brush produces a fill.

- **Rectangle**: This tool allows you to create rectangles and square shapes consisting of both fill and stroke.

- **Rectangle Primitive**: This works similarly to the Rectangle tool, with the distinction of being able to manipulate the corner radius following after creating the object.

- **Oval**: This tool allows you to create ovals and circular shapes consisting of both fill and stroke.

- **Oval Primitive**: This works similar to the Oval tool, with the distinction of being able to manipulate the start angle, end angle, and inner radius after creating the object.

- **PolyStar**: A unique tool that creates a polygonal or star shape where you can determine the number of sides or points accordingly. It creates a shape with both fill and stroke.

- **Line**: This draws a straight line consisting only of stroke.

- **Pen**: This tool works in a similar manner to the **Pen** tool in **Adobe Illustrator** or **Photoshop**. It allows the creation of custom shapes by using anchor points and their related curve handles. It creates a shape consisting of stroke alone, but that can be filled with the **Paint Bucket** tool if the path is closed properly.

Generally, some of these tools will be grouped, and some may not even be visible unless you specifically add them to the toolbar, depending on your chosen workspace.

> Tip
>
> Remember that you can edit the tools that appear in your toolbar or even create smaller tear-off toolbars. Have a look back at *Chapter 3, Settling into the User Interface*, for a refresher!

When a tool is selected, you will be able to adjust the properties of that tool from the **Properties** panel. It is a good idea to set tool properties before creating content with your chosen tool since often, there will be properties that cannot be easily changed with existing objects.

Just make sure to choose the **Tool** tab at the top of the **Properties** panel before you begin using any tool:

Figure 5.2 – Common Shape Tool properties

Shapes in Animate can consist of **Fill**, **Stroke**, or a combination of both. Some of the tools will have special options that you will find lower down within the **Properties** panel since the more common options are generally located toward the top. Once you've settled on a set of properties that make sense to your task, you can go ahead and start creating!

> **Note**
> Fill and stroke can be added or removed from any shape, so long as the requirements for each are met. Look at both the **Paint Bucket** and **Ink Bottle** tools to add each visual aspect to your shape.

In this section, we learned how to create shapes using a variety of shape tools available to us in the software. Next, we'll apply motion to these basic shapes by using shape tweens.

Creating a Shape for Animation

Before we perform any sort of animation, we'll need to create a visual shape to manipulate. Once this shape has been established, we'll perform a specific type of tween that only works with shapes. It will likely come as no surprise to anyone that this type of tween is called a **Shape Tween**.

> **Note**
>
> The term "tween" is shorthand for "in-between" and is a traditional animator's term, describing the frames that exist in-between the main "key" frames that are drawn by a senior animator. These would be filled in by less-skilled junior animators using the "key" frames as a guide. Tweens in Animate work in much the same way!

Let's now create a shape object to perform a bit of animation with:

1. First, create a new ActionScript 3.0 document and set the width to 1280 and the height to 720, with an **FPS** setting of 30. You can verify that you've done this correctly from the **Properties** panel, as shown in the following screenshot:

Figure 5.3 – Document Settings

2. Then, choose a tool to create your shape object with. I suggest keeping it simple for now and using the **Rectangle** tool.

3. Look at the **Tool** tab of the **Properties** panel, set the fill to a medium blue (#0066CC), and disable the stroke by selecting the swatch that looks like a white square with a red line passing from corner to corner:

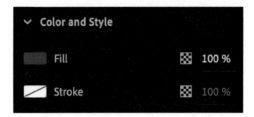

Figure 5.4 – The Rectangle tool's properties with stroke disabled

4. Click on the left-hand side of the **Stage** area, hold down the *Shift* key, and drag to create a square that measures about 200 pixels in both **Width** and **Height**.

5. Choose the **Selection** tool and select the object that was just created. Look at the **Object** tab in the **Properties** panel to ensure that your properties match what has been described. The **X** position value should be 220, while the **Y** position value should be 260:

Figure 5.5 – Our newly created square shape

We now have a simple blue square shape positioned on the stage. In the next task, we'll add motion to this shape through use keyframes and a Shape Tween.

Animating with Shape Tweens

We now have a shape on the **Stage** area, ready to animate. At the most basic level, animation is performed within the timeline through the use of keyframes. Keyframes hold data values for certain properties, such as position, scale, rotation, and opacity. Creating multiple keyframes across time gives the appearance of motion, even though nothing is moving, but your eyes are tricked into processing the change in data between frames as motion.

Traditionally, when using a shape tween or even a classic tween, you manually create keyframes before making a change to the object properties in the **Stage** area. This is normally done by selecting a frame you'd like to create a keyframe on and choosing to insert a new keyframe from the buttons above the timeline, the right-click menu, the application menu by selecting **Insert | Timeline | Keyframe**, or using the *F6* keyboard shortcut. You then select that keyframe and modify the properties of your object in the **Stage** area to create a change between the preceding keyframe and the one you just created.

There is also an **Auto KeyFrame** option that allows keyframes to be created automatically as you adjust object properties across the timeline.

The **Auto KeyFrame** option can be turned on and off as desired from the **Insert Frames Group** drop-down menu:

Figure 5.6 – Auto KeyFrame

When enabled, you get a small, circular indicator that appears above any selected frame. This indicates that a keyframe will be created there if any object properties are changed. For the next task, it doesn't matter whether the **Auto KeyFrame** option is enabled or not as we'll be creating keyframes manually.

Now, let's establish an additional keyframe, change certain properties of our shape in that keyframe, and apply a **Shape tween** to animate our object across the **Stage**:

1. Before doing anything else, we'll want to rename **Layer_1** to something more descriptive. Double-click on the layer's name and type in `Square` as a new layer name. It's important to stay organized!

Figure 5.7 – Renaming your layer

2. Now, click the rectangle beneath the **1s** mark at *frame 30* to select it. It will appear highlighted in blue:

Figure 5.8 – Selecting the 1s mark at frame 30

3. Click the **Insert Keyframe** button, or press *F6*, to insert a keyframe at *frame 30*. A duplicate keyframe will be created with the same properties as the previous keyframe at *frame 1*:

Figure 5.9 – Inserting a keyframe at frame 30

4. Using the **Selection** tool with the *Shift* key held down, move the square shape to the opposite side of the **Stage**. Holding *Shift* will constrain the movement along the *x* and *y* axes. The **X** position should now be 860, while the **Y** position should remain at 260.

5. The keyframes at *frame 1* and *frame 30* now have different position values. To create a **Shape Tween** to fill in the changes between these keyframes across time, click the **Create Shape Tween** button from the **Insert Tweens** group above the timeline, or choose **Insert | Create Shape Tween** from the application menu:

Figure 5.10 – Creating a shape tween between keyframes

The **Insert Shape Tween** option can be located within the **Insert Tweens** group.

6. A **Shape Tween** is established between the two keyframes and an arrow appears between them across the frame span. The frames that make up the **Shape Tween** take on an orange color. This indicates that the tween was created successfully. Go ahead and drag the blue playhead across the frame's span to preview the animation on the stage:

Figure 5.11 – Completed shape tween

The **Shape Tween** works by having Animate fill in the data values between each of the keyframes we have established, based on the properties that have been set at those keyframes. It does so in a completely linear way unless instructed otherwise.

> **Tip**
>
> If the arrow between keyframes appears as a broken or dashed line, this
> indicates a problem with the tween. Ensure that you have at least two keyframes
> and that both keyframes contain shape data and no other object types.

Test your movie by choosing **Control | Test Movie** or by clicking the **Test Movie** button in
the top-right corner of the Animate interface. The animation of our little square will play
back in a small window. Go ahead and close this window when you are finished.

We now know how to perform animation with a basic **Shape Tween** in our projects. Next,
we'll look more deeply into the properties of the tween that can be modified.

Exploring Shape Tween Properties

There are several additional properties of a **Shape Tween** that can be modified once it
has been created. To access these settings, select any frame or keyframe that is part of the
tween and look at the **Properties** panel. Ensure that the **Frame** tab is selected and look
toward the **Tweening** section of the panel:

Figure 5.12 – Shape tween properties

Within the **Tweening** section of the **Properties** panel, you will find the following settings:

- **Ease**: There are two easing choices here: **Properties together** and **Properties
  separately**. When using shape tweens, you can only choose **Properties together**.
  Other tween types are more flexible in this regard.

- **Effect**: This setting allows you to apply different easing effects to your tween. Unless you want completely linear movement, it is recommended that you apply some sort of ease to your tween; the difference is immense! You can apply **Ease Effect** presets or even edit your custom ease through these controls. If you're using a **Classic Ease**, you can tweak the intensity by changing its value from the default of 0.

- **Blend**: This setting determines how the tween frames are calculated by Animate. You have two choices here: **Distributive** or **Angular**.

Each individual **Shape Tween** can have its properties adjusted through this section of the **Properties** panel. You can also remove the tween entirely by clicking the **Remove Tween** button.

Here is an example of our square's movement with a linear, default effect applied to the motion, versus one of the many easing effects available to us:

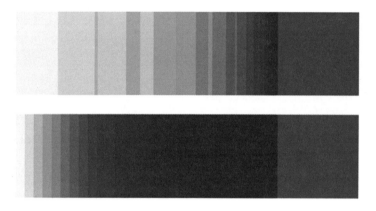

Figure 5.13 – Quint-Ease-Out versus Classic Ease

The bottom square has the default **Classic Ease** applied and moves across the stage at the same linear rate of speed for each of the 15 frames represented in the figure. The top square has a **Quint-Ease-Out** effect applied to it. Because of this, the rate of speed varies across different frames, starting slow and then speeding up.

It is important to know that both of these squares start and end in the same position on the stage and share the same first 15 frames of movement captured by this image. These effects can be used to establish much more natural, physical movements.

When tweening content, you don't have to start from scratch each time when needing to apply the same tween settings to multiple tweens. You can copy and paste tween settings from one tween to another – a huge timesaver!

With a tween selected in the timeline, look to the **Properties** panel for the **Frame** properties and locate the **Tweening** section once again:

Figure 5.14 – Copy and Paste Tween Settings

At the top right of that section is a small gear icon. Clicking it gives you access to additional tween options, which allow you to choose **Copy settings**, **Paste settings**, or even **Reset settings** for the selected tween. This is very convenient when you need the same or even similar settings across multiple tweens.

All right – that's all there is for tween properties. Next, we'll have a deeper look at keyframes and additional shape properties that can be modified over time using the tweening engine.

Manipulating Shape Properties across Tweens

When we established our **Shape Tween**, the only value that differed between each of our keyframes with the shape's **X** position, which is used to create movement from one side of the screen to the next. Using a **Shape Tween**, there are many additional properties that can be tweened!

Let's go ahead and modify the animation to incorporate some of these changes in properties:

1. First, we'll have the square change shape, along with the position. Move the playhead to frame 30 and select the square shape on the stage.

2. Hit the *Delete* key on your keyboard to remove it. Note that in the timeline, there is still a keyframe present, but it is an empty keyframe since there is no longer any content. The tween also appears broken, with a dashed line through it, for this same reason:

Figure 5.15 – The keyframe's contents removed

3. Now, select the **PolyStar** tool and use it to draw a star shape on the stage in roughly the same position that the square shape used to occupy. Set your **Tool** options in the **Properties** panel to use a star **Style** with 5 sides and a point size of 0.5 within the **Tool** tab. Note that we are still at frame 30 in the timeline:

Figure 5.16 – Drawing a five-pointed star

4. Let's have the square change color as it morphs into the star shape. With the star shape selected, change its fill color to a vivid violet (#9900FF).

5. We can even change the scale of our elements if desired by using the **Free Transform** tool. With this tool selected, clicking on the star shape will display a transform box around it, allowing us to scale from any corner, and also perform additional transforms and rotations. Remember to hold down the *Shift* key to constrain proportions as you scale. Note the small white circle in the center of the transform box. This is our **Transform Point**, and any rotation or scaling will be done relative to this point:

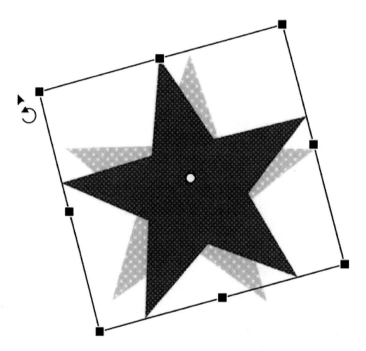

Figure 5.17 – Using the Free Transform tool to change scale and rotation

With these changes in place, either click the **Play** button at the top of the timeline or the **Test Movie** button in the top-right corner of the Animate interface. Whichever choice you've made, you will see how the animation is now very different, with all the various properties being tweened together between the two keyframes.

You may also note that as the square morphs into the star, it does so in a strange way. There are two things we can try to correct this: one is to switch the **Blend** setting in the *Tweening* section of the **Frame** properties between **Angular** and **Distributive**. This may help, but a surer solution is to employ **Shape Hints** to guide the tweening engine into morphing our content more reliably.

Let's now fix our shape morph by adding some **Shape Hints**:

1. Move the playhead back to frame 1. **Shape Hints** work across two keyframes and should be set at the initial frame of any tween.

2. Add a **Shape Hint** by choosing **Modify | Shape | Add Shape Hint** from the application menu. A small red circle with the letter **a** will be added to the center of the square at frame 1:

Figure 5.18 – A shape hint appears as a red circle

3. Move the **a** hint to the top center of the square. We will be placing each hint on the square where each point of the star would be if the two shapes were overlaid, one on top of the other. This will direct Animate to morph the shape in a more controlled manner.

4. Continue to add four additional **Shape Hints** and place them along the square in a sequence that represents our five-sided star:

Figure 5.19 – Shape hints properly positioned

5. Now, move the playhead to frame 30. We need to place our **Shape Hints** at the proper spots on this shape as well so that they correspond with their placement on the square. Notice that we do not have to add any **Shape Hints** at frame 30, as they carry over from frame 1 but are all grouped at the center of our star shape:

Figure 5.20 – The shape hints appear at the center

6. Move each of our **Shape Hints** to their corresponding places on the star shape. Note that they must be placed in the same order to be most effective and that once they are positioned correctly, their color will change from red to green:

Figure 5.21 – Properly positioned shape hints

7. Now, if you move the playhead back to frame 1, you will see that our **Shape Hints** on the square have also changed color, from red to yellow. This indicates that placement is complete on both keyframes:

Figure 5.22 – Verifying that the Shape Hints placement is correct

With that, we can once again preview the animation using the same mechanisms as before. The square will now morph into the star in a much less erratic way. **Shape Hints** are very powerful, but they can be easily broken as well. Always apply **Shape Hints** in an organized and structured way, as we've done here, to avoid any problems.

In this section, we had a comprehensive look at creating and animating shape objects within Animate. Next, we'll look beyond basic shapes and learn how to create and manipulate symbols.

Working with Symbols

As we saw in the previous section, **Shape Tweens** are only applicable to shape objects. They cannot be used on imported bitmap images, compound shape groups, or complex text objects. If you want to bring motion to these additional object types, you'll have to convert them into **symbols** and tween them using a **Classic Tween** or a **Motion Tween**.

We'll now have a look at some of the important topics having to do the various symbol types, including the differences between each type and methods for creating motion through the use of symbols.

Creating Symbols

A symbol in Animate is a special object that can be one of three types: **Movie Clip**, **Button**, or **Graphic**. Symbols exist within the **Library** panel project once created and are used by creating **instances**, which exist on the stage to be manipulated in various ways.

Symbols can be created through the **Library** panel by clicking the **New Symbol** button in the bottom-left corner of the **Library** panel or by choosing **Insert | New Symbol** from the application menu.

In either case, the **Create New Symbol** dialog will appear:

Figure 5.23 – The Create New Symbol dialog

Once you give the symbol a name and select its type, you will be placed directly within the symbol timeline to begin creating visual or motion content within the symbol, since a new symbol will be empty and void of content until you create it.

When you are taken inside a symbol timeline upon its creation, the user interface will reflect this in several ways:

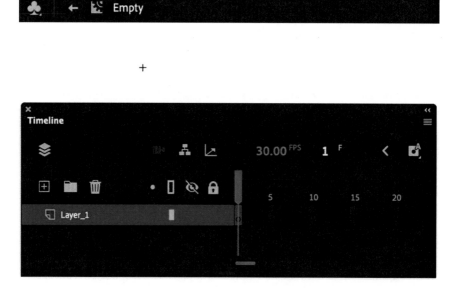

Figure 5.24 – An empty symbol timeline

Note in the previous screenshot how the symbol stage and timeline are empty. The only visible mark on the stage is a small + symbol, indicating the **registration point** of the empty symbol. We can tell we are within a symbol and no longer within the document root by viewing the **edit bar** above the stage. The symbol name appears with a small arrow pointing to the left. Clicking this arrow returns us to the project root outside the symbol.

> **Note**
> The Registration Point of a symbol determines a symbol instance's X/Y position coordinates, once placed on the Stage.

While creating symbols from nothing is definitely a useful workflow in certain circumstances, the more common way of creating symbols is done through a conversion process.

To convert existing content on your project stage into a symbol, you'll first need to select the content to convert:

1. I suggest drawing another square, similar to what we created in the previous section with the **Rectangle** tool.

2. Switch to the **Selection** tool and select the square shape that was just created.

3. With the shape selected, look at the **Object** tab in the **Properties** panel and locate the **Convert to symbol** button:

Figure 5.25 – The Convert to symbol button

4. Click the **Convert to symbol** button for the **Convert to Symbol** dialog to appear. You can also choose **Modify | Convert to Symbol...** from the application menu:

Figure 5.26 – The Convert to Symbol dialog

The **Convert to Symbol** dialog is very similar to the **Create New Symbol** dialog, but since it is converting existing content, it includes the additional option to set the registration point of the converted content. This can be set to the center, any corner, or any side, based on the content being converted.

There are a number of additional settings that are shared between the two dialogs:

- **Name**: This is an identifier that's given to a symbol to locate it within the **Library** panel. No spaces are allowed, and it must begin with a letter.

- **Type**: Choose **Movie Clip**, **Button**, or **Graphic**. You can switch type afterward if you make a mistake, and you can even change the instance behavior on the Stage to another type.

- **Folder**: This specifies the location of your symbol within the **Library** panel for organization purposes. Not specifying a folder will save your symbol to the **Library** root.

- **Advanced**: A set of options that vary according to the chosen symbol type. Most of the time, you can ignore these options as they largely have to do with ActionScript development.

If you would like to explore some of the options in the **Advanced** section of this panel, you will want to be using an ActionScript 3.0-based document type; otherwise, most will be entirely disabled. We'll explore these options in *Chapter 13, Building Apps for Desktop and Mobile*.

> **Note**
>
> If you ever want to adjust these settings, you can do so from the project's
> **Library** panel. Just right-click on a symbol and choose **Properties...** from the
> menu that appears.

Oftentimes, when working in Animate, you'll find yourself having created some engaging content in the main timeline that you then decide should have been created within a symbol instead. One way to turn existing content into a symbol is to create a new, empty symbol in the **Library** panel, then manually cut the layers you need as part of that symbol from the main timeline, and paste these layers into the empty symbol itself. As you might imagine, this can be a messy process that's prone to error. Thankfully, there is a simpler way.

We actually have the ability to select the layers we want to convert into a symbol by opening the right-click context menu from the selected layers and choosing the **Convert Layers to Symbol** option to simplify the entire process:

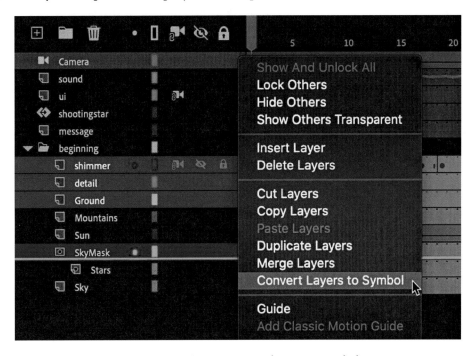

Figure 5.27 – Convert existing layers to a symbol

The **Convert Layers to Symbol** dialog will then appear – it looks exactly like the dialogs to both create an empty symbol or convert existing assets into a symbol, both of which we explored earlier:

Figure 5.28 – Convert Layers to Symbol Dialog

You can provide a symbol name, choose the symbol type, and even set the registration point for your new symbol, as previously detailed.

Once you hit **OK**, the selected layers will be automatically transferred to the symbol's internal timeline and the original layers will be replaced with a new layer containing an instance of the new symbol.

Similarly, you can perform the inverse action on an existing symbol instance. Simply right-click on an instance and choose **Break Apart Symbol to Layers** from the menu that appears:

Break Apart	⌘B
Break Apart Symbol to Layers	⇧⌘B
Distribute to Layers	⇧⌘D
Distribute to Keyframes	⇧⌘K

Figure 5.29 – Breaking Apart Symbol to Layers

New layers will be created, and the contents of the selected symbol will be placed in each layer, with all the properties intact.

Now that we understand how symbols are created, let's look more deeply into the three types of symbols that Animate supports.

Exploring Symbol Types

When we created our symbols, we took note that symbols had to be classified as one of three types: **Movie Clip**, **Button**, or **Graphic**. We'll now have a look at how each of these types differs from one another and when you would want to use one over another:

- **Movie Clip** symbols have internal timelines that are similar to the main timeline and run completely independent of it. This symbol type is ideal for small animations, such as flames, that should run continually in a loop. Even if an instance of this symbol is included in a single frame on the main timeline, its internal timeline will continue to animate, so long as the playhead is on that frame. When previewing your main timeline within Animate, any instance's internal timelines will not play back, and you must perform a test movie to see them in action. Instances of this symbol type can be made interactive, and their timeline can be controlled through code.

- **Button** symbols share some characteristics with movie clip symbols, but their internal timeline is completely fixed to four distinct frames. These frames emulate the states of a traditional button and include up, over, down, and hit. You can change the appearance of each of the first three button states by using the drawing tools. The hit state determines the pixels that will automatically trigger interactions and state switching when engaged with the mouse cursor. Instances of this symbol type can be made interactive.

- **Graphic** symbols have unique behavior in that their internal timeline is locked to the main timeline. There are also robust looping and frame selection mechanisms that are available by manipulating instance properties. Since their internal timelines are bound to the main timeline, previewing the main timeline within Animate will display their internal animation just the same as when a test movie is performed. Traditional animators tend to prefer this symbol type. Instances of this symbol type cannot be interactive.

Whichever symbol type you choose for a specific task, you will work within each symbol to establish its assets and timeline structures and also make use of individual instances of these symbols within your main timeline.

> **Tip**
> When exporting content as an animated GIF file, **Movie Clip** symbol timelines will not be included in the exported animation. If you intend to export your animation as an animated GIF, be sure to use **Graphic** symbols instead.

To create an instance of any symbol, simply drag the symbol from the **Library** panel and onto the stage. This will create an instance that you can then change the properties of, such as its position, rotation, scale, and even more, depending on the symbol type. When you adjust the properties of any symbol instance, these changes only apply to that property, whereas changing anything within the symbol itself will apply to the symbol and all of its instances.

To view the available properties of any symbol instance, select it on the stage and look at the **Object** tab of the **Properties** panel, as shown in the following screenshot:

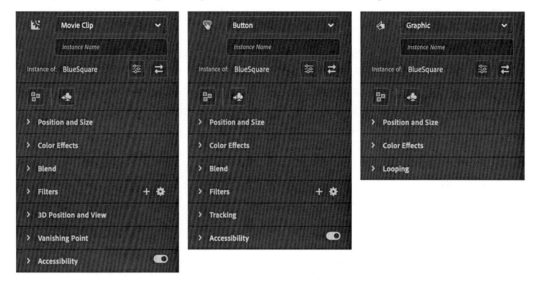

Figure 5.30 – Symbol instance properties

As alluded to previously, instance properties will differ, depending on the symbol type selected.

> **Tip**
> As we mentioned previously, you can override the behavior of any symbol instance by choosing a new behavior from the **Instance Behavior** dropdown. This will not change the symbol type but will change the behavior of that particular instance.

There is a standard set of property sections that are shared across all three types of symbol instances. This can be seen in the following screenshot:

Figure 5.31 – Shared properties

They include the following:

- **Position and Size**: This includes the **X** and **Y** position of your instance on the stage, according to the registration point symbol, as measured from the top-left corner of the stage itself. The width and height of your instance can also be adjusted here.

- **Color Effects**: This property takes the form of a **Color Styles** drop-down selection, where you can choose **None**, **Brightness**, **Tint**, **Advanced**, and **Alpha**. Each selection will present several sliders and other controls that allow you to control the color properties of an individual instance.

The **Movie Clip** and **Button** symbol instances also include properties that pertain specifically to **Accessibility** and are only ever available within ActionScript 3.0 document types:

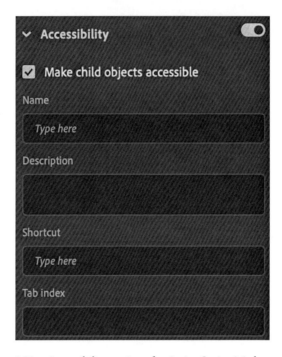

Figure 5.32 – Accessibility options for ActionScript 3.0 documents

These options allow you to include information for screen readers, such as name and description, while also allowing you to define keyboard shortcuts and the **Tab** order.

The **Movie Clip** and **Button** symbol instances also include **Filters** and **Blend** property selections:

Figure 5.33 – The Filters and Blend modes

These property sets allow you to choose from several **Blend Mode** options, including **Normal**, **Multiply**, **Screen**, **Overlay**, **Hard Light**, and more. You can make choices regarding how your instances are rendered when they're published within this section. A variety of filters can also be added, including **Drop Shadow**, **Blur**, and **Glow**, among others. The available filters and blend modes depend on your chosen document type.

Support for specific **Filters** and **Blend Modes** will vary based on the chosen document type. For instance, ActionScript 3.0 remains the most powerful and flexible document type you can choose to work with in Animate. It is a format that grew alongside the software and for a long time, it was the only platform available! Adobe owned the format and could add to or make adjustments however they pleased – making it all very powerful.

HTML5 Canvas is based on web standards and as such does not have a close relationship with Animate, nor the flexibility and power that comes with a proprietary format such as ActionScript 3.0 and the Flash Platform. Because of this, things move much more slowly – and HTML5 Canvas still has a long way to go before it gets even close to what a Flash-based SWF can do in many areas. A good example of this is blend mode support. For a long time, there were only a few blend modes that were available to use when authoring content for HTML5 Canvas.

In newer versions of Animate, this has opened up quite a bit and many more blend modes are now accessible to content authors:

Figure 5.34 – Blend Mode selection in HTML5 Canvas

The list of blend modes when using HTML5 Canvas is now much closer to what we can use when targeting ActionScript 3.0.

The previously supported blend modes in HTML5 Canvas included **Add** and **Normal** – that was it! In the current version of Animate, we have access to **Darken**, **Multiply**, **Lighten**, **Screen**, **Overlay**, **Hard Light**, and **Difference** – in addition to the two that were previously supported. Even with these additions, though, there are a few that will still be disabled when using HTML5 Canvas.

> **Note**
> Blend modes in HTML5 Canvas are still quite limited as they cannot be animated across keyframes. Once set, that is what you are stuck with at runtime!

Button symbol instances have a special **Tracking** property set that includes two options: **Track as Button** and **Track as Menu Item**. The difference here is that when you track as a button, the trigger stops at the button click, and when you track as a menu item, the trigger event bubbles up to additional containing items and can be caught to perform additional actions. It is a subtle difference, but it can be important within certain contexts where you require a secondary action to occur. This feature is only available in ActionScript 3.0 document types.

When using **Movie Clip** symbol instances within an ActionScript 3.0 document, you have access to both the **3D Position and View** and **Vanishing Point** property sections:

Figure 5.35 – 3D Position and View and Vanishing Point properties

The 3D tools within Animate are only ever functional with ActionScript 3.0-based document types and even then, they are of limited use since they only provide the appearance of a third dimension. For true 3D content in Animate, it is suggested to explore **WebGL glTF** documents as they can import and make use of real 3D models.

Finally, **Graphic** symbol instances have a **Looping** section containing properties and tools that pertain directly to animation. We'll explore this section in *Chapter 7, Character Design through Layer Parenting*.

Now that you have a solid understanding of the three types of symbols, how they are instantiated for use in a project, and the differences in capabilities across them all, it's time to start animating!

In this section, we learned how to create symbols and explored the three distinct symbol types in Animate. Coming up, we'll learn how to add motion to these symbol instances using **Classic Tweens**.

Animating with Classic Tweens

When animating with symbol instances, you have two tween options available to you: **Classic Tweens** and **Motion Tweens**. Both of these tweening types work differently from one another, but a **Classic Tween** is handled more similarly to what we saw when using a **Shape Tween** earlier in this chapter, so we'll examine that first. Motion guides will be explored as part of *Chapter 6, Interactive Motion Graphics for the Web*.

We'll now step through the process of animating a symbol instance with a **Classic Tween**:

1. The first thing you need to do is start a new document. I'm going to create a new ActionScript 3.0 document and set the width to 1280 and the height to 720, with an **FPS** setting of 30.

2. Rename your default **Layer_1** layer to something appropriate to the content you intend to create. I've renamed mine Square.

3. The contents of our symbol should be pretty simple for this exercise. I'm going to use a square shape, similar in appearance to the shape we used when performing a **Shape Tween**. Using the **Rectangle** tool, draw a square shape on the stage.

4. Next, you must create a symbol to animate. I'm going to create a **Graphic** symbol. Using the **Selection** tool, select the shape you created and choose **Modify | Convert to Symbol** from the application menu. The **Convert to Symbol** dialog will appear:

Figure 5.36 – Convert to Symbol

5. If you do not have an instance of your symbol on the stage yet, be sure to drag one from the **Library** panel onto the stage. I'm placing mine on the left-hand side of the stage:

Figure 5.37 – Positioning your symbol instance

6. Since the timeline only contains a single keyframe at frame 1 right now, select frame 30 and insert a new keyframe either by using the **Insert Keyframe** button at the top of the timeline or by choosing **Insert | Timeline | Keyframe** from the application menu:

Figure 5.38 – Creating a new keyframe

7. You now have two keyframes. With the playhead positioned at the second keyframe (at frame 30), use the **Selection** tool to move the symbol instance to the opposite side of the stage. This creates a change in position values between the two keyframes:

Figure 5.39 – Modifying the symbol's instance position

8. To create a **Classic Tween** to fill in the changes between these keyframes over time, click the **Create Classic Tween** button from the top of the timeline or choose **Insert | Create Classic Tween** from the application menu:

Figure 5.40 – A completed Classic Tween

Once these steps have been completed and **Classic Tween** is in place, test your animation with the **Test Movie** button. The symbol instance will move across the stage from left to right.

> **Note**
>
> Classic tweens cannot do much of what shape tweens are used for, including morphing between shapes and using shape hints, changing fill or stroke colors, and other similar property changes. Symbol instances are more limited in this respect since their contents are enclosed within the symbol itself.

As you can see, animating with **Classic Tweens** is very similar to doing so with **Shape Tweens**. Once you have a handle on one tween type, the other is easy to pick up and use.

Using Classic Motion Guides

Motion Guides within Animate allow you to direct the change in position during a tween by using a dedicated path. It is almost like placing a mining cart on a rail and just letting it go; the cart will follow any twists and turns that are present.

Say you want your symbol instance to travel in an arc. This is difficult with simple keyframes, but a **Classic Motion Guide** makes it a breeze:

1. The first thing you need is a properly tweened object. We'll use the simple exercise that we completed previously.

2. Right-click on the layer that contains the tween and choose **Add Classic Motion Guide**:

Figure 5.41 – Add Classic Motion Guide

3. A new layer will be added above the selected layer, which will be nested beneath it with a slight indent:

Figure 5.42 – Classic Motion Guide added

4. Using any tool that will create a stroke, such as the **Line** tool, draw a stroke across the stage:

Figure 5.43 – Motion Guide created

5. Now, with nothing selected whatsoever, hover the **Selection** tool over the line you just created and drag it upward to create an arc:

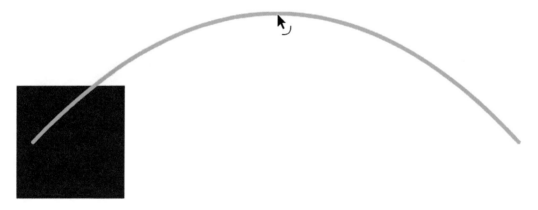

Figure 5.44 – Arcing the Motion Guide

6. You will need to reposition the symbol instance on both frame 1 and frame 30 to be sure that the **Transform Point** property of each asset is overlaying the newly created **Classic Motion Guide** arced line asset.

7. Scrubbing the timeline should ensure that the instance follows the arc of your guide instead of simply moving straight to the other side of the stage:

Figure 5.45 – Completed Classic Motion Guide

If your symbol instance does not follow the arc you've created, be sure that the transform points on all the keyframes align with the visible guide you've drawn! Do not worry about the visible nature of **Classic Motion Guide** within Animate since when you're testing or publishing it, the line is a guide and will not be visible to the user.

> **Note**
> Although they are "classic" motion guides, they are not only to be used in **Classic Tweens**. **Shape Tweens** can also make use of **Classic Motion Guides** in the same way!

Classic Motion Guides are a really useful feature when you want to direct the motion of your animated content across a certain path.

Exploring Classic Tween Properties

As we saw earlier with **Shape Tweens**, **Classic Tweens** have their own set of properties. Even given the similarities between both tween types, there are a few major differences when it comes to the available properties and even how shared properties function.

To view the properties of a **Classic Tween**, select any of the frames that make up the tween span and look at the **Frame** tab in the **Properties** panel:

Figure 5.46 – Classic tween properties with easing separated by property

Locate the **Tweening** section to view the various properties associated with **Classic Tweens**. Let's explore some of the main properties and functions here:

- **Ease**: One of the major differences between the **Shape Tween** and **Classic Tween** easing effects is that a **Classic Tween** can have individual properties, such as position, rotation, and scale, eased in different ways. **Shape Tweens** can only have a single easing effect applied to all properties. Otherwise, this feature has the same behavior across both tween types.

- **Rotate**: You can choose between **None**, **Auto**, **Clockwise**, and **Counter-clockwise**, as well as the number of rotations between keyframes.

- **Snap**: This option will assist in snapping to any guide that might be in use, helping to align the transform point of the instance being guided along a **Classic Motion Guide**.

- **Orient to path**: This option will preserve the orientation of your object as it moves along a **Classic Motion Guide** by adjusting its rotation. This is a really useful option.

- **Color Along Path**: This option can apply the color of the **Classic Motion Guide** shape to your object as a tint.

- **Scale Along Path**: This option can adjust the size of your object, interpreted as scale, via **Classic Motion Guide** being used.

- **Sync Symbols**: This option will force the internal timeline of the symbol to sync frames with the main timeline.

- **Scale**: When selected, the instance will scale across time if the scale has been adjusted within a keyframe. If deselected, scaling will not occur across the tween itself.

- **Remove Tween**: Choosing this button will remove the tween entirely.

There are some major differences between the various properties that are available to us when using different tween types. It's important to know what properties you want to control to choose the right type of tween.

In this section, we had a deep look into the various symbol types available in Animate and how to create motion with them with **Classic Tweens**.

Summary

We covered a lot in this chapter! Beginning with an introduction to the various drawing tools in Animate, we quickly moved on and applied motion to our content using **Shape Tweens** and explored many of the properties associated with this tween type. We then saw how to create symbols from our content and explored the different symbol types that are available to us. Following this, we looked at how to create instances of our symbols and add motion to them using **Classic Tweens**. Finally, we dove into using a **Classic Motion Guide** and the variety of properties available to us through **Classic Tween** properties.

In the next chapter, we will expand on what we've learned here and make use of a third type of tween, the **motion tween**, as we build interactive motion graphics specifically for the web.

6

Interactive Motion Graphics for the Web

In the previous chapter, we explored content creation using the various tools within Animate and focused on animating that content through the use of both **Shape Tweens** and **Classic Tweens**.

In this chapter, we are going to design animated content for publication to the native web using the HTML5 Canvas target platform. As we build out a digital advertisement, we will include externally created content such as photographic bitmap images, design text objects within the project using Adobe Fonts, and animate both by focusing on the third tweening type available to us in Animate: the motion tween. We'll close out this chapter by examining various properties unique to motion tweens and then explore a few ways of writing code to make our project interactive.

After reading this chapter, you'll be able to perform the following functions in Animate:

- Import photographic content to combine with additional object types such as text and shapes within Animate.

- Create and animate symbol instances using Motion Tweens, Motion Guides, and the Motion Editor.

- Effectively animate with Motion Tweens and modify associated tweening properties.

- Develop interactive elements for use on the web by using the **Actions** panel and the **Actions Wizard**.

Technical Requirements

You will need the following software and hardware to complete this chapter:

- Adobe Animate 2022 (version 22.0 or above).

- Refer to the *Animate System Requirements* page for hardware specifications: `https://helpx.adobe.com/animate/system-requirements.html`.

The code in action video for this chapter can be found here: `https://bit.ly/3qLL7FM`

Designing a Document for the Native Web

While we talked in some detail about different document types and publishing platforms in *Chapter 2*, *Exploring Platform-Specific Considerations*, and *Chapter 4*, *Publishing and Exporting Creative Content*, we haven't focused on any particular platform when creating and animating content. This chapter will change that as we will be focusing on the native web in everything we do.

The first step in designing content for the web, such as digital advertisements or interactive infographics, is to create a document that targets these technologies and gets our assets together.

Creating a New Document for Digital Advertising

We'll first create a new document that targets native web technologies from the various presets available to us in Adobe Animate. The **New Document** dialog includes a series of categories containing focused sets of presets to be used. You can access this dialog by choosing **File | New** or by clicking the **Create New** button on the welcome screen.

Whichever method you choose, the **New Document** dialog will appear:

Figure 6.1 – New Document – Ads Category Presets

With the **New Document** dialog open, we are ready to choose a preset. Along the top, you'll find six categories: **Character Animation**, **Social**, **Game**, **Education**, **Ads**, **Web**, and **Advanced**. We've already had a look at the **Advanced** category earlier in this book and will now turn our attention to how the others function.

We are designing a motion advertisement that will be supported on the native web:

1. Choose the **Ads** category and view the many presets that are present there. These presets are useful for both mobile displays and web browsers and are all built to conform to commonly accepted ad sizes.

2. Locate the preset named **Large Rectangle** and select it. It will appear highlighted with a blue border.

3. The sidebar will change to display the details of our chosen preset. Note that the size of our document is 336 x 280, with an FPS value of 30. It's fine to adjust the **Frame Rate** if you find that the playback requires a smoother frame rate or you have too many frames for your needs, but since we are targeting commonly accepted ad sizes through these presets, there is no need to make any adjustments to the width and height.

4. Look below the **Frame Rate** and notice that there is a **Platform Type** selection box. If you interact with this control, you will see two choices: the default of **HTML5 Canvas** and **ActionScript 3.0**. Again, since we are targeting the native web, we want to be sure that **HTML5 Canvas** is selected here.

5. When you are ready to create your document, click the **Create** button. A new document will open within Animate.

6. Be sure to save your new document as a .fla file by choosing **File | Save** from the application menu before moving on.

With that, our new document has been configured, saved, and ready to be worked on:

Figure 6.2 – Our newly created document

A quick look at the **Properties** panel should confirm that all of the choices we've made regarding width, height, FPS, and the target platform have been preserved.

Before moving on, we should note a couple of important things about digital advertising on the web and the standard presets we have based our new document on. If you are new to the field of digital advertising, you may not know there is a set of common ad sizes that almost all ad delivery networks accept.

These range from elongated banners, tall skyscrapers, and a set of sizes that are squarer in aspect. These can be seen in the following diagram:

Figure 6.3 – Common display ad sizes

Some of these sizes should be instantly recognizable by shape alone as they appear all over the internet, on news websites, social networks, and personal blogs – everywhere. The presets within the **Ads** category in Animate are all based on these standard sizes.

> **Tip**
> An extensive list of digital advertising sizes is maintained by Google and can be found at https://support.google.com/google-ads/answer/7031480.

With our new document created and saved, let's turn our attention to the content to be included in our advertisement.

Importing External Content

Up to this point, we've only worked with assets that have been created within Animate itself and haven't used anything external to the software. Many advertisements contain bitmap images such as .jpg and .png files for a photorealistic approach. Animate has no problem using bitmap images within any project, but you must import the files to be used into the project library.

We've prepared a set of photographic images that have been prepared using **Adobe Photoshop** that will be used in different ways within this project. Our example advertisement is going to be for a unique brand of coffee that can only be purchased online.

> **Note**
>
> You can find the images we have used here within the exercise files at `https://github.com/PacktPublishing/Adobe-Animate-2022-for-Creative-Professionals-Second-Edition`.

Let's go ahead and import some bitmap images into our document:

1. Using the application menu, choose **File | Import | Import to Library...** to summon a file browse dialog:

Figure 6.4 – Import to Library...

2. Navigate to the location of your bitmap image files. If your `Bean.png` and `CoffeeBeans.jpg` files are not visible within the browse dialog, be sure and choose **All Files (*.*)** from the **Enable** drop-down menu:

Figure 6.5 – Import image files dialog

3. Select the two files and click the **Open** button.

4. The files will be imported into your project library. You can verify this by opening the **Library** panel. The images will be the only items within it, and you will be able to preview them from here as well:

Figure 6.6 – Imported bitmaps are stored in the library

Alternatively, we could have chosen to import our images directly onto the stage. When choosing **Import to Stage…** from the **Import** menu, your files will be imported into the project library, just as we've done here, but instances of these bitmaps will also be placed on the stage. We are going to handle that part ourselves.

We only want to bring an instance of `CoffeeBeans.jpg` onto the stage at this point, so we can ignore `Bean.png` for now:

1. Ensure your **Library** panel is open and that the stage is in view within the interface as well. Select `CoffeeBeans.jpg` and drag it onto the stage:

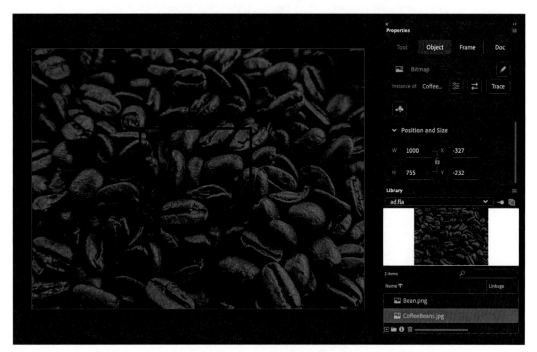

Figure 6.7 – The imported image is much larger than the stage

The image is too large for the stage at its native size is 1,000 pixels in width!

2. Look at the **Object** tab in the **Properties** panel and ensure that the small lock icon between the width and height boxes is active. This will retain the native aspect ratio when the image is resized. Set the image's width value to `425`:

Figure 6.8 – Setting the image's size with width and height constrained

3.   Open the **Align** panel, if it's not already open, by choosing **Window | Align** from the application menu. Ensure that the **Align to stage** checkbox is active and choose both **Align horizontal center** and **Align vertical center**:

Figure 6.9 – Align to stage – vertical and horizontal center

This will center the bitmap instance across the stage. The image will overlap the stage on the pasteboard, as well as on all sides, but that is what we want.

4.   We should always aim to be as organized as possible within our projects. Rename **Layer_1** to CoffeeBeans before moving on.

5. If desired, you can hide the parts of the bitmap image that overlay the pasteboard by clicking the **Clip content outside the stage** button, right next to the zoom percentage above the stage:

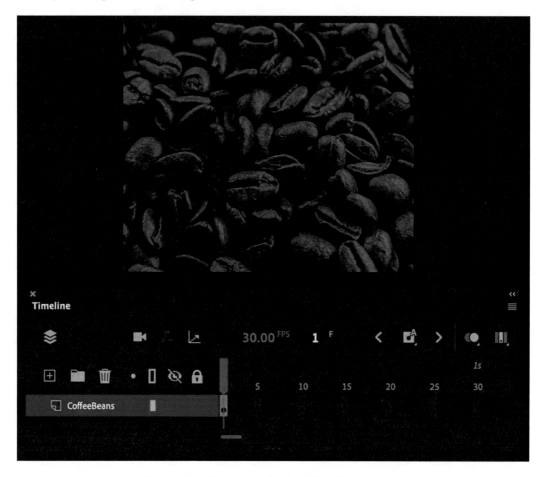

Figure 6.10 – Our background and timeline are ready

We now have an instance of the CoffeeBeans.jpg bitmap file on the stage, resized to allow just a bit to bleed over onto the pasteboard. All of this is contained in a single layer named **CoffeeBeans**, which consists of a single frame.

Next, we'll go ahead and create more objects that will make up the rest of our digital advertisement.

Creating Text Objects

This chapter marks our first time using imported bitmap files in a project, but that won't be our only first. We need some text to include within the coffee advertisement as well and for that, we will put the **Text** tool to work.

Once the text is in place, we will add additional elements to complete the layout portion of this project:

1. We want to keep our text in a different layer from the background image so that we'll be able to animate the image and the text separately. Click the **New Layer** button above the layer stack to add a new layer:

Figure 6.11 – Adding a new layer

2. With a new layer added above the **CoffeeBeans** layer, rename the newly added layer TextMsg. It is always important to name your layers using terms that make sense to the overall project.

3. Select the **Text** tool from the **Tools** panel. Remember that if a tool is not initially present, you can always edit the **Tools** panel to include it:

Figure 6.12 – The Text tool

4. With the **Text** tool selected, look at the **Tool** tab or the **Properties** panel. This allows us to set some properties of our text before even creating it:

Figure 6.13 – The Text tool's properties

We will want to use **Static Text** for this task, so be sure that the **Instance Behavior** dropdown is set to this. **Static Text** is rendered to shape data upon being published, ensuring that even viewers who do not have a specific font installed can see the text using the intended font. We'll look at **Dynamic Text** as part of *Chapter 11, Developing Web-Based Games.*

I've selected an **Adobe Font** for this project called *Neue Haas Grotesk Display Pro*, which can be used by anyone with an **Adobe Creative Cloud** subscription – just visit `https://fonts.adobe.com` and search for it!

I'm going to use a `48pt` value for **Size** and `#FF9900` for my **Fill** color.

To add text to the stage, you can click and begin typing to create an expanding width **Point Text** object or click and drag a textbox with a specific width to create a **Paragraph Text**. We want to control the width of our text objects, so we will create **Paragraph Text**:

1. At the top of the stage, click and drag from one side to the other to create a textbox measuring the width of the stage and type `DARK ROAST` using the previously chosen size and fill values.

2. Modify the **Text** tool properties so that you're using a `15pt` value for **Size** and `#FFD495` for the **Fill** color before adding a secondary piece of text.

3. Once again, click and drag from one side of the stage to the other to create a textbox the width of the stage and type THE ULTIMATE COFFEE EXPERIENCE directly beneath the original text object.

4. Using the **Selection** tool, click on the first text block and look at the **Object** tab of the **Properties** panel. The object's width should be 336 with an **x** position of 0 and a **y** position of 5. Go to the **Paragraph** section and choose to **Center** align the text.

5. Click the secondary text and look at its properties. The width should be 336 and the **y** position should be 63. The **x** position should remain aligned to the left at 0, just like the previous text object. **Center** align this text as well:

Figure 6.14 – Text added to our advertisement

The advertisement layout is beginning to take shape! One of the biggest concerns right now is the legibility of the text across the background image. We can increase the readability of the text message by adding a shape between the text and background.

6. Choose the **Rectangle** tool, set its fill color to pure black (#000000), and disable the stroke. Enable **Object Drawing Mode** so that the resulting shape is easier to handle:

Figure 6.15 – Object Drawing Mode activated

7. Adjust the **Fill** opacity to a value of 80% and draw a rectangle at the top of the stage so that it covers the text completely. Your shape should have a width of 336, a height of 90, and be positioned at an **X** and **Y** of 0.

8. The last step is to send the shape behind your text since it is obscuring it right now. Select the shape and choose **Modify | Arrange | Send to Back** from the application menu. The shape will be sent to the back of the stacking order within this specific layer. If you did not activate **Object Drawing Mode** in the previous step, you will not need to do this as simple shapes will appear beneath text objects:

Figure 6.16 – Shape added for increased contrast and clarity

That looks pretty good! The initial layout for our advertisement is now complete.

With our text objects and the background bitmap image on their layers, this gives us a good starting point to create some animation.

In this section, we assembled imported external bitmap images and created text objects within a new document targeting the native web. Next, we'll begin animating this content by using a tween type called **Motion Tween** – a tween we haven't encountered yet in this book.

Animating with Motion Tweens

Now, let's add motion to the various components of our advertisement. In the previous chapter, we used both shape tweens and classic tweens to create motion, depending on whether our object was a shape or a more complex symbol instance. In this project, we have a bitmap image instance to animate, along with a group of text and shape objects.

We could convert these various objects into symbols and employ a **Classic Tween** – that would work just fine! However, this is the perfect opportunity to introduce the third type of tween that you can use within Animate – **Motion Tween**.

Motion tweens work very similarly to classic tweens in that they are both used to animate symbol instances and not shapes. A lot differs between the two as well – both in how they are created and the various properties available to us.

> **Note**
>
> Classic tweens used to be called motion tweens before motion tweens were introduced to Flash Professional. When that happened, they were given the "classic" moniker and are now known as classic tweens.

We'll have a look at all of this, but the first task in preparing to use a **Motion Tween** is to ensure anything we want to animate is encapsulated within a symbol.

Building Symbols for use in Motion Tweens

Before animating with motion tweens, we will transform the contents of both our existing layers into symbols to tween their instances:

1. Using the **Selection** tool, select the instance of our `CoffeeBeans.jpg` bitmap file within the **CoffeeBeans** layer.

2. Choose **Modify | Convert to Symbol…** from the application menu or choose the **Convert to Symbol** button within **Object** properties. The **Convert to Symbol** dialog will appear. We must convert any bitmap image into a symbol to animate it with a tween as bitmap instances cannot be tweened.

3. Name the new symbol `CoffeeBeans` and choose the symbol type of **Movie Clip**. This symbol type will give us a good amount of flexibility when animating the background and we can also add interactivity to it if the need arises. Click **OK**:

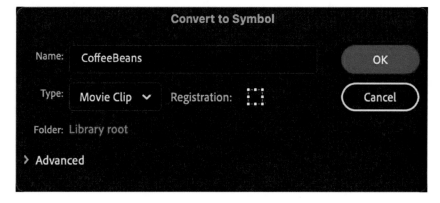

Figure 6.17 – Creating the CoffeeBeans Movie Clip symbol type

Have a look in the **Library** panel and note that the newly created symbol appears there – right alongside the images that have been imported. Both imported files and symbols created in Animate will become part of the project library and you can use as many instances of each as you like.

4. Now, we will focus our attention on the **TextMsg** layer. Clicking the keyframe at frame 1 of this layer will select both text objects, along with the underlying shape object, as they all exist on this single layer. We are going to convert all three into a single symbol to animate them as one object.

5. In the **Properties** panel, the **Frame** tab is currently selected since we clicked on a keyframe. Click the **Object** tab and notice that the object type reads as **Mixed**, indicating that multiple types of objects have been selected:

Figure 6.18 – Object properties show a Mixed selection

6. With this information verified, click **Convert to Symbol** to summon the **Convert to Symbol** dialog.

7. Name the new symbol `TextMessage` and choose the symbol type of **Movie Clip** just as before. Click **OK**:

Figure 6.19 – Creating the TextMessage Movie Clip symbol type

We now have a single **Movie Clip** symbol instance within each of our layers and they can each be effectively tweened in this state. The **CoffeeBeans** symbol contains a single bitmap image, while the **TextMessage** symbol contains multiple objects within it, but we can manipulate them all since they are now part of a single **Movie Clip** symbol.

Now, let's create a **Motion Tween** within each layer to add animation across both symbol instances:

1. Select the keyframe at frame 1 of the **CoffeeBeans** layer and choose **Create Motion Tween** from the **Insert Tweens** button above the timeline:

Figure 6.20 – Create Motion Tween creates a Motion layer

The **Create Motion Tween** command establishes a **Motion Tween** with only a single manual keyframe created. This is very different from shape tweens and Classic Tweens, which both require at least two keyframes to create a tween. This action converts the chosen layer into a special **Motion Layer** and 1 second's worth of frames is added.

2. Do likewise in regard to the **TextMsg** layer so that both become motion layers with active motion tweens. Once the conversions are complete, we can begin animating the contents of each layer.

3. Select frame 30 in the **CoffeeBeans** layer. Right-click and choose **Insert Keyframe | All** from the menu that appears. This will insert a keyframe that holds data values for the **Position, Scale, Skew, Rotation, Color,** and **Filter** properties:

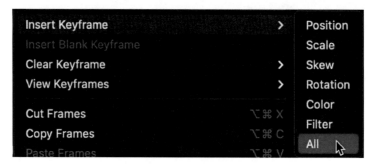

Figure 6.21 – Manual keyframe insertion for motion tweens

Note that these keyframes in the motion tweens appear as small diamonds and not the circular keyframes we are used to:

Figure 6.22 – A diamond-shaped keyframe is inserted

In addition, you do not even have to set a keyframe manually, as we have done here. All you need to do is change any of the supported properties with the playhead at a specific frame; a keyframe representing the change in data will appear automatically. Again, this is quite different from the other tween types as a **Shape Tween** or a **Classic Tween** only behaves this way when the **Auto-Keyframe** option is enabled.

4. The only property we'll be adjusting is the scale of the background image. Move the playhead to frame 1 and use the **Free Transform** tool to scale down the image so that it is closer to the height of our stage:

Figure 6.23 – Scaling the symbol instance

The original scale is preserved in the previously inserted keyframe at frame 30 and a new scale value is present at frame 1. Since we are working with motion tweens, only the scale values are contained within these keyframes. This is because that is the only property that has been changed.

> **Note**
>
> Motion tweens can have specific properties such as scale, position, rotation, and more contained in discrete keyframes, which makes motion tweens very versatile!

5. Now, let's move on to the **TextMsg** layer. Insert a new keyframe with all the properties we used previously at frame 25 and frame 15. All three keyframes hold the same values at this point:

Figure 6.24 – Keyframes Inserted into the motion layer

6. At both frame 1 and frame 15, shift the symbol instance upwards, off the stage so that the **y** position's value is -55. You will notice that a **Motion Guide** appears automatically, which displays the path of motion for our object. The instance will animate in from the top of the stage between frame 15 and frame 25:

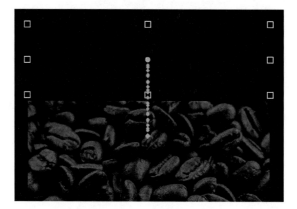

Figure 6.25 – Instance shifted off the stage

7. Our initial animation is rough but complete. Perform a **Test Movie** to view it in the web browser.

Notice that the animation loops endlessly and that there is no pause option at the beginning or end. We will remedy these aspects of our animation before closing out the project.

With two pieces of content animated, we have seen that changing position when using a **Motion Tween** results in a **Motion Guide** on the stage. We'll give this a better look and put it into play with another animated object in the next section.

Including Additional Library Items

To include additional library items, follow these steps:

1. To complete the layout of our advertisement, we'll bring in an instance of the Bean.png bitmap we imported into the **Library** earlier and animate that as well.

2. The first thing we must do is create a new layer to hold our single coffee bean image. This image is a **PNG** file with a transparent background, so all you will see is the coffee bean. Name the layer Bean once you've created it.

3. Drag an instance of the Bean.png bitmap image onto the stage. Place it toward the bottom left. Feel free to use the **Free Transform** tool to scale and rotate the image instance as appropriate:

Figure 6.26 – Scaling the Bean.png bitmap instance

4. Now, let's convert this image instance into a symbol. With the image selected, choose **Modify | Convert to Symbol** from the application menu. Give the **Movie Clip** symbol the name Bean and click **OK**:

Figure 6.27 – Creating the Bean Movie Clip symbol type

5. Now, create a new **Motion Tween** within the **Bean** layer, just as we have done with the previous two. The **Bean** layer will become a **Motion Layer** with an active **Motion Tween** stretching to frame 30 at the 1-second marker.

6. Click on the initial circular keyframe at frame 1 to select it. We are going to shift this over a bit.

7. Hover over the left of the keyframe at frame 1 with your mouse cursor. A small double-headed arrow cursor will appear, indicating that you can shift the frame span by dragging it to the right:

Figure 6.28 – A double-headed arrow appears

8. Go ahead and shift it over until the beginning keyframe is at frame 30. When the mouse is released, the initial keyframe will be relocated and begin at frame 30. The frame span before frame 30 will only contain empty frames.

With the new asset in place on its own layer, let's make some adjustments to the previously included animated content.

Adjusting the Timeline

At this point, we are going to want to adjust the previous animations a bit to allow some padding both before and after the animations. As a common practice in character animation, it's always a good idea to include a bit of anticipation this way, even with motion graphics in advertising.

So, let's fill out our timeline a bit more and perform some additional keyframe arrangements:

1. Insert frames for all the layers, up to and including the 2-second mark at frame 60, using either the **Insert Frame** button above the timeline or **Insert | Timeline | Frame** from the application menu.

2. Let's ensure that the background scaling animation also extends to the entire 2 seconds. Click the diamond keyframe at frame 30 on the **CoffeeBeans** layer so that it becomes selected and highlighted in blue.

3. Now, if you hover over this selected keyframe, you will see the cursor change to include a white box with a dashed line around it next to the cursor. This indicates that you can now click and drag the keyframe to relocate it. Drag the keyframe to frame 60 and release the mouse to relocate it:

Figure 6.29 – Dragging the keyframe to relocate it

The previous scaling animation is preserved but takes up double the time now.

4. Now, let's shift our keyframes in the **TextMsg** layer a bit so that the animation we created previously has a bit more room to breathe at the beginning. Select the block of frames that make up the entire set of keyframes in the **TextMsg** layer:

Figure 6.30 – Block of frames selected

5. Just as we did previously, if we hover over the selection and then drag it across the
    timeline, we can relocate the entire set of frames. To include a pause at the start of
    the timeline, drag the selection over so that it begins at frame 10:

Figure 6.31 – Block of frames shifted to frame 10

Play the animation using the controls above the timeline to view the effect of anticipation.

With these adjustments in place, we can animate the **Bean** symbol instance in the
proper context.

Animating with Motion Guides

It's time to add motion to the **Bean** symbol instance! Right now, it exists at frame 30 and
just sits there. We will have the bean drop in from the top right and settle to its present
location in the lower left:

1. Select the frame at frame 50 of the **Bean** layer and right-click on the selection to
    open the menu. Choose **Insert keyframe | All** from the menu that appears. This will
    duplicate the keyframe information from the previous keyframe.

2. Move the playhead back to the initial keyframe at frame 30 and reposition the **Bean**
    symbol instance so that it's at the top right – completely off the stage. This is where
    the instance will animate in from:

Figure 6.32 – Motion Guide created

Notice that, since the position of our object differs between the two keyframes, a **Motion Guide** automatically appears between the two positions. This is very different from working with a **Classic Motion Guide** since we don't have to do anything special to make it appear.

3. Using the **Selection** tool, we can make all sorts of adjustments to the curve and ease the motion by hovering over our **Motion Guide** until a small arc appears next to the cursor. Pull this down and to the right to give the motion a slight curve and to space the frames more variably:

Figure 6.33 – The curved motion guide path

Each frame in our tween is represented by a small dot along the **Motion Guide** path. This is a great way to visualize easing for the position in our motion tweens.

4. Go ahead and click the **Play** button above the timeline to preview the animation.

Certain aspects of a **Motion Tween** are very different from the two other tween types in Animate, but in terms of execution, they perform in mostly the same way.

Next, we'll examine the properties associated with a **Motion Tween**.

Exploring Motion Tween Properties

Just as with shape tweens and classic tweens, **Motion Tween** properties can be accessed through the **Tweening** section of the **Properties** panel:

1. Go ahead and click on any **Motion Tween** frame and look at the **Frame** tab of the **Properties** panel to access this section and the properties within it:

Figure 6.34 – Motion Tween properties

There isn't a lot here by comparison. That is due to the fact that additional properties are located elsewhere. We'll look into that next, but first, the obvious properties:

- **Ease**: Accepts a value between -100 and 100 with a default of 0, adjusting the intensity of either an ease-in or an ease-out.

- **Orient to path**: This option will preserve the orientation of your object as it moves along the **Motion Guide** path by adjusting its rotation.

- **Rotate**: You can choose between **None**, **Auto**, **Clockwise**, and **Counter-clockwise**, as well as the number of rotations between keyframes and a specific angle.

- **Sync symbols**: This will force the internal timeline of the symbol to sync frames with the main timeline.

- **Remove Tween**: Choosing this button will remove the tween entirely.

  You may have noticed from our initial exploration of **Motion Tween** properties that there are no **Ease Effect** presets like there are in the **Shape Tween** and **Classic Tween** properties. With a **Motion Tween**, you access similar functionality through the **Motion Editor** area.

2. To access the **Motion Editor** area, simply double-click on any existing **Motion Tween**:

Figure 6.35 – Motion Editor

3. The **Motion Editor** area will appear as part of the timeline. On the left-hand side, you will see a list of the various properties that can be tweened. Note that each property of a **Motion Tween** can be tweened individually in this way!

4. You'll also see a graph displayed to the right of this, within the timeline property. Each property has a path here with a set of anchor points and handles that can be manipulated in much the same way as when you edit any path when designing visual content with the **Pen** tool or **Subselection** tool.

5. Below is the location of the ease presets that were missing from the **Tweening** section we previously examined. If you don't want to manipulate each easing curve by hand, clicking the **Add Ease** button will allow you to choose from a list of presets:

Figure 6.36 – Motion ease presets

The **Motion Tween** ease presets are somewhat similar to what can be found in other tween types, but they differ in some ways as well. Double-click on a preset to apply it to any selected property. In addition, certain presets can also have their intensity values adjusted.

Once you apply an ease preset, the apparent ease will be reflected in the easing graph by way of a dashed easing curve alongside the original curve.

To hide the **Motion Editor** area, simply double-click on the associated **Motion Tween** in the same way that you opened it.

As we saw when we looked at the **Shape Tween** and **Classic Tween** properties, motion tweens have their own set to be aware of. In the next section, we'll learn how to make our advertisement interactive using JavaScript code.

In this section, we constructed symbols to animate our text objects and bitmap images. We then brought additional items from the project library onto the stage and prepared the timeline for animating with motion tweens. Taking full advantage of the **Motion Tween** properties, we animated using property adjustments, motion guides, and the advanced **Motion Editor** to complete our motion advertisement. Next, we'll finish everything off by including a bit of interactivity by using JavaScript.

Adding Interactivity with JavaScript

Generally, a digital advertisement like the one we've designed here will need to be interactive as well. Most ads of this kind will respond to user interaction by opening a web page where the user can get more information about, or even purchase, the advertised product or service.

Since we are publishing to the native web using an HTML5 Canvas document type, we will be coding our interactions with the JavaScript language.

Writing Code with the Actions Panel

Animate is a unique piece of software in that it allows both design and development within the same application. This hybrid approach has always been a strong part of the tool and continues to be so, no matter which platform you might be targeting.

Let's go ahead and add some code to our motion advertisement:

1. By convention, and for the purpose of organization, we should keep our code completely separate from any visible assets. Go ahead and create a new layer and name it Actions. All our code will go in this layer to keep things clean.

2. All our code will be on the final frame of the animation, so we must insert a new keyframe at frame 60 in the **Actions** layer. Go ahead and perform these actions.

3. To stop the playhead at the end of our animation, we must use a stop() action. Select frame 60 and open the **Actions** panel from the application menu by choosing **Window | Actions**. The **Actions** panel will appear, with **Script Editor** visible.

4. On line 1 of **Script Editor**, write this.stop(); to stop the playhead once it hits frame 60. This will ensure that the animation will not loop:

Figure 6.37 – Stop action at frame 60 via the Script Editor area

If you know what code to write, you can just start writing directly into the **Script Editor** area here. If you need a more guided approach, we'll tackle that momentarily.

> **Note**
>
> The this keyword refers to the current timeline. We are telling the playhead in the current timeline to stop() as soon as it reaches the current frame.

We want the user to be able to click on our little coffee bean symbol instance to be taken to a website. To make a **Movie Clip** symbol instance interactive, it must be given an **Instance Name** so that the code can identify and address it.

5. Using the **Selection** tool, click on the **Bean** symbol instance to select it and go to the **Object** tab or the **Properties** panel.

6. There is an input field ready and waiting for an instance name to be given. Type coffeebean into the **Instance Name** field. Once you've done this, the instance will be exposed to code:

Figure 6.38 – coffeebean added to a Bean instance

7. Open the **Actions** panel at frame 60 once again if it has been closed. Instead of editing code in the **Script Editor** area, we will make use of the **Actions Wizard** area to construct the code. Click the **Add using wizard** button above the **Script Editor** area to open it.

8. The editor will disappear and be replaced with the wizard. **Step 1** asks you to **Select an action** from a long list of possible actions. Locate the action named **Go to Web Page** and click it.

9. You'll notice that a preview of the code you are building has been added to the tiny code editor at the top of the panel. Replace the highlighted URL with one of your own and then click the **Next** button to move on to **Step 2**.

10. **Step 2** asks you to **Select a triggering event** from a list of events. Choose **On Mouse Click** for your event so that *Step 3* activates.

11. In **Step 3**, you are asked to **Select an object for the triggering event**. Notice that the given **Instance Name** of `coffeebean` appears as part of this list! Choose this object and click the **Finish and add** button to complete these steps and build the final code:

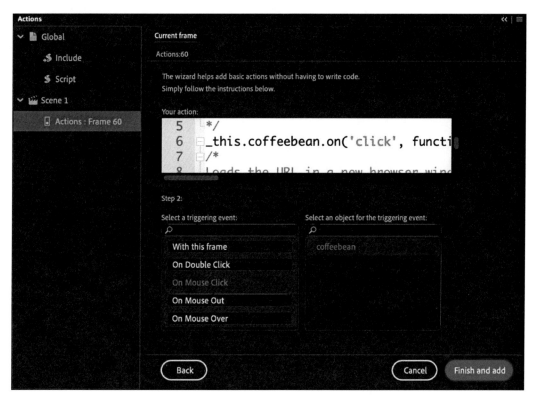

Figure 6.39 – Click trigger added via the Actions Wizard

12. You can close the **Actions** panel and perform a **Test Movie** to view the animated advertisement and interact with it by clicking the little bean at the end.

The resulting JavaScript code that's been created by the **Actions Wizard** area is included here:

```
var _this = this;
_this.coffeebean.on('click', function(){
window.open('https://josephlabrecque.com', '_blank');
});
```

The code is defining a variable, `this`, to preserve scope, followed by registering an event listener on our `coffeebean` object. If a `click` event is detected, the function to open a URL in the web browser is executed. Passing in the `'_blank'` argument opens the URL in a new window or tab. Pretty simple stuff!

In this snippet of code, all the comments have been removed for clarity.

> **Note**
>
> We will be looking at a lot more JavaScript in *Chapter 11*, *Developing Web-Based Games*, and *Chapter 12*, *Producing Virtual Reality Content for WebGL*.

In this section, we had a look at the features of the **Actions** panel and used both the **Script Editor** area and the **Actions Wizard** area to add interactivity to our digital advertisement.

Summary

In this chapter, we focused on creating a web-based digital advertisement using the HTML5 Canvas document type and introduced several new topics while doing so. We learned how to import bitmap images, create text objects, convert object types into symbols, and animate those symbol instances by using motion tweens. Building on that, we also had our first look at the **Actions** panel and made our content interactive.

In the next chapter, we will have a look at an even newer way of animating content in Animate by using Layer Parenting.

7
Character Design through Layer Parenting

In the previous chapter, we built an animated digital advertisement that targeted the native web and spent a lot of our energy focused on doing so through the use of **Motion Tweens**.

This chapter will focus on a newer animation technique for characters and any other complex jointed mechanisms known as **Layer Parenting**. We'll begin by exploring **Advanced Layers** mode and then examine how to design a hierarchical character rig by establishing parent-child relationships across multiple layers through the **Layer Parenting** workflow. We'll then delve into animation using **Layer Parenting** structures and learn how to add an additional flourish to our animation by adding audio and automated lip syncing.

After reading this chapter, you'll be able to do the following in Animate:

- Understand the benefits and potential drawbacks of using **Advanced Layers** mode
- Build a set of parent-child relationships across your layers through layer parenting
- Create character animation using layer parenting mechanisms
- Import audio files and configure a set of visemes for use with automated lip-syncing mechanisms

Technical Requirements

You will need the following software and hardware to complete this chapter:

- Adobe Animate 2022 (version 22.0 or above).

- Refer to the Animate system requirements page for hardware specifications: `https://helpx.adobe.com/animate/system-requirements.html`.

Working with Advanced Layers Mode

In this section, we'll have a look at **Advanced Layers** mode, how it differs from **Basic Layers** mode, and the benefits of using **Advanced Layers** mode within your Animate projects.

As we've seen in previous chapters, the use of layers in an Animate project allows us to organize artwork, animations, and other elements within the document. They also influence the stacking order of visible assets that appear on the stage. Layers keep things neat, tidy, and in their proper place.

If you want to animate through **Layer Parenting** mechanisms, you must be able to use **Advanced Layers** mode within your Animate document. This is a special document setting that is on by default when you're using the current version of the software and provides numerous advanced capabilities, such as **Layer Parenting**, **Layer Depth**, the use of **Camera**, **Layer Filters**, and **Layer Effects**.

We'll first have a look at the two different layer modes available in Animate and a couple of items you should be aware of when choosing one over the other.

Assessing Layer Mode Benefits and Gotchas

While **Advanced Layers** mode is now enabled by default with any new document you create, there may be projects where you would prefer to work in **Basic Layers** mode instead. Additionally, you should be aware that you are changing the fundamental structure of any document when you switch from one mode to another. These decisions will affect workflows and may invalidate any code that you may have written.

Let's provide a brief overview of the various layer modes and what they can be used for:

- **Basic Layers**: This could almost be thought of as a classic mode of working in Animate as it is basically how things have functioned for nearly 2 decades. When using this mode, you will not have access to certain newer workflows, such as **Layer Parenting**. Writing code that interacts with various symbol instances that are present on the stage, however, is a bit easier to accomplish.

- **Advanced Layers**: When using this mode, each layer will be transformed into a **Movie Clip** symbol, allowing for more advanced workflows, such as **Layer Parenting**, in addition to all the workflows available in **Basic Layers** mode. The biggest problem when using this mode is when you are also writing code that targets certain, specific symbol instances, as these instances may now be nested within an additional instance that's been created from the layer and named accordingly.

To illustrate the potential issues with code, consider the following Animate project:

Figure 7.1 – Advanced layers and code considerations

Notice that we have a layer named `Face_Layer` and that, within that layer, is a Movie Clip symbol instance with an **Instance Name** of `face`.

When dealing with code, there are two possibilities. If we want to target the face instance and stop its internal timeline, we will normally write the following code (ActionScript, in this example):

```
this.face.stop();
```

However, under certain circumstances, with **Advanced Layers** mode, since layers may be rendered as Movie Clip symbol instances themselves when using **Advanced Layers** features, you may need to include the name of the layer as well:

```
this.Face_Layer.face.stop();
```

Most of the features of **Advanced Layers** mode are geared toward visual effects more than anything code-based, but it is good to keep this in mind as a possibility as you work through various projects.

> **Note**
>
> There is an optimization in recent versions of Animate that will not publish container symbols based on layers if no advanced layer feature is in use. Because of this, we can often use the shorter syntax without referencing the containing layer, even when we're using the **Advanced Layers** mode.

Advanced Layers mode enables the following features in Animate documents:

- **Layer Parenting**: This feature allows you to establish a parent-child hierarchy between layers in the timeline. These relationships are retained even when you're animating the various assets associated with these layers, which allows you to create a rigging system. This feature is the focus of this chapter and will be covered in depth shortly.

- **Layer Depth**: This feature can be used to manipulate the **z-depth** of various timeline layers, apart from their actual order. Using this feature, you can have objects pass in front of or behind one another, and even use layers set at different depths to control a parallax camera effect in your animation. We will explore layer depth further in *Chapter 10, Working with the Camera and Layer Depth*.

- **Camera**: The **Camera** document exists on the main timeline and can be zoomed, rotated, and panned just like a real camera. It allows for many more expanded cinematographic elements within your animated content. We will explore the **Camera** document alongside **Layer Depth** in *Chapter 10, Working with the Camera and Layer Depth*.

- **Layer Effects**: This feature allows you to make use of effects and filters on entire layers, similar to what you would normally apply to individual **Movie Clip** symbol instances. This feature is only available in **ActionScript 3.0**-based documents.

Now that we have a better understanding of what **Advanced Layers** mode does, we'll have a look at how to switch between that and **Basic Layers** mode within an Animate document.

Switching Between Layer Modes

As mentioned previously, **Advanced Layers** mode is enabled by default in any new document you create. For older documents, you can always enable it if desired once the document has been opened in a newer version of Animate.

> **Note**
>
> In *WebGL glTF*-based documents, you cannot disable the **Advanced Layers** mode as the checkbox to do so is non-functional.

In older versions of Animate, the switch to toggle between layer modes was located in the timeline. In newer versions of Animate, you will find this option within the **Document Settings** dialog. To access **Document Settings**, click the **More Settings** button in the **Document Settings** section of the **Doc** tab within the **Properties** panel or choose **Modify | Document…** from the application menu.

The **Document Settings** dialog will then appear:

Figure 7.2 – Enabling Advanced Layers in Document Settings

There are several important settings within this dialog. Many of them, such as **Frame Rate**, **Stage Color**, **Width**, and **Height**, are available from within the **Properties** panel as well. Below all of these settings, toward the bottom of the dialog, you can find the **Use Advanced Layers** checkbox.

Any modifications that are made to this checkbox will cause an alert to appear immediately, letting you know what will happen based on your choice:

Figure 7.3 – Advanced Layers warning dialogs

It is immensely important to understand the repercussions that you may need to deal with when you switch between these various layer modes. It is best to have an understanding of what you want to accomplish in any project and choose the best layer mode at the beginning, so you don't have to deal with the hassle later on.

In this section, we explored the two available layer modes within Animate and gained an understanding of the differences, benefits, and drawbacks of each choice. Next, we'll put one of the advantages of **Advanced Layers** mode to use in the form of **Layer Parenting**.

Animating a Character with Layer Parenting

Layer Parenting is a feature of **Advanced Layers** mode that allows us to establish nested parent-child relationships between actual layers within the timeline of a document. The benefit of doing so is that we can create a rig across our layers in this way, through which the manipulation of any parent layer will also apply to its children and grandchildren.

A good way to envision this relationship is to visualize a human arm. If you want to move the hand without any other arm parts, it can easily be rotated at the wrist and will not affect the lower or upper arm. Moving the lower or upper arm, however, will also change the position of the hand since it has an attachment to both of those additional structures. **Layer Parenting** works in much the same way but allows no incidental movements across other structures as more natural physical motion would.

> **Note**
>
> Animating through **Layer Parenting** is very precise in that the rotations, positioning, and other manipulations only affect the layer whose properties are being changed and attached child layers in precise ways. There is a more natural, less precise method of rigging called **Inverse Kinematics**, which we'll look at in detail in *Chapter 8, Animating Poses with IK Armatures*, as well as a third way of rigging animated content, which we will explore in *Chapter 9, Manipulating Warped Objects Advanced Rigging*.

We'll now have a look at how to set up an Animate document for **Layer Parenting** through the import and configuration of prepared visual assets.

Preparing Assets for Layer Parenting

When you're setting up the assets in your project to be used for **Layer Parenting** workflows, all of the basic considerations still apply. You'll want to have layers named in a meaningful way and organized appropriately, with each object that will receive animation through tweening on a layer of its own.

> **Note**
>
> We've already prepared an FLA file for use in this project that contains assets that are suitable for rigging with **Layer Parenting** workflows. You can find this, along with all the files, at `https://github.com/PacktPublishing/Adobe-Animate-2022-for-Creative-Professionals-Second-Edition`.

Let's have a look at our existing document, named `WoodenDoll.fla`, and modify it for **Layer Parenting**:

Figure 7.4 – The wooden doll

You will immediately notice a human-like figure that appears very similar to the type of posable wooden dolls that are used by sketch artists and sculptors. The doll is positioned within what appears to be a plain room, with a floor and single wall visible.

Upon inspecting the timeline, you'll notice that the document has two layers named **Room** and **Doll**:

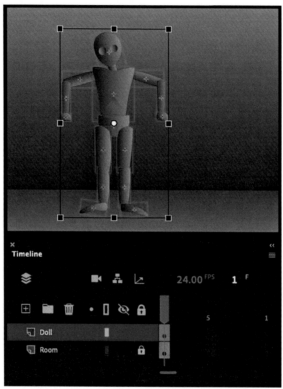

Figure 7.5 – The document Timeline and Stage

The **Room** layer contains the background assets and is locked. The **Doll** layer includes a set of 15 individual movie clip symbol instances that make up the various parts of the wooden doll we will be rigging and animating through **Layer Parenting**. Since we will be animating these objects using Classic Tweens, it is very important to ensure that they are all symbols that have been given identifiable names.

Now that you are familiar with how the document is set up, let's organize things a bit better:

1. Since **Layer Parenting** involves creating parent-child relationships between different layers, we'll need to move all 15 objects out from the single **Doll** layer they are currently placed within and create a unique layer for each. To do this easily, simply select all 15 objects in the stage within the **Doll** layer by drawing a selection rectangle around them with the **Selection** tool.

2. Right-click on the selected objects and choose **Distribute to Layers** from the menu that appears:

Figure 7.6 – Distribute to Layers

This will remove all 15 instances from the current layer and generate a new layer for every instance, automatically placing each inside its own layer.

3.   With so many layers now part of the timeline, it may help to dock the entire
      Timeline panel to the side of the stage instead of beneath it:

Figure 7.7 – Assets arranged across layers

Notice that each of the new layers has a meaningful name as well. This is because the
Distribute to Layers option will automatically name each layer with the same name
that was given to the object that the layer is being generated for. Pretty convenient!

Our character assets have now been imported into the stage and assembled into a
meaningful layer structure within the timeline.

One important thing to know is that each of these body parts has been assembled to form
a visual representation of the entire doll. The head is where a head should be, while the
various arm and leg pieces are positioned as you would expect for a full doll.

Related to this is the fact that the **transform point** of each doll part, indicated by a white circle, has been positioned at the various natural joints along the body:

Figure 7.8 – The transform point acts as a joint

So, with the lower arm, for instance, the transform point is positioned at the elbow, where an arm would naturally rotate. You can always reposition any transform point by using the **Free Transform** tool to click and drag it to different locations. This will become very important once we rig our layers together and begin making adjustments and animations with it.

> **Tip**
> You may want to rearrange the automatically generated layer order if items are not grouped in a meaningful way; for instance, making sure that all the parts of the arms or legs are grouped alongside one another so that they are easy to find concerning their visual placement on the doll's body.

We'll organize these layers into a hierarchical structure using the **Layer Parenting** view as part of our next task.

Establishing a Layer Hierarchy

With the various objects that make up our figure delegated to individual layers, we can now activate **Layer Parenting** and create our rig. When using **Layer Parenting** within Animate, each layer can be a parent or child of another layer, and while parent layers can have multiple child layers, child layers can only have a single parent layer.

Let's go ahead and establish our rig through **Layer Parenting**:

1. Our first task will be to open the **Layer Parenting** view. This can be done by toggling the small **Show Parenting View** button above the timeline.

    It appears as a small square with lines extending to two additional boxes below it:

Figure 7.9 – The Layer Parenting view enabled

With this option enabled, a new column within the layers view will appear. This new column is where we can establish parent-child relationships to construct our rig.

Before clicking anything else, we should identify our root layer. This is the layer that will be the parent, grandparent, or even great grandparent to every other layer in our rig. With a human figure, the torso often makes the most sense.

2. To establish a parent-child relationship and begin building your rig hierarchy across the wooden doll layers, you must identify layers that will serve as children and drag them to their parent layers.

Starting with **RUpperLeg**, drag the area of that layer with **Parenting View** activated onto the **Pelvis** layer:

Figure 7.10 – Pulling wires to establish relationships

Note that a small line connects across layers as you drag, which indicates that you are pulling a child toward a parent to establish this relationship. The workflow is always adding child layers to parent layers, and never parent to child.

3. Now, continue to pull the children to their parents in this same way. The **Pelvis** layer will become the child of **Torso**, our root layer:

Figure 7.11 – A series of parent-child relationships

The root layer is never dragged to another layer since it is not the child layer of any other layer whatsoever.

4. Move more children to continue testing how dragging the child layers to the parent layers affects everything to establish a fully formed rig. For instance, **LFoot** is a child of **LLowerLeg**, which is a child of **LUpperLeg**, which is a child of **Pelvis**, which is a child of **Torso**. **Head** is a child of **Torso** as well, as are **RUpperArm** and **LUpperArm**.

Create the remaining relationships in this manner:

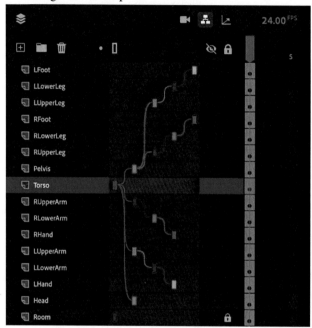

Figure 7.12 – Completed branching Layer Parenting rig

5. You can now test your rig and see how everything functions. Select the **Free Transform** tool and rotate different parts of the doll. Notice that as you rotate any parent object, such as an upper arm, both the lower arm and the hand also rotate along with it:

Figure 7.13 – Rotating parts of the completed rig

Again, note that the arm rotates around the transform point of the object, as indicated by a small white circle when the **Free Transform** tool is active.

With our layer hierarchy established through the use of the **Layer Parenting** view, we can easily add motion to the objects within each layer to take full advantage of these parent-child relationships.

The next step will be to perform some animation using our new **Layer Parenting** rig.

Animating using Layer Parenting

Now that we have our **Layer Parenting** relationships established across the timeline layers, we can animate our content with any tween type we would like to, so long as we adhere to the constraints and capabilities of each type.

You can animate your doll however you like, but here is a standard workflow when using **Layer Parenting**:

1. Arrange your various objects into a starting pose. I've set my wooden doll to appear to have been seated upon the floor and against the wall. You can do something similar by using the **Selection** or **Free Transform** tool:

Figure 7.14 – Choosing a starting position for the wooden doll

As you manipulate the various parts, notice how the parent-child relationships affect which specific parts need to be animated, and which others follow along as a result of these relationships.

2. Once you have settled on the initial position, scale, and rotation of your parented objects, you can start inserting keyframes in each layer, just as you would for a normal tween, and continuing to adjust object properties:

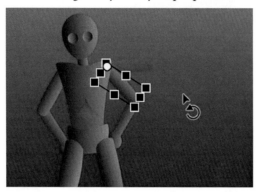

Figure 7.15 – Rotating and repositioning both the parent and children

Tweening works the same way as always here. The only difference is that Animate will interpret any change in parent properties and automatically make the same interpretation about any child and grandchild layers down the branch.

3. The various keyframes can be staggered across the timeline in whatever way works best for your particular animation:

Figure 7.16 – The Layer Parenting rig with classic tweens

It's a good idea when animating in this way to take things step by step, and to test and tweak regularly! Keyframes can always be moved backward and forward as needed to create more natural motion and easing effects, and other tween adjustments can be made as you go.

When finished, you can always visualize the animation by using **Onion Skin Advanced Settings**:

Figure 7.17 – Advanced onion skin settings

This can be accessed from the controls above the timeline. These settings allow you to view a range of frames concerning the current playhead's position so that you can tune your motion. I find viewing outlines in place of fully rendered fills provides a clearer view of the action.

By default, when using outline mode, the current frame is a red outline. Any frames before the playhead's position will be blue, and any upcoming frames will be shown in green:

Figure 7.18 – Motion visualization via onion skinning

My wooden doll is pulling himself up from a sitting position to a standing one. This can be easily understood by using the **Onion Skin** mechanisms. This is just one of many tools available within Animate to help you achieve your best animation.

In this section, we learned how to use **Layer Parenting** to establish a hierarchical relationship among the layers that compose a full character and then apply animation to that character once successfully rigged. Next, we will explore some additional considerations and features when performing character animation of this kind.

Exploring Additional Character Animation Features

While rigging a full character through the use of **Layer Parenting** and performing animation through various tweens certainly demonstrates the versatility of this rigging method, there are additional features that we can make use of to enliven our animation even further.

The next method we will highlight, will examine how to add recorded audio to your character and perform automated lip sync using Graphic symbol looping properties.

Making use of Graphic Symbols

In *Chapter 5, Creating and Manipulating Media Content*, we mentioned that Graphic symbol instances have a special **Looping** section within their **Object** properties. Let's examine these settings in more detail.

To view the **Looping** properties, select any Graphic symbol instance within a project and look at the **Object** tab of the **Properties** panel:

Figure 7.19 – Graphic symbol instance looping

Looping determines how the Graphic symbol instance should handle playback and which frame playback should begin and end on. The options that are included are as follows:

- **Play Graphic in Loop**: This option will loop the symbol timeline, so long as there are enough frames in the containing timeline.

- **Play Graphic Once**: This option will loop the entire symbol timeline up to its final frame, so long as there are enough frames in the containing timeline.

- **Play Single Frame for the Graphic**: The playhead will hold upon the specified frame within the symbol timeline. There is no movement until another keyframe is added to the main timeline with additional instructions.

- **Play Graphic Reverse Once**: This option will loop the entire symbol timeline in reverse up to its initial frame, so long as there are enough frames in the containing timeline.

- **Play Graphic in Reverse Loop**: This option will loop the symbol timeline backward, so long as there are enough frames in the containing timeline.

The **Frame Picker** button will open the **Frame Picker** dialog, which displays each frame within the symbol, allowing you to choose the initial frame to start the looping option at, or hold the motion at a specific frame, visually.

Similarly, the **First** option beside the **Frame Picker** button provides the same functionality, but strictly by numeric input. Either mechanism will allow you to choose the starting frame for playback at that keyframe, with 1 being the default. The **Last** option directly beneath it is blank by default. Specifying a **Last** frame for your loop provides you with full control over which specific portion of the internal timeline will be included in the loop.

The final option here is the **Lip Syncing** button, which is used by Animate to automate a properly prepared Graphic symbols sync option through **Adobe Sensei**, Adobe's cloud-based artificial intelligence.

Next, we will set up our project to use the **Lip Syncing** option to give our character a chance to speak.

Importing Audio for Stream Sync

As a feature-rich, multi-media authoring tool, Adobe Animate provides support for many media formats. Most document types have full audio support as well. The greatest support for audio can be found in ActionScript 3.0, HTML5 Canvas, and the various AIR document types. All three of these platforms can make use of a feature called **Auto Lip-Sync**, which automatically interprets included voice-based audio and determines which mouth shapes (or visemes) to insert at specific points in the voice performance. The first step to any of this is to record and import a suitable audio file.

In the files for this chapter, we have included an audio file named `DollSpeak.mp3`:

Figure 7.20 – Audio file properties

This file is a 16-bit stereo recording that's been encoded for full compatibility with Animate at 44.1 kHz and with a sample MP3 rate of 128 kbps. It is a recording of the wooden doll "speaking" to the viewer across a brief period of 6 seconds. You can use this in your project or record your voice using **Adobe Audition**.

> **Note**
>
> Animate can make use of various sound encodings and formats but to avoid problems, it is best to use audio files encoded as 16-bit at 44.1 kHz. A good sample rate for an encoded MP3 is 128 kbps. These settings represent a solid standard when working in Animate and deviating into something such as 24-bit or 32-bit audio or 256 kbps is highly discouraged.

Now, let's import the MP3 audio file and make use of it within the timeline:

1. Choose **File | Import | Import Audio…** from the application menu and browse to the location of your audio file. Alternatively, you can drag the file from your filesystem directly into the **Library** panel. Either way, the MP3 file will now be displayed within the project library:

Figure 7.21 – The imported audio file in the project library

From here, you can view the audio waveform and preview the audio playback.

2. Like just about everything else in Animate, audio must reside within the timeline, attached to a keyframe. In your timeline, just above the **Head** layer, add a new layer and name it Audio.

3. With any frame of the **Audio** layer selected, look at the **Frame** tab of the **Properties** panel and examine the **Sound** section:

Figure 7.22 – Stream Sync type

Select the DollSpeak.mp3 file from the **Name** dropdown. Any audio files in your project library will appear in the dropdown for you to select.

4. Before moving on, it is very important to also set the **Sync** type to **Stream**. This is necessary for the audio to work with the automatic lip-syncing feature, as **Stream Sync** will bind audio to each of your frames along the timeline, ensuring that the audio will neither drift nor lag. It also allows you to preview the audio by scrubbing the playhead.

5. Now, look back to the timeline and examine the **Audio** layer. The chosen audio file is now assigned to this layer and the waveform appears across the frame span:

Figure 7.23 – A waveform appears in the audio layer

6. Scrub the playhead along the timeline to hear how the audio synchronizes across the assigned frame span.

> **Tip**
> For an even better view of the audio waveform, right-click on the layer's name and choose **Properties**. From the dialog that appears, you can set the layer's height to, at most, 300%.

With our audio file imported and assigned to a layer within our main timeline for **Stream Sync**, we can start setting up the various mouth parts to switch out according to the sounds that are detected within the speech.

Configuring our Graphic Symbol Frames

With the audio file imported and configured within our project's main timeline, we will turn our attention to the head of our doll to establish various mouth shapes, which we will use to simulate speech. Perform the following steps:

1. Open the **Library** panel and locate the **Head** movie clip symbol. Right-click on the symbol's name and choose **Properties...** to edit the symbol's properties.

2. Automated lip syncing can only be used with Graphic symbols since this symbol type is the only one with dedicated **Looping** properties. In the dialog that appears, change **Type** to **Graphic** and then click the **OK** button:

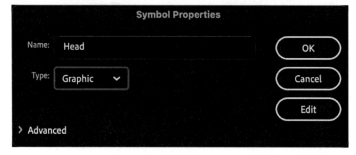

Figure 7.24 – Symbol changed from Movie Clip to Graphic

This action will not change the behavior of existing instances on the timeline. We will take care of that later.

3. At this point, you must import a version of the **Head** symbol with all the layers and shapes already completed with the appropriate mouth parts. Choose **File | Import | Open External Library...** and browse to the file named Head.fla within the exercise files.

4. The Head.fla file opens as another **Library** panel alongside the project library and only contains the **Head** graphic symbol. Drag the **Head** symbol from the imported library into the library of the current document.

5. Animate will ask you what you want to do since there is already a symbol named **Head** in the library. Choose **Replace existing items** and then click the **OK** button:

Figure 7.25 – The Resolve Library Conflict dialog

The **Head** symbol has now been replaced within the project library with the one you brought in from the external library.

6. Double-click on the Graphic symbol icon next to the **Head** symbol to edit its contents. We will be taken inside the symbol, where we can now manipulate the stage and timeline of the symbol itself:

Figure 7.26 – The Head timeline with mouth parts and labels

Examine the **Head** timeline to discover a set of layers that include the static doll head visuals, a set of mouth and tongue shapes across two layers, and a layer dedicated to labels. The **Labels** layer will help us identify each frame when we map the frames as visemes later.

Explore each frame and notice how the various mouth and tongue shapes overlay the head visual and how they conform to the sound labels that have been given to them. I've kept the first frame without any mouth whatsoever so that we can keep it blank when desired.

7. Exit the symbol and return to the main timeline by clicking the left-facing arrow in the top-left area above the stage:

Figure 7.27 – Returning to the main timeline

Back on the main timeline, note that the modifications we've made to the symbol have no immediate bearing on any existing instances along the timeline. We will remain on the main timeline to perform our next set of tasks.

> **Note**
>
> The mouth shapes and labels that were used here represent a standard set of vocal sounds that conform to established mouth forms called visemes. Of course, you can always draw your own mouth shapes if you like. The prepared Head symbol timeline can act as your guide if you wish to do so, though there are detailed examples to be found on the internet as well, in a variety of styles.

With our Graphic symbol property configured for use alongside the automated lip sync feature, next, we'll assign the various frames to a proper viseme grid for lip sync interpretation.

Assigning Visemes and Automating Lip Syncing

Earlier in this chapter, we converted our **Head** symbol in the project library from a Movie Clip symbol into a Graphic symbol to prepare it for automated lip sync. As you may recall, we noted that this action would not change the behavior of any of the pre-existing symbol instances on the stage. If you select any **Head** symbol instance on the stage and look at the **Object** tab in the **Properties** panel, you will see that the behavior of the instance remains a Movie Clip in the **Instance Behavior** dropdown.

Before we even attempt to set up our visemes and employ **Lip-Syncing** for our project, we must either create a new instance of the **Head** symbol or change the existing instance behaviors to use the Graphic symbol.

To change the behavior of any symbol instance, select it and make a new selection from the **Instance Behavior** dropdown in the **Properties** panel:

Figure 7.28 – Behavior changed to Graphic

No matter what behavior it previously exhibited, the symbol instance will now behave according to the behavior it has been assigned.

> **Tip**
> Even though you can change instance behavior between symbol types in this way, it is a best practice to change the actual symbol type in the project library as well, for clarity and consistency. As you may recall, we've already done this.

Now, let's prepare our timeline and enter the automated lip-syncing workflow:

1. The first thing you must do is decide where in your existing animation you want the audio playback to start. I suggest starting the audio playback directly after any existing animation, or even removing your previous animation entirely for a clean start:

Figure 7.29 – Ensuring a clean start

In either case, shift the starting keyframe in your **Audio** layer to the point where the audio playback should begin (if necessary) and add a corresponding keyframe within the **Head** layer so that they both align.

2. Scrub to the end of your timeline to ensure that you have enough frames for the audio waveform to complete. My audio file is 6 seconds in length, so I need to add enough frames to ensure there are at least 6 seconds of playback:

Figure 7.30 – Adding the required number of frames

If you need to add additional frames, go ahead and do so. Don't forget to add these extra frames across all your layers!

3. Select the **Head** instance on the stage that aligns with the start of your audio file and look at the **Object** tab of the **Properties** panel. **Instance Behavior** should be **Graphic**. Change its behavior to **Graphic** if it is either **Movie Clip** or **Button**.

4. With the **Graphic** behavior verified, look at the **Looping** section of the **Properties** panel and click the button. The **Lip Syncing** dialog will appear.

5. The first task is to set up our visemes. You will see a grid of possible visemes, but each is identical at first. You must click each viseme and assign it to an appropriate frame derived from within the selected Graphic symbol. Since we also labeled each of our frames, this makes the assignment very simple.

   Go ahead and assign each viseme to each corresponding frame from within the **Head** graphic symbol until they have all been matched up:

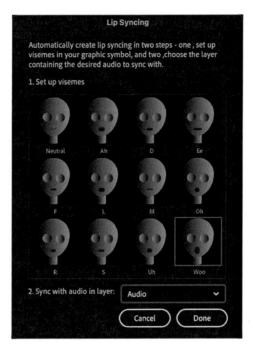

Figure 7.31 – Assigning visemes and the audio layer

6. The second task is to choose which audio layer we will use in the automation process. Since we only have a single layer with audio assigned to it, the **Audio** layer should be selected. If not, select the **Audio** layer from the dropdown.

7. With our visemes mapped and our audio layer selected, click the **Done** button to begin the automated syncing process.

   This process should not take long, and when it's finished, your **Head** layer will include a set of automatically generated keyframes with specific visemes applied across the timeline, as per the sounds that were detected from within the spoken audio file:

Figure 7.32 – Keyframes automatically assigned

8. You can use the playback controls above the timeline to test out the lip syncing and ensure that it has been applied to your satisfaction:

Figure 7.33 – The completed lip sync animation

Now, you can add some additional animation across the wooden doll body part layers, by utilizing the existing **Layer Parenting** relationships, to go along with the spoken audio and produce a fully realized character animation.

> **Note**
>
> If you need to adjust any viseme that was automatically assigned in error, you can always use the frame picker to select an alternative viseme for any keyframe.

In this section, we took the animated content we created with **Layer Parenting** and gave our wooden doll character a voice and the mouth animations to go along with it through automated **Lip Syncing**.

Summary

In this chapter, we began with an overall exploration of **Advanced Layers** mode and why we would want to use it over **Basic Layers** mode for various projects. Following that, we put **Advanced Layers** mode into practice by constructing a complex hierarchy of parent-child relationships using **Layer Parenting**. We also animated our newly created **Layer Parenting** rig through all the normal tweening mechanisms we've come to understand when animating symbol instances across the timeline. Finally, we added voice-based audio to our project and performed automatic lip syncing against that audio through a set of properly configured visemes and the **Lip Syncing** dialog.

In the next chapter, we will explore another type of rigging – **Inverse Kinematics** through the employment of armatures to be animated across various poses within an animated project.

8

Animating Poses with IK Armatures

In the previous chapter, we explored how to use **Layer Parenting** to establish a parent-child relationship among the various layers in an Animate document. This helps us create a type of rig that we can use to animate a character's body parts with ease.

In this chapter, we will explore animating with **Inverse Kinematics** workflows by using fully rigged **IK Armatures**. Armatures in Animate are established by creating **IK Bones** using the **Bone tool** and exist on a single **Armature Layer**. We will build a multi-object armature and explore the various properties associated with each node to establish a solid and refined rig. We will then explore how **Poses** are managed by creating animation through **Inverse Kinematics**. Finally, we will learn how to package a rig for sharing and reuse.

After reading this chapter, you'll be able to do the following in Animate:

- Use the **Bone tool** to establish a rig and understand the concepts behind inverse kinematics.
- Adjust node properties such as joint constraints and physics on the established IK rig.
- Create animated IK content and manage rig poses across the timeline.
- Export a completed rig through the **Animate Asset** file type for sharing and reuse.

Technical Requirements

You will need the following software and hardware to complete this chapter:

- Adobe Animate 2022 (version 22.0 or above).

- Please refer to the Animate system requirements page for hardware specifications: `https://helpx.adobe.com/animate/system-requirements.html`.

Building an Armature using Inverse Kinematics

Previously, we learned how to animate a character across layers with **Layer Parenting** mechanisms using **Advanced Layers** mode. While they are simple enough to use, there are some limitations to consider while constructing your rig using that method, and dealing with so many layers can be a chore. Another rigging mechanism exists in Animate that is capable of similar results, but with a completely different workflow and set of tools. Animate is capable of producing animation through an **Inverse Kinematics** workflow by using the **Bone tool** and special **armature** layers. This will be the focus of the current chapter.

First, we'll address how these two approaches differ from one other and then build a rig using inverse kinematics.

Understanding Inverse Kinematics vs. Forward Kinematics

Just like in the previous chapter, we'll be using the wooden doll artwork to construct our alternate rig. As with all the files referenced in this book, you can locate this file at `https://github.com/PacktPublishing/Adobe-Animate-2022-for-Creative-Professionals-Second-Edition`.

> **Tip**
>
> If you would like to see the animation that we will create using IK, you can always open the `Animated_WoodenDoll.fla` file and perform a **Test Movie** to see it in action before we get to work! Just remember to close it before moving on.

Locate the `WoodenDoll.fla` file and open it within Animate. Just as in the previous chapter, there are two layers within this document: the **Room** layer, which is simply a background image, and the **Doll** layer, which contains a set of body parts that comprise our wooden doll.

Take a moment and refamiliarize yourself with these assets:

Figure 8.1 – The wooden doll starter document

Both **Layer Parenting** and **Inverse Kinematics** share several aspects. For instance, either one can be used effectively to produce complex, jointed character animation.

Layer Parenting is by far the simpler workflow to adopt as you have control over each object, and changing the properties of any object will not affect any additional object, so long as it is not a designated child of the modified object. It is easier to understand for beginners since layers are retained and animation takes place through normal tweening mechanisms.

Inverse Kinematics is a more complex approach as there are many more aspects to consider and tools to master. Alongside the technical aspects, modifying any object along the chain will have an immediate effect on the entire armature rig, affecting even the parent objects physically. More thought has to be put into every aspect of armature rigging since each piece directly influences the other objects making up the armature, and they can all have specific physical properties applied to them that differ from other parts of the rig.

Let's go ahead and compare both of these models, point by point.

Aspects of Layer Parenting

We learned how to use **Layer Parenting** in detail in *Chapter 7, Character Design through Layer Parenting*. This type of animation is sometimes referred to as **Forward Kinematics**, as you change the rotation and position of each joint from the top down. When animating an arm to wave at the viewer, for instance, you would begin by rotating the upper arm, then the lower arm, and finally the hand.

Keep the following aspects of layer parenting in mind:

- It works across many layers through parent-child relationships.
- Manipulating a child object will never influence a parent object.
- It is wholly controlled through **Parenting View** on the timeline, along with the **Free Transform** tool.
- It lacks any sort of constraint mechanism.
- It requires **Advanced Layers** mode to be activated.
- It makes use of normal tweening mechanisms to achieve motion.

Aspects of Inverse Kinematics

Inverse kinematics allows you to create a skeletal structure known as an **armature**, which is then animated as a single object that's influenced by a set of physics-based parameters that make use of various **Poses** over time. This is the primary subject of this chapter. When you're animating an arm to wave at the viewer, you could begin by manipulating any aspect of the arm as rotating the upper or lower arm will influence the other part. You must be very careful!

To implement the various aspects of inverse kinematics with those of layer parenting, consider the following:

- It works on a single, special layer type known as an **Armature Layer**.
- Manipulating a child object has a physical influence over the angle and rotation of the parent objects.
- It is controlled through special tools that can be accessed from the toolbar, such as the **Bone tool**, in addition to the **Free Transform** tool, the management of **Poses** within an **Armature** layer, and special bone properties through the **Properties** panel.
- It lets you constrain aspects of each joint by rotation, position, and more.

- It can be used with either **Basic Layers** mode or **Advanced Layers** mode.
- It makes use of special pose mechanisms, along with individual physical properties, to achieve resultant motion through **Spring** properties.

This information should provide some general ideas regarding the differences that are inherent between both rigging models. We are intentionally using the same assets across both this and the previous chapter to make the best comparison possible between rigging models.

With this background information around both models fresh in our minds, let's move on to rigging using **Inverse Kinematics** and the **Bone tool**.

Using the Bone Tool to Rig Symbol Instances

The **Bone tool** is the tool within Animate that we use to create **Inverse Kinematics** (**IK**) armatures from either a collection of symbol instances or simpler vector shapes, depending on our needs. First, let's explore how to use this tool with a collection of symbol instances, as arranged within the sample document.

To access the **Bone tool**, you will likely need to edit the available tools by utilizing the **Drag and Drop Tools** panel.

You can open this panel by clicking the **Edit Toolbar…** button at the bottom of the toolbar:

Figure 8.2 – Locating the Bone tool

The **Bone tool** and its associated **Bind tool** are located together, toward the bottom of the panel. Drag them onto the toolbar to make them available for working with your document.

> **Note**
>
> The **Bone tool** does not include any **Tool** properties that can be accessed from the **Properties** panel. You must create an armature first before setting various properties associated with IK.

You can use the **Bone tool** to construct an IK rig from separate symbol instances by placing bones across the individual body parts of the wooden doll:

Figure 8.3 – The Bone tool

This action will connect all the associated parts as a single **Armature** and also act as a complete rig that can then be adjusted and animated.

You can use the **Bone tool** by dragging an initial root "tail" bone, followed by additional bones that branch off from the root, to assemble a rough IK structural rig. Think of the rig as a tree, starting with the trunk and then expanding from that across branches and roots. The various bones and joints can then have their properties adjusted through the **Properties** panel, which creates a more refined IK rig for use.

> **Tip**
>
> When you're using the **Bone tool**, I highly recommend that you disable snapping entirely. This can be achieved through the application menu by choosing **View | Snapping | Edit Snapping...** and unchecking all the options shown in the dialog box that appears.

Now, let's look at the **Bone tool** in action as we create an IK rig for our wooden doll:

1. Ensure that the **Bone tool** is selected in the toolbar.

2. Click the top center of the doll's torso and drag a bone up to the neck area. Release your mouse to establish your initial "tail" bone:

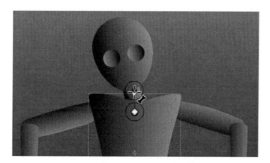

Figure 8.4 – Creating the tail bone connecting the torso and the head

As you start creating additional bones, note how the tail bone of your rig has a slightly different appearance than any other bone you create.

3. It is now possible to click and drag from the origin point of the tail bone to create additional bones. Click and drag a bone from the torso to the upper left arm, at the shoulder. A secondary bone will be created.

4. From the shoulder of the upper left arm, drag another bone to the elbow of the lower left arm:

Figure 8.5 – Branching the bones from the initial tail across the arms

5. Complete the arm branch by dragging a final bone from the elbow to the wrist.

6. Now, you'll need to create additional branches until the entire rig is established:

Figure 8.6 – Fully rigged rough IK armature

The fully rigged armature should include the following:

- A branch from the torso to the head
- Branches across both the right and left arms
- A branch from the torso down to the pelvis
- Secondary branches from the pelvis down the left and right legs

---

Tip

If you have trouble dragging bones to the correct symbol instances to connect them, you can either rearrange things so that the **Armature_1** layer appears below the existing **Doll** layer or arrange the various instances so that the one you need is not obscured by any other.

Notice that as you go through the process of creating your IK rig, the individual instances from the original **Doll** layer are removed from that layer and merged with the automatically created **Armature_1** layer as they are added to the armature itself.

The previous layer has been completely removed:

Figure 8.7 – Newly created armature layer

An **Armature layer** is a special type of layer in Animate that is only used with IK rigging. The keyframes appear as small black diamonds, very similar to what we've seen with motion layers in the past. The layer icon changes to show a human figure in motion and the frame span's background becomes green.

With our IK armature created in this initial state, next, we will establish some refinements for the rig, ensuring that it will behave the way we want it to during manipulation.

Refining the Rig Properties

Once an armature has been created, the **Selection** tool can be used to modify the appearance of the armature by moving its various body parts around. In its initial, rough state, you can get some rather odd results before you start adding constraints and other refinements.

Using the **Selection** tool, click and drag the arms of the armature to create a different pose:

Figure 8.8 – Adjusting unconstrained armature limbs

This isn't very good! The joints have no constraints, so the arms bend around in unnatural ways. In addition, the arm can fly away from the shoulder altogether, making a real mess of our hard work.

A lot of beginners will simply rig up their assets with the **Bone tool** and think that's all there is to it. It is worth taking the time to inspect the properties of both the IK armature itself and also the individual **IK Bone** properties. We'll go ahead and do this now.

First, let's look at the **IK Armature** properties. The armature is bound to the layer, so you'll want to click on any of the frames that make up that layer and refer to the **Frame** tab of the **Properties** panel:

Figure 8.9 – The armature's Frame properties

You'll immediately notice that you are editing **IK Armature** properties. We can provide a meaningful name to our armature here and choose to hide or reveal editing controls and hints that overlay the armature itself on the stage.

Looking further down, you'll find the **Ease** section:

Figure 8.10 – The armature's Ease properties

The **Ease** properties consist of a **Strength** slider, which accepts values from -100 to 100 and defaults to 0. This is just like the easing intensity values we've seen in some of the various tween types covered in previous chapters.

You can also select the type of ease from the **Ease Type** dropdown. This is similar to selecting an ease effect as part of a **Classic tween** or **Shape tween** and the options include **None**, **Simple**, and **Stop and Start**. Each of these two choices has four versions: **Slow**, **Medium**, **Fast**, and **Fastest**. By default, **None** is selected.

I'm going to set my **Ease** properties to a **Strength** of -40 and use **Simple (Medium)** for my **Type** selection. This will provide some weight to the actual motion that's created between the poses of this armature.

We will also find an **Options** section further down the **Properties** panel:

Figure 8.11 – The armature's Options

From here, you can define your armature to have an animation type of **Authortime** or **Runtime**. **Authortime** allows you to use the tools within Animate to design the motion of our IK armature, while **Runtime** makes it so that you can change poses by interacting with the armature at runtime by using the mouse cursor.

> Note
>
> Runtime armatures are only available when you're using ActionScript-based document types targeting Flash Player or AIR.

The **Armature Style** setting determines how the bone overlays appear on the stage as you modify the armature. The default setting is **Solid**, but you can also set this to **Wire**, **Line**, or **None**. This setting does not affect any functionality and is purely a personal preference as to how the various overlay controls appear. I tend to keep mine set to **Solid**.

The last setting in this section is a checkbox that allows you to **Enable springs** when selected or disable springs when deselected. Springs are attributes of individual **IK Bones**, and I suggest leaving this enabled for most armatures. We will go into more detail regarding this feature when we look at individual bone properties.

To view properties specific to any individual bone, use the **Selection** tool and click on the bone itself, not the underlying asset, to select it.

An unselected bone will appear in violet, and a selected bone will be shown in light green:

Figure 8.12 – Bone selection

With a bone selected, we can now explore the **IK Bone** properties. Note that in some of the screenshots, we've hidden the **Room** layer to focus on the individual bones and related controls.

Be sure that the bone is still selected and go to the **Object** tab of the **Properties** panel to view the **IK Bone** properties for the selected bone:

Figure 8.13 – IK Bone properties

The first thing you'll want to do is rename each bone in a way that makes sense. I've selected the bone that is aligned to the upper left arm, so I have named the bone **LeftUpperArm**. Similar to the overall **IK Armature** properties we saw earlier, we can also choose to hide or reveal editing controls and hints directly from each bone in this way. You will want to name every IK bone for organizational clarity.

At the bottom of the section, notice four buttons with directional arrows on them pointing left, right, up, and down. This is a navigational feature that lets you easily traverse the entire armature, bone to bone, by clicking these directional buttons instead of using the **Selection** tool to select each IK bone.

> **Tip**
>
> Depending on the structure of your armature, some of these directional buttons may be disabled. It all depends on the construction of your rig concerning the currently selected bone.

The **Location** section follows this and contains not just location properties, but several additional settings as well:

Figure 8.14 – Location properties

You can view the x and y positions of the bone from here, as the section header indicates, but you can also gauge the length of that **IK Bone** and its present angle. All of these settings cannot be adjusted from here; you need to interact with the armature directly for that.

There are also two settings here that can be manipulated. The little stopwatch icon indicates relative **Speed** and is measured from 0% to 100%. Modifying individual bone speed will provide additional variations of movement when the armature is animated. For instance, perhaps the upper arm moves more slowly than the lower arm because it is closer to the torso and doesn't have as far to travel.

The second setting is the **Pin** checkbox. Enabling this will lock an individual bone in place, freezing all movement. This ensures that the movement of your entire armature is not too wild and can be used to ground the entire armature in place while allowing movement through the other bones.

The **Joint: Rotation** section is very important for realistic movement:

Figure 8.15 – Joint: Rotation properties

You can disable rotation entirely by toggling the switch in the top-right corner of this section to its off position, but it is often best to set angular constraints to each joint instead. If you enable the **Constrain** feature, you can set the angles of constraint through the **Left Offset** and **Right Offset** settings.

Since we are dealing with the upper arm, the joint in question is that of the shoulder. Without a constraint set, the arm can rotate all the way around; the same goes for the lower arm. That's not how the human body works at all!

We can see the constraints visually expressed on our armature as well:

Figure 8.16 – The difference that proper rotation constraints make is huge

The left screenshot shows the initial state of our arm joints with no rotation constraints. The right screenshot shows a more refined rig, with angular constraints at both the shoulder and elbow. This will enable more natural poses for our armature. You will want to perform these constraints across all IK bones.

The next sections, **Joint: X Translation** and **Joint: Y Translation**, are both very similar to **Joint: Rotation** in practice:

Figure 8.17 – Joint: X Translation and Joint: Y Translation properties

Unlike with **Joint: Rotation**, these settings are all toggled off by default and if you want to use them, you will need to hit the toggle switch. **Translation** refers to the amount of movement across a certain number of pixels across all four directions on both the x and y axes. This is not normally something that can be applied to a human figure such as this, but it is often used when rigging machinery. Think of the up and down movement of a set of engine pistons, for example. We won't be using this for our armature, but it's there in case you ever need it!

The final section has to do with **Spring**:

Figure 8.18 – Spring properties

As you may recall, we mentioned **Spring** earlier when we looked at the **IK Armature** properties. **Spring** provides a physical springiness to your motion, even after the object has come to rest. The greater the **Strength** property of **Spring**, the more residual movement will occur. **Damping** is a way to dampen or buffer **Spring** and determines how long it takes for the effects of **Spring** to lessen and finally dissipate. Think of a tree branch following a gust of wind and how the movement slowly winds down over time. This is what can be expressed through **Spring**.

Now that you know how to refine your **IK Armature** and IK bones by using these properties, you'll want to take some time to do so. Be sure to name each bone and set proper constraints where necessary, using the human form as a guide.

There are several tricks you can use when adjusting and testing your armature at this phase. Keep the following in mind as you refine your rig:

- Holding down the *Shift* key while adjusting your rig parts with the **Selection** tool will isolate joint rotation to that specific bone.

- Holding down *Option/Alt* as you click and drag body parts with the **Selection** tool will allow you to relocate assets while keeping the rig intact.

- You can even adjust the transform point of each part using the **Free Transform** tool to modify the joint's position.

- Don't forget to use the **Arrange** options as well to ensure the proper stacking order of the various parts.

When complete, change the name of the armature layer from **Armature_1** to `WoodenDoll`. Be sure to save your `.fla` document as we'll be taking a slight detour in the next section before returning to our wooden doll.

Next, we'll have a brief look at using the **Bone tool** within shapes before moving on to IK animation.

Using Bone Tool to Rig Shapes

So far, we've built our armature out of a collection of symbol instances. We can also create an armature as part of a shape. It is worth going into this a little bit to close out this section before animating our previously created wooden doll.

Creating an IK armature with an **IK shape** is very similar to creating an **IK Armature** with **Movie Clip** symbol instances. The main difference is that you can build this using only a single shape object, while we previously made use of a set of different objects bound together using an IK armature.

Let's explore how to use inverse kinematics using a single shape:

1. Create a new document of any size and use one of the shape tools to draw out a basic shape. I'm simply going to create a long, rounded rectangle for this example:

Figure 8.19 – Basic shape created

2. Select **Bone Tool** and drag out a bone to one end of the shape, covering about one-fifth of the entire shape. This is the initial "tail" bone for your IK shape-based armature:

Figure 8.20 – Dragging the tail bone

3. With the tail created, we can now drag out branching bones from this tail bone to create either a linear or multi-branch armature within the shape. Continue laying down additional bones across the IK shape until you reach the other end:

Figure 8.21 – Shape-based armature created

4. At this point, the shape has been converted into a special type of object in Animate called an **IK Shape** and contains a complete armature. Using the **Selection** tool, drag one end of your armature around to see how the bones affect the shape itself:

Figure 8.22 – Shape armature movement

The shape will morph along with the internal bone structure you've created.

> **Note**
>
> You can still refine this armature by using the **IK Armature** and **IK Bone** properties, such as joint rotation constraints, joint translation, and spring, which we examined previously. All these settings work the same, no matter what style of armature you create.

You may notice that as you modify the armature with the **Selection** tool, sometimes, the edges of the shape become odd. We can control such behavior by using the **Bind tool**, which we will cover in the next section.

Using Bind Tool to Refine Shapes

Only applicable to **IK Armatures** created with shapes, we can use the **Bind tool** to modify connections between existing bones and the shape control points that define the overall path. If you are having extreme and unwanted distortion in your shape as you adjust the armature, this tool can help you refine and eliminate these oddities.

The **Bind tool** is likely going to have to be added to the toolbar through the **Edit Toolbar...** button at the bottom of the **Tools** panel. If you didn't add this tool alongside the **Bone tool** earlier, you'll want to do this now.

Its appearance is similar to the icon for the **Bone tool**, but with an additional little target reticle alongside it:

Figure 8.23 – The Bind tool

The **Bind tool** is used for control point management within shape-based armatures.

If you select any IK bone in your armature, you will see the various control points attributed to that particular bone highlighted in yellow:

Figure 8.24 – Bone selected with the associated control points

Control points are the shape path anchor points but, within an IK armature, they are additionally associated with particular bones so that the overall shape can be morphed as the armature shifts around.

You can also select any control point to highlight any of the bones associated with that point by clicking a control point with the **Bind tool** selected. This gives you a good idea of which points are controlled by which bones.

To change control point associations, you can select a bone and then hold down the *Shift* key to select additional control points you want to associate with the selected bone. To remove associations, you can hold down *Option/Alt* and click any of the currently highlighted points.

> **Tip**
> Managing various control points and bone associations can help remedy any extreme morphing when dealing with IK shapes, although it can be very finicky to work with and we should be extra cautious when using this workflow.

In this section, we learned how to build IK armatures using the **Bone tool** and refined our armatures using the various properties and settings available. We explored the construction of armatures using both symbol instances and shapes and learned how to constrain joint rotation and translation to achieve a solid, capable rig. Next, we will explore how to create animation using our IK armature by using **Poses**.

Animating an IK Armature

Now that we have created our armature and refined its various properties, it's ready to be animated. The motion of an IK armature is not animated using any of the tweening methods we've seen up to this point. Instead, we can define various poses across the timeline and Animate will automatically fill in the frames between each pose. It can do this without creating any additional tween as the layer is already an **Armature Layer**, similar to how Motion Layers work when establishing a **Motion Tween**.

Let's define some additional poses so that we can animate the wooden doll figure jumping into the air.

Creating Additional Poses

Looking at the **WoodenDoll Armature Layer** as it is right now, there is a single pose at frame 1. A pose is signified by a small diamond shape along the timeline. As expressed previously, we can animate IK armatures by defining poses as various spots along the timeline. A pose behaves very similarly to a keyframe, except that a keyframe contains the properties for a single object, while a pose contains the properties for all the objects that make up your armature and is all handled through the single pose.

For this animation, we want our figure to jump into the air and then land again. We will require a set of four distinct poses for this animation to occur:

Figure 8.25 – The four necessary poses

You can think of the four poses in this way, and in this order:

- **Resting**: A pose where the figure is standing at a comfortable resting position.
- **Anticipation**: A crouching pose where the figure prepares to jump.
- **Active**: This is where the figure is up in the air, at the apex of an active jump.
- **Recovery**: The figure hits the ground and, from this point, can go back to the resting or anticipation poses, depending on how many times you'd like it to jump.

Let's go ahead and create these **Poses** now. You can refer to the previous figure of all four **Poses** as a visual guide:

1. The first pose we need to create is our resting pose. This pose exists on frame 1 and, as shown within the timeline, the pose itself already exists:

Figure 8.26 – The initial pose at frame 1

Use the **Free Transform** tool to position and rotate each of the body parts so that the pose appears similar to the resting example:

Figure 8.27 – The resting pose

2. To create an animation, we need more than a single frame on the timeline. Extend the current frame span to the 3 second marker at frame 72 (assuming you have a 24 FPS document setting) so that we have a good amount of time to plot our poses across.

3. Now, let's create our second pose. Recall that poses are represented by small diamond-shaped keyframes along the timeline. Move the playhead to frame 12 and use the **Free Transform** tool to adjust the various body parts so that the figure is crouching in preparation to jump, similar to the anticipation pose example:

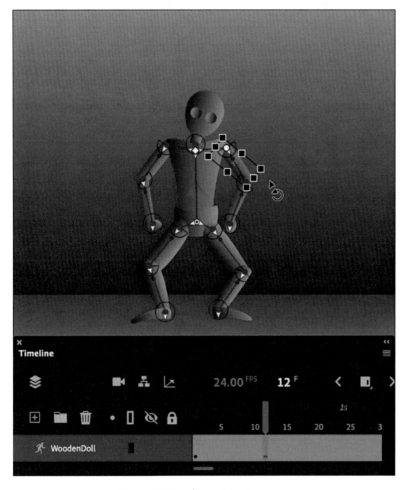

Figure 8.28 – The anticipation pose

With two poses established, scrub the playhead along the timeline and see how the figure animates automatically between each pose. Each time we add a new pose, the frames in-between the poses will update, just as though we were using a tween.

4. Move the playhead to frame 18 to create a new arrangement representing the proposed action pose. Use the **Free Transform** tool to place the legs together and the arms stretched out wide. You'll also need to shift the armature's position higher on the stage to fully realize the jumping motion:

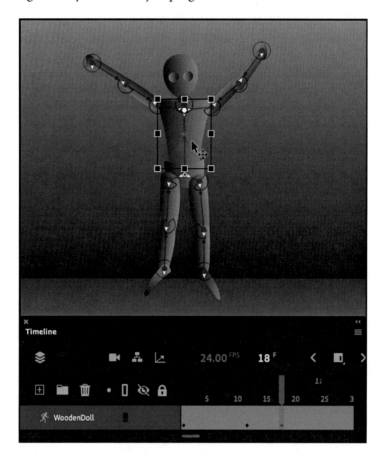

Figure 8.29 – The active pose

5. The final pose represents the figure having jumped, now landing on the floor in a recovery position on frame 22. Ensure that the figure is securely planted on the floor by changing the armature's overall position. Using the **Free Transform** tool again, bring the arms down a bit and ensure that the feet and legs look appropriate concerning the floor beneath:

Figure 8.30 – The recovery pose

6. Test your animation by playing it back with the timeline playback controls or through the **Test Movie** command.

If anything needs to be adjusted, you can go back and adjust the IK armature, the IK bones, or the individual poses to make everything as smooth and realistic as possible.

We now have a single jump cycle composed of four distinct poses, but we can go further than this! Let's learn how to manage the various poses we've established in different ways.

Managing Armature Poses

Once you have created your **IK Armature** poses, it is very simple to then copy and paste them wherever they're needed to produce a full animation. In this section, we'll refine our overall animation and reproduce the completed animation cycle for our wooden doll figure.

Since we've already created our various poses, it is now just a matter of arranging them at different points along the timeline:

1. The first thing we want to do is place a hold on our initial resting animation for a few frames. Select the pose on frame 1 and right-click to summon the menu. Choose **Copy Pose** from the menu items that appear:

Figure 8.31 – Copying an existing pose

2. Now, select frame 7 and right-click again. Choose **Paste Pose** from that same menu to create identical poses across these frames, essentially creating a pause in the action:

Figure 8.32 – The pasted pose creates a pause

3. With the initial pose still present in the system clipboard, move to frame 25 and select it.

4. Right-click once again and choose **Paste Pose** from the menu that appears. This will bring the wooden doll back to a resting position following the anticipation, action, and recovery poses. We now have a full animation cycle defined within our timeline.

5. To repeat this cycle, we can copy and paste full spans of frames, including poses. Select frames 7 – 25:

Figure 8.33 – Frame span selected to copy

Right-click to summon the contextual menu for frame selections.

6. Choose **Copy Frames** from the menu that has appeared.

7. Select frame 30 and summon the right-click menu once again.

8. This time, select the **Paste and Overwrite Frames** option to paste the frame span without extending the overall timeline:

Figure 8.34 – The pasted frame span produces a repeated cycle

The frame span has been added to our existing animation cycle as a separate armature frame span and, upon playback, the figure jumps twice. Notice the vertical lines that appear as part of the layer. These indicate where each armature span begins.

Since we have multiple armature spans now, we can manage these armature spans through the frame selection right-click menu by choosing **Join Armature** or **Split Armature**.

You can now continue adding additional jump cycles in this way and even go back and tweak the various poses to add some variability to the entire animation. It's entirely up to you!

> **Note**
>
> You can also choose **Clear Pose** from the right-click menu on an existing pose, which will remove it from the timeline in its entirety. The **Insert Pose** option, which is right above **Clear Pose**, will insert a new pose at the selected frame manually.

In this section, we explored how to animate our IK armature using poses and how to manage those poses across the timeline. In the next section, we'll wrap this chapter up by examining how to share our carefully crafted rig as an **Animate Asset**.

Sharing a Completed IK Rig

While we can copy and paste frames and even entire layers from one document to another, it can be a bit cumbersome to do so and is very unorganized in practice. Animate comes equipped with a workflow for sharing rigged objects through **Animate Asset** (.ana) files.

Let's learn how to export these files to either preserve them in an organized way, share them with colleagues, or make them available as a persistent resource through the **Assets** panel.

Saving a Rig for Reuse

If you've created an IK armature and you'd like to save it so that you can use it on additional assets in the future, Animate has a workflow that can be used to generate your rig as an **Animate Asset** for sharing or for direct use from the **Assets** panel.

If we want to preserve our wooden doll armature as a rig, we need to wrap it within a symbol, as follows:

1. Right-click on the **WoodenDoll** layer and choose **Convert Layers to Symbol** from the menu that appears.

2. In the **Convert Layers to Symbol** dialog, name it **WoodenDoll** and choose **Graphic** as the symbol type:

Figure 8.35 – Converting your armature into a Graphic symbol

We are using a **Graphic** symbol so that the armature animation can be viewed within the authoring environment timeline. If we created a **Movie Clip** symbol, the only way to preview would be via **Test Movie**.

3. When you're ready, click **OK** to perform the conversion. The full **IK Armature** layer will be wrapped within the symbol and an instance will be placed within the timeline, replacing the layer that was there previously:

Figure 8.36 – The IK armature layer has been replaced

Once you have created your symbol with a fully rigged armature within it, locate the symbol you want to export as a rig from the **Library** panel. We'll use the **Library** panel to export our rig as an **Animate Asset** (.ana) file.

To export a symbol from our document to use as a sharable asset, perform the following steps:

1. Select the symbol in the **Library** panel and open the menu by right-clicking it:

Figure 8.37 – Exporting an asset from the Library panel

You'll find two options here: **Export Asset…** and **Save As Asset…**. Either one will create the rig, but if we want to save to a .ana file, we'll need to choose **Export Asset…** and make a few selections in the dialog that follows.

2. Once **Export Asset…** has been chosen, a dialog will open and present you with several options:

Figure 8.38 – Saving a rig for reuse as an Animate asset

These dialog options include providing the asset with a **Name** and choosing which aspects of the asset you want to include: **Objects**, **Bones**, **Motion**, or **Audio**. Only those aspects of the asset that are available for packaging can be chosen. As we have no audio, that option is not available.

Depending on your checkbox selections, the **Type** property of the asset to be saved will be displayed. In this case, I'm saving an **Animated Rigged Object**. You can also input a set of **Tags** here to help locate your asset once within the **Assets** panel through the integrated search mechanism.

3. Click **Export** and save your asset as a `.ana` file:

Figure 8.39 – An Animate Asset file

The Animate Asset now exists as a `.ana` file on your hard drive, which can now be distributed to others or added to your version of Animate through the **Assets** panel.

Next, you'll learn how to import a `.ana` file from your local filesystem into Animate.

Importing a Rig within the Assets Panel

Let's close out this chapter by importing the .ana file we created into our **Assets** panel for reuse. Of course, if the option to **Save As Asset...** was selected from the **Library** panel menu instead of **Export Asset...**, your asset would immediately be added to the **Assets** panel and no .ana file would be generated.

The first step of importing an exported **Animate Asset** file is to open your **Assets** panel and click the **Custom** tab:

Figure 8.40 – Importing an Animate asset

Depending on whether you have added any assets previously, some may be present here; otherwise, your panel will be empty. There is a small button in the bottom-left corner of the panel that looks like a big plus symbol. This is the **Import Assets** button. Clicking this will open a file browser, which you can use to locate the .ana file you want to import.

Once you have chosen the file you want, it will be added to the appropriate category within the **Assets** panel:

Figure 8.41 – Imported rigged object within the Assets panel

You should also perform a search from the panel based on the tags that were input when you exported the asset. Once imported, an asset such as this can be used across Animate documents as a persistent resource.

> **Note**
>
> You can also import assets by using the **Assets** panel options menu in the top-right corner by choosing **Import**. You can manage your custom assets through this menu since you have access to options such as **Delete**.

Aside from **Rigged Objects**, you can also save **Rig** alone, to be applied to existing artwork. Rigs can be included in the **Custom** tab of the **Assets** panel but are also available in the **Default** view. Rigs can be applied to existing artwork by using the **Rig Mapping** panel.

The **Rig Mapping** panel can be opened from the application menu by choosing **Window | Rig Mapping**. This panel will also open automatically when you're selecting a **Rig** for use within the **Assets** panel. This is because you must identify individual movie clip symbol instances to apply to specific bones of the rig armature:

Figure 8.42 – Locating Rigs within the Assets panel

To apply a **Rig** from the **Assets** panel to a symbol instance, you must double-click the instance to enter the symbol itself. Dragging and dropping a rig onto the stage will then open the **Rig Mapping** panel, where you can map certain visual elements, such as the torso, arms, legs, and so on, to the **Rig** itself.

You simply click each bone in the **Rig Mapping** panel and then choose individual movie clip symbol instances within the containing symbol to associate each bone with a symbol instance. This will allow the system to recreate the full armature:

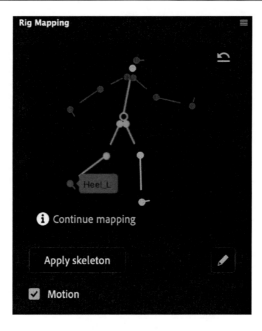

Figure 8.43 – Applying a pre-built rig

Be sure to start from the root node and then branch off from there. Rigged bones will appear green, while unrigged bones will appear gray.

Once you've mapped all the necessary visuals to the rig, choosing **Apply skeleton** will create an armature – with full animation if the **Motion** checkbox is selected – for your symbol instance.

Once a skeleton has been completely applied to a set of objects, **Rig** will appear pink.

Tip

There is also a way to automatically map a rig to your symbol instance and avoid the manual mapping process. For this to work, be sure that each of the movie clip symbol instances that make up your visuals include **instance names** that are identical to those from the rig itself. This method bypasses the visual **Rig Mapping** panel workflow altogether but is very specific.

In this section, we looked at how to preserve, share, and apply our IK armature rigs, motion, and assets by creating and using **Animate Asset** files. These files can be used to preserve important assets or share them with colleagues and the wider world!

Summary

In this chapter, we took a deep dive into one of the most mystifying workflows in all of Animate – **Inverse Kinematics**. This is truly a professional-level animation workflow and one that can easily be done incorrectly if you don't have a good understanding of all the different aspects involved in IK armatures, IK bones, poses, and the various settings attributed to each. You can now confidently rig an armature using inverse kinematics in a refined and believable way, as well as animate the character or figure attributed to your armature by creating and managing poses across the timeline.

In the next chapter, we are going to look at the most modern and flexible method of creating rigging for your animated content; that is, by using **Warped Objects**.

9
Manipulating Warped Objects through Advanced Rigging

In the previous chapter, we saw how to build complex **Inverse Kinematics (IK)** armatures and create fully animated figures using the tools and workflows present within the software. In this chapter, we will examine workflows associated with the **Asset Warp** tool and the creation and management of **Warped Objects**.

This chapter presents an introduction to the **Asset Warp tool** and how to use it to create Warped Objects out of our vector or bitmap-based artwork through the placement of **pins**. We'll also see how to manipulate these pins across time and create animation through tweening property differences between keyframes. We then explore more advanced uses for these workflows through **modern rigging** and the creation of rich armatures, with the ability to manipulate **bones** and **joints** as part of our Warped Objects. Finally, we'll perform animation with an armature that makes use of **hard bones**, **soft bones**, **freeze joints**, and more!

After reading this chapter, you will have learned how to do the following:

- Use the **Asset Warp** tool to create Warped Objects.
- Use the **Asset Warp** tool to build modern rigs within Warped Objects.
- Make use of various pin, bone, and joint options within Warped Objects.
- Animate content using Warped Object meshes and armatures.

Technical Requirements

You will need the following software and hardware to complete this chapter:

- Adobe Animate 2022 (version 22.0.2 or above)
- Refer to the Animate system requirements page for the hardware specifications: `https://helpx.adobe.com/animate/system-requirements.html`

Warped Objects and the Asset Warp Tool

Using the **Asset Warp** tool, we can create a special kind of object—a **Warped Object**—out of vector shapes or bitmap images. This object type includes the underlying artwork within a container that exhibits a distortion mesh. This allows the mesh to influence the artwork within through the use of **Pins** and **Bones**. Warped Objects are somewhat similar to symbols, but they will not appear within the Library as symbols do. They can, however, be animated like symbols through the use of keyframes and Classic Tweens.

> **Tip**
> Be sure that you do not attempt to use the **Asset Warp** tool on a symbol instance—it simply will not work.

Initially, Warped Objects and the **Asset Warp** tool were added to Animate 2019 in October 2018. Despite the feature being part of the application for nearly 3 years, not much had been done to expand upon the workflows originally introduced with the tool since then. This has all changed with the release of Animate 2022, however, as the feature set has been greatly expanded with additional properties that allow the inclusion of hard and soft bones as part of the distortion mesh, frozen joints, and more!

> **Note**
>
> Newer features involving the creation of bones and modern rigging were not included in the initial released version of Animate 2022 (22.0.0) but were originally intended for it. They were actually released during a follow-up version (22.0.2). If you do not see these options in your installed version of Animate 2022, check for an update!

The **Asset Warp** tool itself appears as a pushpin icon in the Animate toolbar:

Figure 9.1 – The Asset Warp tool

Once you select this tool, you can set the general **Tool** properties through the **Properties** panel, and once you establish a Warped Object through the use of this tool on vector shapes or a bitmap image, you'll be able to define properties specific to the whole object, pins, bones, and more via the **Object** tab in the **Properties** panel:

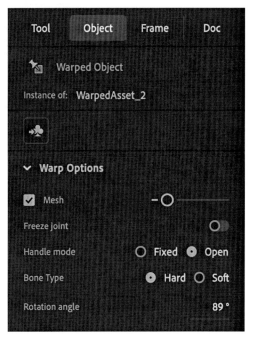

Figure 9.2 – Asset Warp tool properties versus Warped Object properties

A Warped Object has a couple of unique properties that can be exploited within the **Warp Options** section of the panel. The availability of these options will depend upon whether you are observing **Tool** properties or **Object** properties. The various properties are explained here:

- **Mesh**—This is a toggle switch that will display the mesh when active or hide the mesh when not active. It is active by default.

  The complexity of the mesh can be controlled through manipulation of the associated **Mesh Density Slider** when a Warped Object has been selected.

- **Create Bones**—Allows the creation of bones when toggled on, and if toggled off, will create simpler distortion pins instead.

- **Freeze Joint**—This allows you to select an existing joint and freeze it so that it is not displaced as the rest of the armature is shifted about.

- **Handle Mode**—An **Open** handle is the default mode and is more impactful to the surrounding mesh fragments:

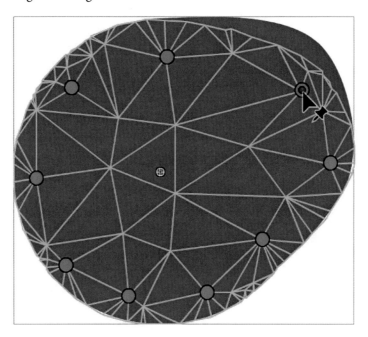

Figure 9.3 – Moving pin locations modifies the mesh

A **Fixed** handle is less impactful but also allows you to rotate the mesh around it:

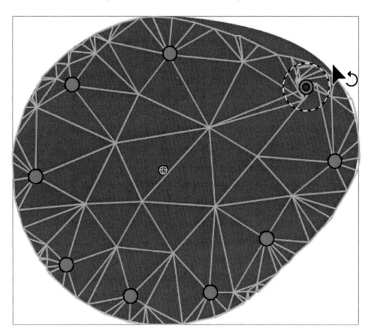

Figure 9.4 – Fixed handle mode can rotate around pins

Play around with both handle modes to see what works best for your chosen assets. The most important thing is to make decisions about which handle modes to use before any animation is attempted.

- **Bone Type**—Choosing **Hard** will make the bone behave similarly to what we've seen in IK armatures, while choosing **Soft** will allow the bone and the attached artwork to bend and squish.

- **Rotation Angle**—Provides a convenient way to adjust the rotation angle of a pin or bone through numeric values instead of on the stage.

> **Note**
>
> You may want to also refer to *Chapter 1, A Brief Introduction to Adobe Animate*, for additional information about the **Asset Warp** tool and its new capabilities.

We'll explore the use of bones within Warped Object meshes in an upcoming section of this chapter. For now, let's focus on using pins to distort Warped Object meshes and influence the contained artwork.

Creating Distortion Meshes using Pins

We'll now explore the creation of Warped Objects and the use of the **Asset Warp** tool to create distortion meshes through pins. We first need to either import a bitmap image or design a vector graphic to establish the Warped Object upon.

Let's design a spooky little ghost character in Animate for this example:

1. Create a new ActionScript 3.0 document and save it to your local hard drive. As this format is native to Animate, we can use the full range of tools and features of the software.

2. Set the width and height of the stage to a value of 800px. This will be a 1:1 ratio and will form a square, suitable to publish to social networks such as Instagram. When exporting or publishing, you can always scale the resolution up or down to match specific social network standards such as Instagram's recommended 1080px – it's all scalable vector content, after all! The **frames per second** (**FPS**) value should be 30.

3. Set the background color of the document to something like an autumnal orange or tan color. I'm using a value of #D06401 for mine.

4. Ensure that **Snap to grid** is activated from the **View | Grid | Edit Grid** menu selection:

Figure 9.5 – Grid settings

5. Set the grid cell size to 40px at each dimension. This will ensure that the shapes we draw will be easily snapped to the dimensions we want to align to when drawing.

6. Now, select the **Rectangle** tool and disable the stroke. Choose a spooky violet color for the fill. I've chosen a value of #6666CC. This will be the color of our ghost:

Figure 9.6 – Tool settings established with Object drawing mode off

Ensure that **Object Drawing Mode** is disabled in order to create simple shapes and not Drawing Objects.

7. Draw a square upon the stage that measures 360x360 pixels. Use the grid snapping to help you along with this task.

8. Select the **Oval tool** and note that the stroke and fill settings are retained from the **Rectangle** tool. Draw a circle that also measures 360x360 pixels alongside the square but ensure they do not overlap. The result should look like this:

Figure 9.7 – Square and circle shapes are established

9. Switch over to the **Selection tool** and drag the circle shape to the top of the square shape so that the center of the circle aligns with the very top of the square and both objects are perfectly vertically aligned.

Figure 9.8 – Creating a compound shape

Once again, the grid snapping should assist you in placing these objects correctly.

10. Select the **Oval tool** once more and change the fill color to solid black. Draw a set of elongated ovals to serve as the ghost's hollow eyes. The sizing and shape of the eyes are really up to you. Here's what my example looks like:

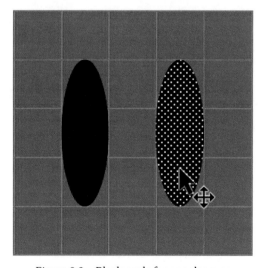

Figure 9.9 – Black ovals for spooky eyes

11. Select both eyes and place them upon the ghost shape in order to complete the ghost character.

Figure 9.10 – The completed ghost character

12. Double-click the ghost to select the ghost along with its black eyes. Now, use the **Align panel** to center the character both horizontally and vertically to the stage.

13. We no longer require the grid to be visible now that the ghost is complete. Hide the grid by unchecking **View | Grid | Show Grid** from the application menu and save your work.

So easy to create a little ghost, right? While the edges and angles of the ghost character are very straight and clean right now, we'll want to make additional changes to provide a more ephemeral and cloth-like appearance to this ghost… especially when it comes to the bottom portion. We can accomplish all of this through the use of a distortion mesh, and we create such a mesh through the use of the **Asset Warp** tool.

We will now convert the set of vector shapes that make up our ghost into a Warped Object and will add a number of pins in order to provide these qualities to our ghost character. To do that, follow these steps:

1. Select the **Asset Warp tool** from the tools panel and click anywhere on the little ghost to select it:

Figure 9.11 – Selecting an object with the Asset Warp tool

The mouse cursor changes to add a little plus (+) sign next to it, indicating that the next click will add a pin to the selected object.

2. With the **Asset Warp** tool still selected, click the lower-right corner area of the ghost to set your initial pin:

Figure 9.12 – The shape is transformed into a Warped Object

A distortion mesh is applied to the shape and it is transformed into a Warped Object.

3. Create a set of pins across the ghost in any way you like. I've simply created them along the outside edge all around:

Figure 9.13 – The completed distortion mesh

4. Try playing with the **Mesh Density Slider** to see how it changes the mesh you've created. I suggest keeping the mesh fairly simple for this small project.

5. When you are ready, begin using the **Asset Warp** tool to select and drag pins slighting in different directions to create a visible distortion to the ghost shape. You can influence the straight lines we created to make them wavier, as you'd expect from a spooky ghost like this:

Figure 9.14 – The underlying artwork is distorted by the mesh

6. Continue adjusting the pins and various properties until you are pleased with the result.

With our Warped Object established, we'll next have a look at animating between mesh states, as established through regular keyframes.

Animating Warped Object Meshes

As mentioned previously, when you convert a bitmap or shape into a Warped Object, it doesn't become a symbol and cannot be found within the **Library** panel. Despite this, a Warped Object can behave very much like a symbol and can be animated through the use of Classic Tweens in a similar way to symbol instances.

> **Tip**
> Even though it doesn't appear in the project library, you can still edit the underlying artwork of a Warped Object by right-clicking upon it and choosing **Edit Selected** from the menu that appears.

We are now going to establish keyframes across the layer containing our Warped Object and will make use of Classic Tweens to animate between these keyframes. Any variation in the mesh between keyframes will cause a distortion effect similar to moving cloth or morphing shapes that can be tweened across time.

1. The first thing you'll want to do is give your layer a proper name. Double-click the existing layer you've been working on and name it ghost.

2. Next, create a new keyframe at frame 15. We will be adjusting the pins at this keyframe in order to create our animation:

Figure 9.15 – A keyframe is created at frame 15

3. Create a third keyframe at frame 30. This will exhibit the same properties as the keyframe at frame 1, completing a looping animation:

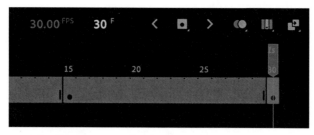

Figure 9.16 – A keyframe is created at frame 30 that is equal to the one at frame 1

4. Move the playhead back to the keyframe at frame 15 and shift the various pins in order to distort the mesh in a different way.

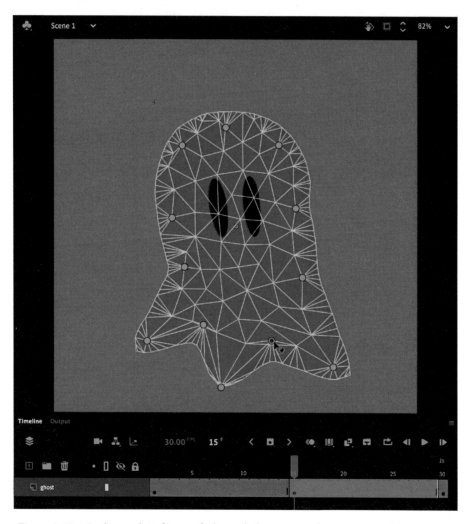

Figure 9.17 – As the mesh is distorted, the underlying artwork is represented accordingly

5. Changes in pin properties across keyframes can be tweened just as with symbol instance property changes by using a Classic Tween. Selecting frames across both frame spans, create a Classic Tween:

Figure 9.18 – Creating a Classic Tween across both frame spans

6. To complete the motion, we'll add an easing preset to both tweens. Apply the **Sine** preset from the **Ease In Out** category to each of them to create a floaty effect to the ghost's movement:

Figure 9.19 – Applying the Sine preset from the Ease In Out category

7. Perform a **Test Movie** to watch the smooth, looping animation of the hovering ghost.

You can apply such mesh distortions and resulting tweened animation to all sorts of content—both vector shapes and imported bitmap images. This sort of animation based upon mesh distortion is great for things that have subtle movements, such as cloth, hair, or—of course—spooky little ghosts.

In this section, we got an overview of the **Asset Warp** tool and how to use it to create Warped Objects using pins and mesh deformations. We also produced a short, looping animation through the use of pin property changes and Classic Tween animation with our Warped Object. Next, we will explore an exciting new set of capabilities with the **Asset Warp** tool and Warped Objects through the construction of bones and modern rigging techniques.

Animating Warped Objects using Armatures

Before we begin building armatures with the **Asset Warp** tool, you'll likely be wondering how this type of armature differs from the IK and layer parenting rigs we've explored in previous chapters.

Rigging with **Inverse Kinematics** and the **Bone** tool is meant to be very physics-based but still quite precise as everything conforms to the IK bones that are established as part of the rig. The largest obstacle here is that IK is a more advanced type of rigging that takes a while to do correctly because you have so many options over each bone and joint.

Rigging through **Layer Parenting** is unique again, in that it affords a simple mechanism for tweening layer content through the use of familiar workflows possible with the **Selection tool** tool and **Free Transform** tool. Layer parenting is simple to pick up for those who are already familiar with basic tweening workflows, but the motion generated can be very mechanical and stiff as it does not have the rich physics properties associated with an IK rig.

Rigging with **Warped Objects** is also quite easy for newcomers to pick up but works through the same mesh deformations we've seen in the little ghost project. This type of rigging is more fluid and has a completely different appearance than the other two but still can provide precise control through the use of bones and joints.

Building armatures and then animating them is what Adobe has termed *modern rigging* and is meant to be more accessible to newcomers but also offers a different type of result than the other rigging options. Adobe also views the capabilities that exist in this type of rigging to be just the beginning of the modern rigging feature set. It is also important to note that this is not a replacement for any other rigging type—it is simply another option in your toolbox.

To get started with modern rigging, we'll make use of some starter files that have been prepared for this purpose. Locate the downloaded files and look within the folder for this chapter to make use of the appropriate file.

> **Note**
>
> The gnarly tree assets that we will use in this section can be downloaded from `https://github.com/PacktPublishing/Adobe-Animate-2022-for-Creative-Professionals-Second-Edition.`

Open the `SpookyTree.fla` file to get started:

Figure 9.20 – The Warped Object armature starter file

There are two layers present—one for the tree, and another for the background elements. The file is a 16:9 resolution at `1920 x 1080` and includes no animated content whatsoever. The frame rate is set to `30` FPS.

We will be creating a series of complex armatures for the tree and rope swing using the **Asset Warp** tool by transforming the gnarly tree bitmap instance into a Warped Object. Once the armatures are established, we'll perform some dynamic animation to simulate the tree being buffeted about by strong winds, with the rope swing likewise disturbed.

Creating Armatures using Warped Objects

As we've seen in our previous experiences with the **Asset Warp** tool, there exists an option to either create pins or bones through the use of a simple toggle switch in the **Tool** tab of the **Properties panel** with the **Asset Warp tool** selected.

Let's begin by creating our Warped Object:

1. First, we'll select the **Asset Warp** tool and ensure that **Create bones** is toggled to the on state within the **Tool** tab of the **Properties** panel:

Figure 9.21 – Create bones must be toggled on

We will keep **Bone Type** set to **Hard** for now.

2. Let's begin creating our armature. Click the bottom trunk area of the tree once to select the bitmap and click a second time to establish an initial pin and transform it into a Warped Object:

Figure 9.22 – A pin is added and a distortion mesh created

3. Move your cursor up the truck of the tree about halfway and click to produce a joint. A hard bone is automatically created between the two joints:

Figure 9.23 – Bones appear as sticks between joints

4. Proceed in a branching pattern up each section of the tree to create a full armature. To create bones from additional joints and establish more branches, simply select the joint you'd like to have bones originate from:

Figure 9.24 – Selected joints exhibit a red dot

Do not create any bones for the branch with the swing just yet, as we'll do that in a special way once the initial armature is established.

Before proceeding, let's examine some tips that may help you work with the joints you've laid out so far:

- To help visualize the armature you are building and unclutter the screen, you may want to turn off the mesh overlay. To do so, simply uncheck the **Mesh** checkbox in the **Warp Options**.

Figure 9.25 – Turning off the mesh overlay

- Again, to branch out from any joint along the armature, simply select an existing joint, and any additional bones you create will originate from the selected joint.

- You can delete any bones by selecting the associated joint and pressing the *Delete* key on your keyboard:

Figure 9.26 – Deleting bones in an established armature will create multiple armatures

- If you select an existing joint and hold the *Option* or *Alt* key on your keyboard as you click another joint, a hard bone will be created between them. You can even use this to connect two separate armatures.

- To relocate any joints, you can hold the *Option* or *Alt* key on your keyboard before dragging the joint to a new location:

Figure 9.27 – The cursor will change to let you know the joint is movable

Go ahead and build out your armature to match the branching structure of the tree, using the tips and tricks previously mentioned to guide you. Remember to leave the branch with the swing alone for now.

The initial structure should look similar to the figure below:

Figure 9.28 – The initial tree rig will appear similar to this

Use the **Asset Warp** tool to move the armature around and get a feel for how these bones work across the mesh distortion to affect the underlying artwork:

Figure 9.29 – Shifting the armature through joint movement

We've only used rigid, hard bones in this armature so far. These bones are suitable for the branches of a tree, but you can imagine that if the wind is going to make these rigid branches move and sway, it has to have a greater influence on the rope swing attached to one of the lower branches. Additionally, the thicker parts of the tree are not going to be swayed by any wind and should be frozen in place.

We'll now grow and modify our rig to take all of these concerns into account:

1. Using the **Asset Warp** tool, create a set of bones for the remaining limb that will appear similar to what you see in the following figure:

Figure 9.30 – Bones along the rope-swing limb

It is important that a joint exists between the two ropes, as we will create a soft bone from here to influence the swing.

2.   Create a new bone from the joint in between the two ropes that extends to the swing seat below, and in the **Properties** panel change the **Bone Type** to **Soft**.

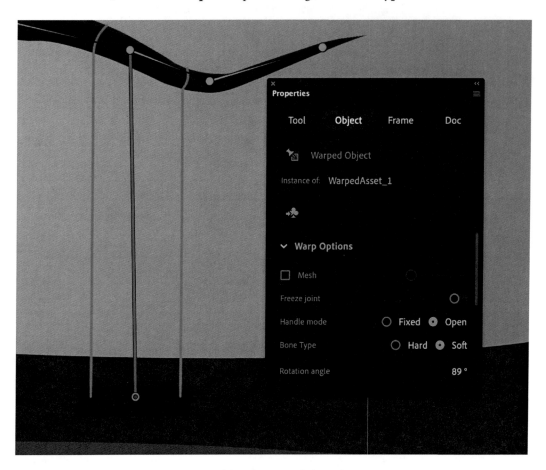

Figure 9.31 – A soft bone is created along the rope swing

3.   Test out the differences in the use of soft bones by dragging the joint at the base of the swing up toward the tree:

Figure 9.32 – Soft bones have a different appearance from hard bones

The ropes distort with a soft bone, just as you would expect they might in reality, bending and twirling in the wind. Soft bones are great for objects and materials of this nature.

4. We'll complete our rig by making use of **Freeze Joints** along the thick trunk. Select one of the joints along the thick part of the trunk and toggle the **Freeze joint** option in the **Warp Options** to the *on* position I've frozen two of the joints along my trunk:

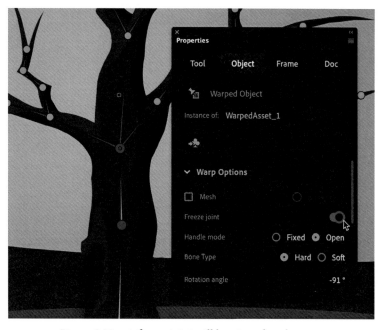

Figure 9.33 – A freeze joint will be pinned to the stage

Remember that you can always re-enable the mesh and use the **Mesh Density Slider** to increase or decrease the complexity of the deformation mesh. Before moving on, give the slider a go in order to get a feel for how it impacts the influence of what we've built.

When you feel you are ready to move on, compare the rig you've created with the one in the following figure. Note that the number of joints, their placement, and the mesh complexity will likely be different from what you see in my image, and that is fine! The important things are around how the rig functions as a whole.

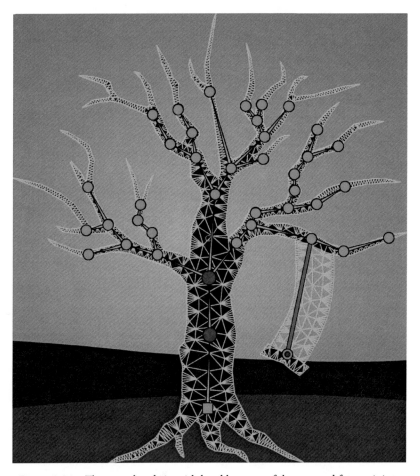

Figure 9.34 – The completed rig with hard bones, soft bones, and frozen joints

Now that we have our rig established, we'll next look at creating some animation through keyframing and Classic Tweens to have the tree and rope swing blow about in the wind.

Animating with Modern Rigging Techniques

We've already seen how to animate a Warped Object through the use of basic pins, but we now have the ability to create bones-based armatures within Warped Objects as well. This is what Adobe has termed *modern rigging* within Animate and is a brand-new feature with Animate 2022 (version 22.0.2).

1. Let's start by extending the frame span across all layers. Select the frames across both the `Ground` and `SpookyTree` layers at frame 90 and insert frames in order to create a 3-second timeline:

Figure 9.35 – Extending the overall frame span to 3 seconds

2. Using the **Asset Warp** tool, modify the rig to exhibit the starting pose however you like. We'll be creating a number of poses for the tree and swing across these 3 seconds, and they will all vary according to how you envision them.

3. Insert a keyframe somewhere before the 1-second marker. In this example, I'm creating a keyframe at frame 15:

Figure 9.36 – Inserting a new keyframe along the timeline

4. Move the playhead to the new keyframe and use the **Asset Warp** tool to position the various branching elements of the gnarly tree rig ever so slightly, as if driven by the wind.

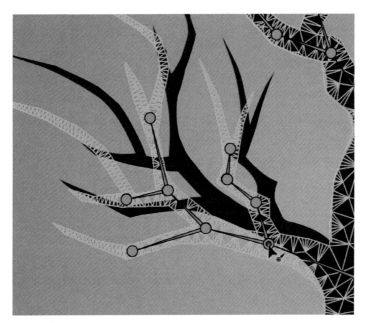

Figure 9.37 – Manipulating the hard bones of the rig branches

5. Modify the position of the rope swing as well for each keyframe you create.

Figure 9.38 – Adjusting the soft bone associated with the rope swing

6. Continue placing keyframes every 10-15 frames along the timeline and adjusting the branches slightly for each keyframe. Do not forget to tweak the position of the rope swing as well. It is up to you how many keyframes and associated poses you create, but I would suggest around seven to eight, overall.

7. At the final frame—frame 90—insert a blank keyframe:

Figure 9.39 – A blank keyframe is inserted at frame 90

8. Move the playhead to frame 1 and select the tree Warped Object on the stage.

9. Copy the Warped Object at frame 1 and move the playhead to the blank keyframe at frame 90 once again.

10. Right-click upon the stage and choose **Paste in Place** from the menu which appears, to insert an identical Warped Object into frame 90 from frame 1. The Warped Objects at frame 1 and frame 90 are now identical.

11. Select the entire set of frames on the SpookyTree layer, as illustrated in the following screenshot, and create a series of Classic Tweens across the entire timeline:

Figure 9.40 – Creating Classic Tweens across the timeline

If we leave the content at frames 1 and 90 identical as they are now, our loop will visibly repeat the same content, causing a stutter to the otherwise seamless motion. We will adjust for this.

12. Add a new keyframe at frame 89 and delete all content from the final keyframe at frame 90 to establish a blank keyframe:

Figure 9.41 - Adding a keyframe at frame 89 and deleting the keyframe content at frame 90

13. Select the keyframe on frame 89 and drag it to frame 90. This will create a seamless loop with no repeating frames since frame 1 and frame 90 are no longer identical:

Figure 9.42 - Dragging the keyframe at frame 89 to frame 90

14. Perform a **Test Movie** to view the resulting animation.

The tree branches are buffeted in the wind and the rope swing tosses wildly about the air. The tree trunk remains fixed in place throughout all this turbulence due to the frozen joints.

After viewing the animation, you may want to make further adjustments to the rig to make everything more believable and realistic. Make use of onion skinning to assist with this. You can also add easing presets to the tweens to introduce further physicality to your structural motion.

Figure 9.43 – Onion-skin controls can help you adjust the rig positions

In this section, we explored modern rigging through the use of bones created with the **Asset Warp** tool and Warped Objects. This is a natural extension of the existing mesh deformation functionality and is sure to expand in features as it matures further.

Summary

In this chapter, we had an in-depth look at how to create Warped Objects by establishing a distortion mesh through the use of the **Asset Warp** tool. We created a little spooky ghost character and used pins to animate it floating about the stage. We then explored the use of modern rigging and established a set of branching armatures with a gnarly old tree. Lastly, we made use of various bone and joint properties to give the tree some intense motion as though being blown about by a strong wind.

In the next chapter, we are going to put the focus on advanced layers once again, this time exploring the document **Camera**, **Layer Depth**, and **Layer Effects**!

10

Working with the Camera and Layer Depth

In the previous chapter, we spent time working with the **Asset Warp** tool to establish mesh distortions while defining both hard and soft bones within **Warped Objects** for complex rigging and animation.

In this chapter, we will examine the **Camera**, **Layer Depth**, and **Layer Effects**. All of these features rely on **Advanced Layers** mode, which we first put to use in *Chapter 7, Character Design through Layer Parenting*. Using these features, we can create some pretty amazing parallax animations by making just a few alterations to the depth of our layers and by manipulating the document-level camera. In the following sections, we'll explore various properties and workflows associated with the camera and learn how to animate smoothly between various camera states. Once that has been covered, we'll learn how to apply filters, effects, and blend modes across entire layers within our animation.

After reading this chapter, you will learn the following:

- Learn the basics of adding the document camera and manipulating its various properties.
- Understand how to change the camera's state and produce smooth movement.
- Invoke the **Layer Depth** panel and explore the relationship between **Layer Depth** and the camera.
- Apply effects and filters to your layered animations.

Technical Requirements

You will need the following software and hardware to complete this chapter:

- Adobe Animate 2022 (version 22.0 or above).
- Refer to the Animate system requirements page for the hardware specifications: `https://helpx.adobe.com/animate/system-requirements.html`.

Understanding the Camera

While we've done a lot of animation so far with individual layers and objects, the document-level camera in Animate allows us to achieve even more. We can use it to zoom, pan, and rotate the entire contents of the stage as though we are using a real camera on our animation. Not only that, but we can still layer and nest animated content as usual through the normal methods to create multiple levels of animation across any project.

One of the most common uses of the camera is to zoom in on a scene:

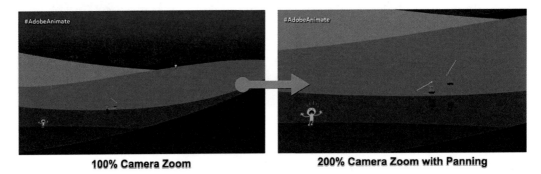

Figure 10.1 – The camera adds zoom, pan, and rotation to a scene

This can be an animated zoom or even a simple cut from one zoom level to another.

> **Note**
> The camera can only be used at the document level and not within individual symbol timelines.

We'll be using the camera in this chapter to add all sorts of interesting motion and effects to our content.

Examining the Starter Project

To make use of the camera right away, we have a starter project specifically for this chapter that you can use to follow along with as we go over the different concepts involved. You can always use your files if you wish to as these concepts can be applied to just about any content.

> **Note**
> You can find the starter file we are using here within the exercise files at https://github.com/PacktPublishing/Adobe-Animate-2022-for-Creative-Professionals-Second-Edition.

If you open CameraStarter.fla, you'll notice that the stage has been laid out, with several varied assets ready to go:

Figure 10.2 – The starter project stage

The scene is that of a vast desert with rolling sand dunes. Far away are a set of rocky outcroppings and a steep cliff face. The sky appears free of clouds and a strange haze hangs over the horizon. The view is expansive with no obstructions apart from the dunes themselves.

Set across the various dunes of sand are animated characters that have been brought into our project through the **Assets** panel. They are all symbol instances that contain internal animations with **Graphic** or **Movie Clip** behaviors.

Looking at the timeline, you will see that these various objects have been organized into layers according to how close or far away they are from the viewer:

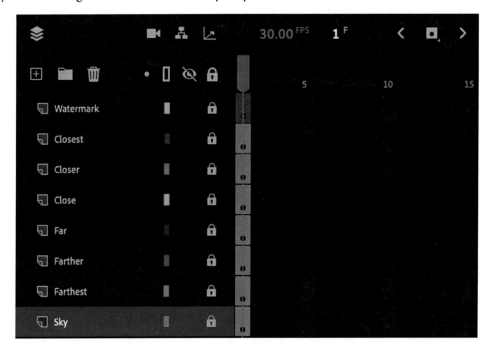

Figure 10.3 – The starter project's timeline and layers

These layers have a particular order to them, with the closer layers being toward the top of the layer stack and the layers that are more distant being closer to the bottom. At the very top of the stack is an empty **Watermark** layer, which we will use later to add some text to our animation. At the very bottom of the stack is the **Sky** layer, which contains the background sky elements.

In between these two are the layers that focus on scenic content. Most of them only contain various shapes that make up the levels of the sand dunes, but there are a few layers with additional character elements that you should take note of:

- The **Closer** layer includes an instance of the **Complainer** movie clip symbol instance.
- The **Close** layer includes an instance of the **Cat Fight** graphic symbol instance.
- The **Far** layer includes an instance of the **Boy and Flower Monster** movie clip symbol instance.
- Finally, the **Farthest** layer includes no sand dunes but a rocky outcropping with a dead tree and an instance of the **Bunny Hop** graphic symbol instance.

None of the layers include any motion. We are focusing on the camera in this chapter and will be using that mechanism alone to provide motion for our project, apart from any internal symbol animations.

Go ahead and click the **Test Movie** button to see the current state of the project. With only a single frame included as part of the main timeline, we only see movie clip symbol instances exhibiting any animation. Graphic symbol instances require additional frames to be in the main timeline for playback, so our graphic symbol instances only display a single frame, thus no animation. It's a fairly lifeless scene!

It doesn't have to stay that way, though. We'll explore how to activate and use the camera next.

Activating and Manipulating the Camera

To use the camera within our document, we must be using **Advanced Layers** mode, as described in *Chapter 7, Character Design through Layer Parenting*. This is the default layer mode within all recent versions of Animate, so you will not need to do anything to enable this mode. With the camera available, you must activate it to use it in your document, as the camera is not activated by default.

> **Note**
>
> The camera is not available in WebGL-based documents, including VR document types.

The camera can be activated by clicking the **Add Camera** button at the top of the timeline:

Figure 10.4 – The Add Camera button

Once the camera has been activated within a document, the same control is switched to a **Remove Camera** button. When you're toggling this button to add or remove the camera, it is only activating or deactivating the camera. If you deactivate and then reactivate the camera at any time, all of your changes and settings will still be present!

> **Note**
>
> You can also activate the camera by selecting the **Camera** tool from the toolbar. You may need to edit the toolbar to be able to access this tool.

With the camera active, several changes across the Animate interface will become immediately apparent.

Across the timeline, a new **Camera** layer will be added at the very top of the layer stack:

Figure 10.5 – The dedicated Camera layer

This layer, indicated by a small camera icon and with the fixed layer name of **Camera**, is dedicated to the document **Camera**. The layer must exist at the very top of the stack and it cannot be moved. You also cannot add any content to this layer as it is meant to hold the camera; nothing else is allowed. In addition, the layer cannot be locked, have its visibility disabled, or be placed in outline mode as normal layers can.

You'll notice that a new icon has been added to the timeline that appears as a small camera with a chainlink attached. We'll see what this option does shortly.

Another big change to the interface occurs on the stage. A control overlay appears over the stage's content, toward the bottom:

Figure 10.6 – Camera overlay controls

The camera overlay includes a slider for either zooming in/out or rotating the camera. This mode can be changed by activating either the rotation or zoom options, which appear to the left of the overlay. Moving the slider to either side will adjust the selected property and snap it back to the center once released, allowing for additional adjustments.

In addition to the overlay, if you hover over the stage, you will see the cursor change to indicate the ability to pan the camera. If you click and drag anywhere on the stage with this icon visible, you can pan the camera.

> **Tip**
> When you pan the camera, the actual view moves the opposite way to the camera's pan direction. This may feel a bit odd at first but try to imagine you are actually moving a camera and not moving the stage content and it will likely feel more natural.

With the camera activated and the **Camera** tool selected, we can view the various properties associated with it in the **Tool** tab of the **Properties** panel:

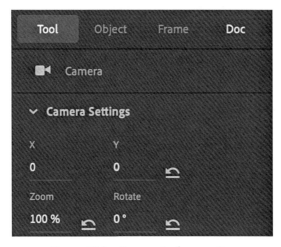

Figure 10.7 – Camera tool properties

The **Camera** properties entail everything you'd expect from a virtual camera. The settings include X/Y position, zoom, and rotation values. Each of these properties can be set in either the overlay controls or through the **Properties** panel. Setting them this way is more precise, and each setting includes a button for quickly resetting each property to its default.

> **Note**
> There are also color effects and filters that can be set within the **Camera** properties, but these are only available when you're using an ActionScript 3.0-based document.

It is also important to mention that these property settings are bound to keyframes across the timeline. So, if you want to change a camera property at any point, you can simply insert a new keyframe and make adjustments through the overlay controls or the **Properties** panel – whichever works best for your current task.

In this section, we looked at the starter document and learned how to activate the camera and make adjustments to its properties. Next, we'll look at the layer depth settings and prepare our starter document to make use of this feature.

Understanding and Manipulating Layer Depth

In this section, we are going to learn how to manipulate the depth of layers within an Animate project. While panning and zooming the camera can be very effective, we can enhance everything we do with the camera by using another feature of **Advanced Layers** mode in the form of **Layer Depth**. This feature allows us to place specific layers closer or farther from each other and the camera to simulate a difference of depth across each. The result is that as the camera changes property setting values across time, the view shifts across the variety of depth settings, providing a feeling of enhanced immersion.

Let's explore the mechanism that allows us to adjust the depth settings of our various layers. Then, we'll use it to modify the depth of the layers that are currently within our project.

Activating the Layer Depth Panel

By default, the **Layer Depth** panel is visible in the **Essentials workspace** area, minimized to the icon view along the right-side column, along with several additional panels. It can be difficult to locate this way. You can also invoke the **Layer Depth** panel by choosing **Window | Layer Depth** from the application menu, but a more direct method is to invoke it from the timeline itself.

The simplest way to invoke the **Layer Depth** panel is to click the **Toggle Layer Depth** button at the top of the timeline:

Figure 10.8 – Invoking the Layer Depth panel

Wherever the **Layer Depth** panel resides, it will then appear and allow us to visualize and manipulate the depth settings of our various layers.

Let's have a look at some of the features of the **Layer Depth** panel to become more familiar with its layout and function:

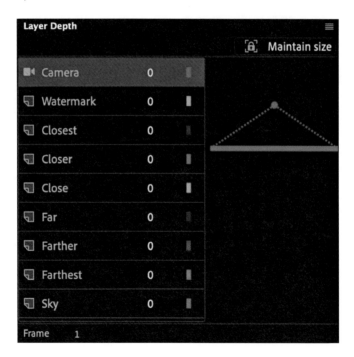

Figure 10.9 – The Layer Depth panel

With the **Layer Depth** panel open, you can view the current depth setting for each layer and even visualize how close or far layers are from one another with the current settings. Since we haven't made any alterations yet, all the layers have a depth of 0 and are equidistant from the camera itself.

Within the **Layer Depth** panel, there are several important things to note:

- **Left Column**: Contains all the layers in the order that they appear on the timeline. The data value is the depth setting and the layer's color corresponds to the visual depth indicator in the right column.

- **Right Column**: This is a visual representation of the layer's depth regarding the depth values expressed in the left column. Each layer is represented as a line and shares its color with the layer itself. The camera is also represented here as a blue dot with two dashed lines emerging from it.

- **Frame Number**: Just as with the **Camera** properties, the **Layer Depth** values are tied directly to keyframes. This number represents the playhead position along the timeline for quick reference.

- **Maintain Size**: This changes the depth of the selected layer without affecting the sizes of the objects embedded within the layer. If this is not selected, the layer's content may scale as per the modified depth value.

All of these settings can be manipulated within the **Layer Depth** panel, but we should also keep a close eye on both the timeline and the stage as we do so. It will be easy to spot mistakes as changes are immediately reflected within the stage.

> **Tip**
> Normally, you need to click the **Maintain size** button each time you want to change the layer's depth. This can become tedious. If you hold down the *Alt* or *Option* key while dragging the layer depth values, Animate will maintain the size of the layer without needing to interact with the button each time.

With that, we have provided an overview of the **Layer Depth** panel. Next, we'll learn how to use the various settings within it to modify the depth of our layers across the timeline.

Modifying Layer Depth

While you can make adjustments to the depth of a layer at any time, it is best to do so before making any adjustments to the camera settings. As we're working through these concepts, have you noticed how we haven't done any work with the camera yet aside from exploring its various settings? This is because we want to establish the initial layer depth settings first. With the **Layer Depth** panel open, let's go ahead and assign a depth setting to each layer. Using the panel controls, there are two different ways of setting the depth of any layer.

The first way to adjust the layer's depth is to either manually enter a number into the value field beside the layer's name, or simply drag the value to either increase or decrease it:

Figure 10.10 – Numeric depth control

When making slight adjustments, dragging across the value field works well to nudge the layer, but if you're changing the depth by a larger number, you will likely want to simply click the value and type a new one in manually.

The second method of adjusting the layer's depth values is to do so visually, by selecting a layer and dragging the highlighted layer marker up or down:

Figure 10.11 – Clicking and dragging layer markers

You can keep an eye on the value that's been attributed to the selected layer to monitor its actual depth setting.

Positive numbers indicate that the layer is far from the normal field of view and more distant, while negative numbers indicate that the layer sits between the normal field of view and the camera's position. If the layer is set to a depth that is behind the camera, as indicated by the blue dot intersected with dashed lines, then that layer is no longer in view at all as it is behind the camera.

> **Tip**
> If you have layers arranged as part of a layer folder, the folder will appear within the **Layer Depth** panel as well, allowing you to modify the depth of all the contained layers simultaneously.

Let's set our layer depth values from top to bottom:

- **Camera**: We will not be modifying the camera's position, but it is something you could do to achieve a camera pass-through animation. Instead, we'll adjust the camera pan and zoom settings as that will provide more control. Keep this at 0.

- **Watermark**: This should be at least 1 unit more toward the camera than all the other layers since we want it to be visible atop all the layers, no matter what. We'll set this to -151.

- **Closest**: Set this layer to -150. Note that this is only one unit farther away than the **Watermark** layer.

- **Closer**: The layers closest to the camera are all being set to negative numbers since they fall between the camera itself and the normal field of view. This layer will be set to a value of -100.

- **Close**: Leave this at 0. This layer remains at the normal field of view, so it is the default depth value. It isn't necessary to have any layers at 0, but we have done so here to illustrate the differences between the positive and negative depth values.

- **Far**: The next four layers, including this one, all contain positive numbers. Set the depth value of this layer to 200.

- **Farther**: The next layer will have a depth value of 400 since as we get farther away from the normal field of view, the distances are greater.

- **Farthest**: The layer that includes the craggy outcropping and cliff face should be given a value of 650.

- **Sky**: The background imagery should be farthest away from everything else, so we will give it a value of 1000.

Your completed depth settings within the **Layer Depth** panel should look like this:

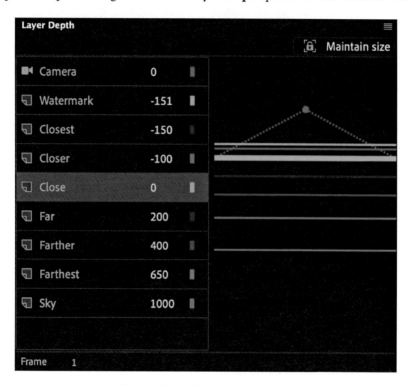

Figure 10.12 – Layer Depth settings

Notice that in our example, the layer's order in the timeline and the **Layer Depth** stacking order both share the same general order. They do not have to, though, as **Layer Depth** overrides the normal layer order in the timeline. We will see an example of this shortly.

A good way to see the effect that these depth settings have on our layers is to use the camera to pan around the stage:

Figure 10.13 – Layer depths visualized

You will see the various layers all moving at different speeds, depending on how far or close they are. Once you have finished playing around with the camera, be sure to reset any of the values to their defaults.

With that, we have set up all our layers in this project to utilize the layer depth settings, along with the camera. We can also modify the depth of the layers across time without using the camera to create additional effects. We'll have a look at that workflow next.

Using Layer Depth without the Camera

As alluded to earlier in the chapter, you don't have to enable the camera to use **Layer Depth**, and you don't have to have the layers in any proper order either since the depth setting overrides the layer order.

Take a look at the exercise file named `NoCameraDepth.fla` for a quick example of this:

Figure 10.14 – The rocket passes before and behind the moon

In this example, we have two objects on the stage: a rocket ship and a moon. In the timeline, there is a layer for each of these objects and the rocket is animated in such a way that it travels behind the moon first and then returns to pass in front of it.

The **Rocket Ship** layer is always above the **Moon** layer, though, so how does the rocket pass behind the moon at all? Via the **Layer Depth** settings, of course!

Notice that the **Moon** layer isn't animated at all but includes two keyframes along the timeline:

Figure 10.15 – The Layer Depth values are bound to keyframes

At frame 1, the **Moon** depth value is set to -10, while the **Rocket Ship** depth is set to 0. This brings the moon closer to the viewer than the rocket. At frame 36, both layers have a depth of 0 and since their timeline order has the **Rocket Ship** layer above the **Moon** layer, the rocket is visible above the moon. This technique can be used in many cases to swap depths across time for similar effects.

In this section, we explored the fundamental properties of the camera and explored how to manipulate the **Layer Depth** settings in a variety of ways. Next, we'll put all of this into practice as we create different camera states and animate between them.

Animating the Camera

The camera is integrated into the timeline just like any other object in Animate, with certain restrictions. For instance, it is contained within its own layer and this special layer does not behave as the other layers do. However, certain aspects of a normal layer workflow precipitate onto the **Camera** layer as well. Primary among these is how motion is handled.

In this section, we'll establish camera states through keyframes and animate between these states using the techniques we've already addressed in this book.

Setting Camera Keyframes

As the document exists now, we have a single frame across all layers. To have any actual motion occur, camera-based or otherwise, we need additional layers.

First, be sure to lock all the existing layers. It's a good habit to lock and unlock specific layers as needed. The **Camera** layer can never be locked. Add frames up to and including frame 540 across all of the layers, including the **Camera** layer.

We now have 18 seconds of total frames across all layers:

Figure 10.16 – Frames extended across all layers

With our frame spans fully extended, we'll add keyframes at specific points along the **Camera** layer and make adjustments to the **Camera** properties, such as zoom and pan. It is best to set the zoom value first, followed by the panning adjustments.

Let's plot out the keyframes to signify specific key points across the animation:

1. An initial keyframe exists at frame 1, with the camera's position at 0 along both the **X** and **Y** positions and the zoom level at 100%.

2. Add a keyframe at frame 20 to place a hold between these two keyframes:

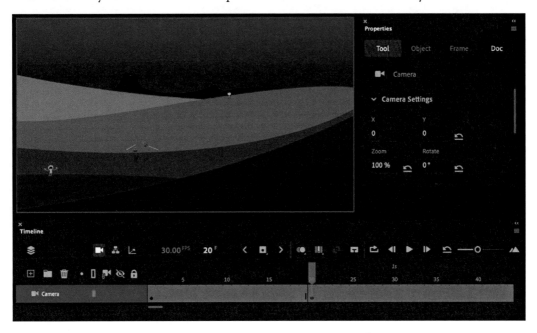

Figure 10.17 – Starting with the camera's defaults

3. Now, add another keyframe at frame 60 and set the **Camera** properties so that the **Zoom** value is 565 with an **X** position of 2110 and a **Y** setting of -850.

The focus for this keyframe is on the **Complainer** animation:

Figure 10.18 – Focusing on the Complainer animation

4. Now, add a keyframe at frame 90 for a short hold with these same settings.

5. Place the next keyframe at frame `140` with a **Zoom** value of `1026`, an **X** position of `-2025`, and a **Y** position of `1100`.

This will focus the camera on the **Boy with Flower Monster** animation:

Figure 10.19 – Focusing on the Boy with Flower Monster animation

6. Insert another keyframe at frame `200` to hold on the **Boy with Flower Monster** animation a bit. Then, add another keyframe at frame `230` with a **Zoom** value of `325`, an **X** position of `362`, and a **Y** position of `-513`.

This will zoom out somewhat and reposition the camera to focus on the **Cat Fight** animation:

Figure 10.20 – Focusing on the Cat Fight animation

From the **Cat Fight** animation, we'll pan up and zoom toward the base of the craggy cliff face in the distance.

7. Insert a keyframe at frame 280 and set a **Zoom** value of 1000, an **X** position of 4560, and a **Y** position of 1430.

    You will begin to notice that the more extreme the zoom becomes, the more variable the numbers you input will be. Don't worry if Animate changes the values by a few units each time you change the camera settings – this is expected.

8. Place the next keyframe at frame 320. This will allow us to pan the camera upward to view the **Bunny Hop** animation at the top of the cliff. Include a **Zoom** value of 3290, an **X** position of 14280, and a **Y** position of 11120.

    Notice that we've zoomed in a huge amount and can see all the details of the cliff, such as the tree and stone present there. At 100% zoom, this is almost impossible to see:

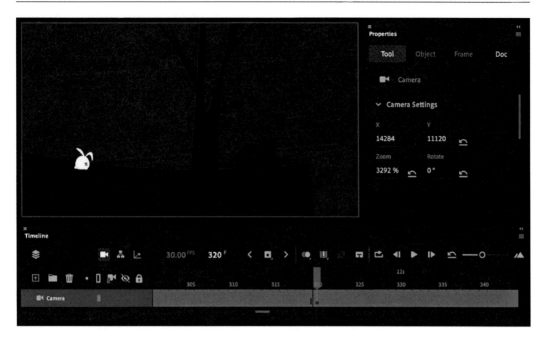

Figure 10.21 – Focusing on the Bunny Hop animation

9. Finally, add a keyframe at frame 380 as a hold on the **Bunny Hop** animation. The last keyframe will sit at frame 450, where we will pull back on the camera zoom to get a larger picture of the entire scene once more.

10. Adjust the camera settings at frame 450 so that the **Zoom** value is 150, the **X** position is 0, and the **Y** position is also 0.

If we play our project at this point, it will consist of a collection of quick cuts as each keyframe is encountered. While a jumpcut like this can work in certain scenarios, we require a smoother motion from keyframe to keyframe.

Now that we have keyframes across the **Camera** layer holding specific camera settings at each, we can add tweens and eases to establish smooth motion between them.

Adding Motion and Easing to the Camera

Motion can be applied to the **Camera** layer by using either **motion tweens** or **classic tweens**. We will be using classic tweens in this project since it is simpler to plot out camera settings in keyframes beforehand and the ease effect presets can be interpreted and applied easily.

> **Tip**
>
> To achieve believable, smooth camera movement, **Ease Effect** presets are a must!

Our **Camera** layer currently contains keyframes for each camera state. Certain frame spans are meant to hold the camera at a specific position and zoom level, while others are meant to contain movement from one keyframe to the next. We will be adding classic tweens and ease effect presets to those that are intended to feature camera movement.

Additionally, following the focus on certain character animations, we will insert keyframes into the layers that contain them and remove the characters from the stage. This will be good practice for toggling the camera off and on to best select each character for removal.

For each of the following frame spans, add a classic tween and the indicated ease effect preset:

- **Frame span 20 – 60**: Use the **Quad Ease-In** effect preset.

- **Frame span 90 – 140**: Use the **Sine Ease-In-Out** effect preset.

- Additionally, add a keyframe to the **Closer** layer at around frame 140 and remove the **Complainer** character.

- **Frame span 200 – 230**: Use the **Sine Ease-In-Out** effect preset.

- Additionally, add a keyframe to the **Far** layer at around frame 230 and remove the **Boy with Flower Monster** character.

- **Frame span 230 – 280**: Use the **Quad Ease-In** effect preset.

- **Frame span 280 – 320**: Use the **Quad Ease-Out** effect preset.

- Additionally, add a keyframe to the **Close** layer at around frame 320 and remove the **Cat Fight** characters.

- **Frame span 380 – 450**: Use the **Quart Ease-In-Out** effect preset.

Once you've done this, your timeline should look similar to the following:

Figure 10.22 – Timeline with camera tweens and keyframes

Note that the frame spans of the **Camera** layer that are meant to serve as a motion hold do not contain tweens and certain additional layers include keyframes to remove characters following their focus.

The bulk of our camera animation is now complete. Perform a test movie to see it in action!

Creating Text and Attaching Layers to the Camera

As you may recall, we still have an empty layer right below the **Camera** layer named **Watermark**. This layer will be used to display a small, text-based #AdobeAnimate hashtag identifying the animation as having been created in Adobe Animate.

Let's create this text object now:

1. The first thing we need to do is select the **Text** tool:

Figure 10.23 – The Text tool

2.   With the **Text** tool selected, go to the **Tool** tab of the **Properties** panel:

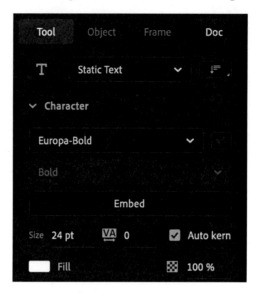

Figure 10.24 – Text Tool properties

Be sure to choose **Static Text** from the dropdown. We'll explore additional text options, including the use of dynamic text, in *Chapter 11*, *Developing Web-Based Games*, and *Chapter 13*, *Building Apps for Desktop and Mobile*.

3.   Choose a bold font to use for the text – I've selected **Europa**, which can be synced to your computer from Adobe Fonts at `https://fonts.adobe.com/fonts/europa` with a Creative Cloud subscription.

4.   Set the size value to `24 pt` and the fill color to pure white (`#FFFFFF`).

5.   Unlock the **Watermark** layer if it is currently locked and select frame `1`.

6.   Click in the top-left area of the stage and type in `#AdobeAnimate`:

Figure 10.25 – The text object has been created

7. Select the text object and go to the **Object** tab of the **Properties** panel to ensure the text object is positioned 40px at both the **X** and **Y** positions.

8. With the **Watermark** layer content in place, play the project back. Note that the text immediately zooms past the camera and offscreen.

    We want the text to stay exactly where it is, no matter what the camera does. To do this, we have to attach the layer the text exists within to the camera. This will have the layer ignore anything to do with the **Camera** layer and its various settings.

9. To attach the **Watermark** layer to the camera, simply activate the **Attach Layer to Camera** option:

Figure 10.26 – The Attach Layer to Camera option

Playing the project now will exhibit completely different behavior when it comes to our text overlay. It stays put throughout the animation, unaffected by the camera.

In this section, we looked at establishing camera states and animating the camera across the timeline. We also spent a good deal of time adjusting our tweens and additional layer frame properties to achieve an interesting, dynamic animation, using nothing but the **Camera** and **Layer Depth** settings. Next, we'll finish this animation by adding some camera effects and layer filters.

Applying Layer Effects and Filters

Another advantage of **Advanced Layers** mode is that you can have effects and filters applied directly to a layer, which, in turn, affects all the objects within that layer without you having to modify the objects themselves. You can also add effects directly to the camera in a similar way.

> **Note**
>
> Layer effects, filters, and camera effects are all only available when you're using ActionScript 3.0-based document types.

We are going to add some effects to the camera to simulate a fade in/fade out to black and add a filter to our **Watermark** layer to add some drop shadow to the text within it.

Adding Effects to the Camera

The camera effects and layer effects both work very similarly, with the only difference being that camera effects are applied via the **Camera** tool properties and the layer effects are applied through the **Frame** properties.

Let's add both a fade in and a fade out to our **Camera** layer:

1. First, add a keyframe at frame 10 within the **Camera** layer.

2. Move the playhead back to frame 1 and select the **Tool** tab within the **Properties** panel. You will see a section for **Color Effects** below the normal **Camera** properties, such as zoom and position.

3. From within the **Color Effects** section, choose **Brightness** from the dropdown and set the **Bright** value to -100:

Figure 10.27 – Adding a camera effect

The entire stage will go black except for any of the layers attached to the camera. This is the first step in creating a fade in from black.

4. Apply a classic tween to the **Camera** layer between frame 1 and frame 10 and add the **Sine Ease-Out** preset from the **Properties** panel.

5. Move the playhead to the end of the timeline at frame 500 and add a keyframe.

6. Add another keyframe at frame 530 and access the **Camera** tool properties, setting **Brightness** to -100 on this keyframe as well to establish a fade to black.

7. Create a classic tween between frame 500 and frame 530 and add the **Quad Ease-In** preset from the **Properties** panel to complete our fade effects.

If you preview the animation, you'll see that the movie begins by quickly fading in from black, proceeds as normal, and then fades out to black before completion.

In the next section, we'll finish this project by adding a layer filter to the **Watermark** layer.

Adding Filters to a Layer

Layer filters and layer effects are both added through the **Frame** tab of the **Properties** panel. We want to have our text within the **Watermark** layer pop out against the background. So, for this, we will add a drop shadow to the entire layer via the **Filters** section of the **Properties** panel.

To add a filter to the **Watermark** layer, perform the following steps:

1. Select the **Watermark** layer and choose the **Frame** tab of the **Properties** panel.

2. Locate the **Filters** section at the bottom of the panel and expand it if it is closed.

3. Click the **Add Filter** button at the top right of the panel to invoke the filter selection overlay and choose **Drop Shadow**.

4. The **Drop Shadow** filter will be added to the selected layer, making the text stand out even more:

Figure 10.28 – The Drop Shadow filter added

At this point, you can modify any of the settings of this filter. The filter's settings will differ between each filter type, but for any that allow a **Quality** selection, I normally choose **Medium**.

Looking at the timeline, notice that the keyframes within the **Watermark** layer now appear white instead of black as they normally do. A white keyframe indicates that a filter or effect has been added to that layer.

In this section, we looked at how to add effects to the camera that affect all the layers and filters for individual layer effects. Both of these features are available as part of **Advanced Layers** mode and help us perfect our overall animation.

Summary

In this chapter, we learned how to animate an entire project by using the document's **Camera**, without that content itself being animated within the main timeline. We also explored how to manipulate layer depth and learned how to work with both the camera and layer depth to create some amazing dynamic parallax movement within our animation. We wrapped everything up by implementing both camera effects and layer filters to add a feel of completion to our animation.

In the next chapter, we'll begin working with additional platforms and have a look at writing JavaScript code to target **HTML5 Canvas** in the form of a simple web-based game.

Section 3 – Exploring Additional Platforms

For the final section, we will focus less on motion design and instead explore some advanced concepts and techniques associated with specific target platforms, such as coding JavaScript to develop web-based games and virtual reality experiences and using ActionScript to write a fully functional application for desktop and mobile devices. We will then wrap up by having a look at how to extend Animate's capabilities through the creation of custom in-app tutorials, internal scripting, and the use of third-party extensions.

This section comprises the following chapters:

- *Chapter 11, Developing Web-Based Games*
- *Chapter 12, Producing Virtual Reality Content for WebGL*
- *Chapter 13, Building Apps for Desktop and Mobile*
- *Chapter 14, Extending Adobe Animate*

11
Developing Web-Based Games

In the previous chapter, we took a deep dive into **Camera**, **Layer Depth**, and several additional features available as part of the **Advanced Layers** mode in Animate.

We'll begin this chapter by providing an overview of our game concept and the HTML5 Canvas starter document, which already has several assets laid out concerning the techniques we learned about in the previous chapters. We will then prepare various assets on the stage and assets within the project library for interactivity. We'll also create all-new dynamic text assets for our gameplay screen that can display game data through our use of JavaScript. The majority of this chapter will be spent in the code editor as we build out the logic for our entire game bit by bit across the timeline and by using global scripts.

After reading this chapter, you'll be able to perform the following functions in Animate:

- Create a game using both designer and developer workflows in Animate.

- Configure and manage interactive content, game states, and data variables.

- Write JavaScript code to generate assets dynamically from the project library.

- Develop logic to control the game's flow and manage all aspects of gameplay.

Technical Requirements

You will need the following software and hardware to complete this chapter:

- Adobe Animate 2022 (version 22.0 or above).

- Refer to the *Animate System Requirements* page for hardware specifications: `https://helpx.adobe.com/animate/system-requirements.html`.

The code in action video for this chapter can be found here: `https://bit.ly/3nmrIJ3`

Understanding the Game Concept

The game we will build in this chapter makes use of one of the strongest aspects of Adobe Animate, and that is the ability to create assets with visual tools and then program them with code directly within the same application. The game concept is very simple: you control a kitty that can walk back and forth across the screen and shoot energy balls upward. Enemy pigs are dropping from above and the kitty must ensure that none reach the ground by blasting them out of the sky. If three pigs get past the kitty, it's game over.

We'll be dealing with a lot of code in this chapter. If you've never written much code, don't worry! We will be stepping through the visual aspects of the game first and will slowly build up to the programming aspects. Even when in the thick of development, all the code will be provided and explained piece by piece.

Starter Document Overview

An HTML Canvas document named `GameStarter.fla` is available from the file downloads, and for this chapter, you are highly encouraged to download it. Once you have the Animate file on your local system, open it up and have a look at what has been prepared.

> **Note**
> You can find the starter file we use here within the exercise files at `https://github.com/PacktPublishing/Adobe-Animate-2022-for-Creative-Professionals-Second-Edition`.

The starter project is an **HTML5 Canvas** document and will target the native web so that it can be run on any modern web browser. As we discussed in *Chapter 2, Exploring Platform-Specific Considerations*, an **HTML5 Canvas** document will specifically make use of the `<canvas>` element of HTML to render any static or animated content. However, it is also interactive, making it the ideal platform for web-based games.

The document itself exhibits a stage width of 640 and a height of 480:

Figure 11.1 – Document Settings

This is a 4:3 aspect ratio, which often works well for games. The timeline is set to run at 24 frames per second and the background is black (#000000).

Before we get into the contents of the document, let's go over how we'll be programming the content. Since we are targeting the native web, we'll be using **JavaScript** to write all our code. JavaScript is fairly easy to pick up and start working with – especially since it can run within any standard web browser. JavaScript can be used within Animate when targeting HTML5 Canvas documents, as we are doing in this chapter, but it can also be used to the **WebGL glTF Extended**, **VR Panorama**, and **VR 360** document types.

> **Note**
>
> A great resource for writing JavaScript is the following documentation, which is located on the Mozilla Developer Network: https://developer.mozilla.org/en-US/docs/Web/JavaScript.
>
> If you'd like to have a comprehensive resource for learning JavaScript in the form of a book, I recommend *The JavaScript Workshop* from Packt: https://www.packtpub.com/product/the-javascript-workshop/9781838641917. I contributed a few chapters to this book and served as the lead author.

In addition to vanilla JavaScript, we'll also make use of the **CreateJS** JavaScript library within HTML5 Canvas documents. CreateJS is a set of libraries that includes EaselJS, TweenJS, SoundJS, and PreloadJS. Each of these libraries fulfills a different role in CreateJS but they all work together in making the HTML <canvas> element much easier to work with. Again, refer to *Chapter 2, Exploring Platform-Specific Considerations*, for a refresher.

> **Note**
>
> For deeper insight into how the **CreateJS** libraries function, you can access the **CreateJS** documentation from their website at `https://createjs.com/docs`.

With the general document settings and platform considerations covered, let's move on to examine how the document has been assembled.

Exploring the Timeline and Stage

Taking a look at the timeline, you'll notice two layers. Each of them has been divided into three sections separated by keyframes. These will serve as the three screens that make up our game.

Have a look at the starter document timeline:

Figure 11.2 – Starter document timeline

The **Backgrounds** layer contains a bitmap image for all three of the timeline sections. In the first and third sections, we have a shape overlay to dim the background a bit and make any additional assets stand out. In the middle section, the background is presented as-is since this will serve as the gameplay screen. In the **Assets** layer, we have several assets that overlay the background imagery and vary from text to shapes to symbol instances, depending on the section.

The sections of the timeline can be referred to by different names for clarity. This is how things have been configured:

- **Start Screen**: Covers frames 1-3 and represents the game's start screen and title.
- **Game Screen**: Consists of the next three frames (4-6) and is where actual gameplay will occur.
- **End Screen**: This is the game over screen once you've lost the game and covers frames 7-9. There is no way to win the game.

Let's have a look at each of these screens in detail, beginning with **Start Screen**:

Figure 11.3 – Start Screen

We have our background image dimmed with a semi-opaque rectangular shape covering the stage. An instance of the player-controlled **Kitty** movie clip symbol instance appears on the left but has no interactivity associated with it. An animated **KittyOrb** movie clip symbol instance with a text overlay of **PLAY!** is present but also non-interactive at this time. Finally, we have the title, **KITTY WARS**, rotated slightly with a black shape behind it.

Next, we'll focus on **Game Screen**:

Figure 11.4 – Game Screen

This is the screen where all of the gameplay will happen but since we haven't written any code yet, it is the most minimal visually. Our background is present without any overlay obstruction and an instance of the player-controlled **Kitty** movie clip symbol instance appears, standing on the ground. That's it! We will be doing most of our work on this screen, adding dynamic text and writing the majority of our code to manage assets and game mechanics.

Finally, let's examine **End Screen**:

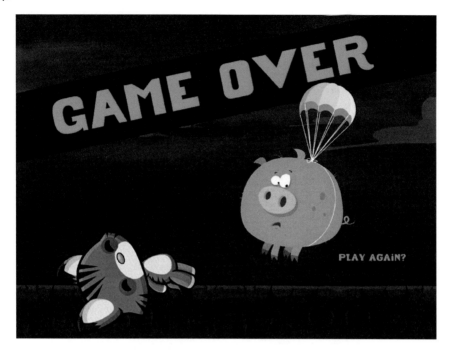

Figure 11.5 – End Screen

This screen is very similar in functionality to **Start Screen** but while that screen is presented to the user initially, this one is presented when the game is over. It includes the background image dimmed with a semi-opaque red shape. There is also a version of the kitty that appears defeated and laying on the ground. An instance of the **PigEnemy** movie clip symbol is present as well to further illustrate that the game has concluded. Instead of the game title, we have a banner that reads **GAME OVER**. There is a small text prompt in the bottom-right corner that prompts the user to **PLAY AGAIN?** if desired. Of course, none of this is interactive at all just yet.

With that, we are pretty familiar with the layout and functionality of each screen and how the timeline has been segmented to represent them. The last thing we need to look at is the project library and see what assets have been prepared.

Exploring the Project Library

Some of the library's content, such as the **Kitty**, **PigEnemy**, and **KittyOrb** movie clip symbols, have already been shown on different screens. We also know that there is a background image that's used across all three scenes. Some of these assets have been laid out on the various screens already, but others will need to be instantiated for more dynamic, gameplay-focused usage – even many of the assets currently being used statically. It's good to keep this in mind as we explore the project library.

Open the **Library** panel and have a look at the assets within it:

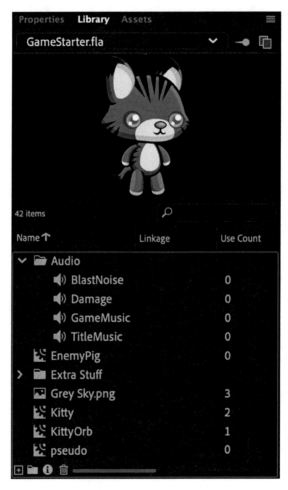

Figure 11.6 – The Library panel

The assets you see within the **Library** panel have all been gathered from the **Assets** panel and have been somewhat reconstructed or rearranged to fit our needs for this game.

All the assets we need for our game are included within the **Library** panel:

- A folder of audio files for music and effects.
- A set of movie clips for the player, enemies, clickable areas, and projectiles.
- A background image in the form of a bitmap PNG.

There is also a folder called `Extra Stuff` that can be ignored – this contains some of the simpler assets that our more complex assets are constructed of. Some text and additional shape content have been constructed and placed on the stage that does not exist within the library.

Within the **Library** panel is a set of columns. In the preceding screenshot, we can see columns for **Name**, **Linkage**, and **Use Count**. These are all important when building a game in this way. The functionality of the **Name** property of the symbol is obvious – this is the name we provide when the symbol is created. **Use Count** shows how many times a particular asset appears in some form on the stage, but this only counts objects that are manually placed on the stage, like everything we've seen so far in our start document. **Linkage** is very important for our game. This field, which is currently empty for all objects, can be used in conjunction with code to dynamically instantiate symbols from the library for use in the game at runtime. It is a very powerful feature and one we will be making use of shortly.

In this section, we opened the starter document and explored the timeline, stage, and library to familiarize ourselves with the assets and constructs that have been arranged for the game we'll be writing. Next, we'll make further preparations across all three of these aspects before writing our JavaScript code.

Preparing the Game Timeline, Stage, and Library

As we've seen, a lot of asset gathering and preparation has gone into our game already. The concepts that are involved in preparing these assets are tasks you are already familiar with after reading the previous chapters, and the pre-arranged content serves as a jump-start and foundation for actually building the game.

So, what else needs to be done? Elements such as layers to hold identifying labels and code must be created. Space for user interface elements such as dynamic text to relay information to the user during play should be included as well. Finally, clickable elements to start the game from the **Start Screen** area or restart it from the **End Screen** area should be added. Additionally, we need to make the various items within our library addressable through code.

We will accomplish all of this as we work through this section!

Labeling the Timeline

When developing a game, we need to be able to switch between certain screens, whether we are starting the game, playing the game, or have reached the end of the game. One of the ways we can do this with Animate is through the use of frame labels. When we provide a keyframe with a label, we are able to target that frame by its label name through code.

We also need a layer dedicated to the code itself. It is best practice when programming in Animate to have a layer – often named **Actions** – that contains all of our code and keeps it separated from any visual or animated elements. In this project, we are going to combine both the **Actions** layer and our labeling into a single layer, since they are so closely related.

Let's go ahead and modify the timeline, preparing for the insertion of frame labels:

1. Create a new layer and name it `Actions`. Add keyframes at frame 4 and frame 7:

Figure 11.7 – Actions layer added with keyframes

This conforms to our previously established screen structure across the timeline. We'll be able to add frame labels to each of these keyframes, which represent each screen, and also include code specific to individual game states.

2. To add a frame label to a specific keyframe, select that frame and look at the **Frame** tab of the **Properties** panel.

3. Locate the **Name** field within the **Label** section to input your label identifiers:

Figure 11.8 – Adding a frame label

Using the **Name** field of the **Label** section for any keyframe, we can direct the playhead to that specific frame through code. Be sure to set **Type** to **Name** using the drop-down selection below the **Name** input.

Set the following label names across the timeline:

- **Frame 1**: Create a new keyframe and add a frame label of `startscreen`.
- **Frame 4**: Create a new keyframe and add a frame label of `gamescreen`.
- **Frame 7**: Create a new keyframe and add a frame label of `endscreen`.

Notice how the frame labels you've entered appear along the timeline, attributed to each screen we've defined:

Figure 11.9 – Our Actions layer with defined frame labels

When we write JavaScript code to move between the different screens in our game, frame labels will help us direct the playhead to the correct frame, regardless of the assigned frame number. We also have specific keyframes to write our code in, directly bound to each screen.

Before moving on, be sure to lock all your layers. This will ensure that we don't mistakenly modify the content or add any visual assets to our **Actions** layer, which should contain only code.

With our **Actions** layer created and specific keyframes configured and labeled, we can start adding user interface elements to each game screen.

Creating Dynamic Text and Clickable Overlays

We'll now focus our attention on the more dynamic components of our game. We need to create a new layer to that will contain dynamic text objects that we can write game data to on our **Game Screen**, such as health and stats, and also set up some clickable elements on our **Start Screen** and **End Screen**.

Let's prepare a layer that will be specifically used to hold our UI elements:

1. Create a new layer and name it UI. This will contain all the user interface elements of our game:

Figure 11.10 – UI layer added

2. Additionally, add a set of new keyframes at frames 4 and 7, just like we have for every other layer in this project. We will include different interface elements bound to each keyframe. With the three keyframes established, we can now go ahead and add different elements to each screen.

With the UI layer prepared, we can work on building up the associated elements within this layer. We'll include clickable areas that overlay the existing prompts and dynamic text elements to inform the player as to how they are doing during gameplay.

Let's begin with the **Start Screen** area:

1. Select frame 1 of the **UI** layer.

2. You may have noticed a weird symbol in the **Library** panel named **pseudo**. This element is meant to exist as a non-visual, hit-enabled overlay. Drag an instance of this symbol onto the stage atop the **PLAY!** message.

3. Use the **Free Transform** tool to adjust the size and rotation of this instance so that it covers the visual elements of the blast and text:

Figure 11.11 – Using the Free Transform tool on the overlay

4. With the instance selected, look to the **Object** tab of the **Properties** panel and locate the **Color Effects** section. Take the **Alpha** property down to 1%, rendering it invisible. To make it clickable when you're using HTML5 Canvas, the object must not have 0% **Alpha** transparency!

5. Now, let's provide an instance name to be able to address this object through JavaScript code. Give this object an instance name of startbutton:

Figure 11.12 – Instance name given

The **Start Screen** area is now complete. Next, we'll move on to the **Game Screen** area to add dynamic text fields to inform the user of both the player's health and the number of enemies they've destroyed.

Let's build up our **Game Screen** user interface elements by adding dynamic text objects:

1. First, move the playhead to the middle section of the timeline representing our **Game Screen**, which is composed of frames 4, 5, and 6. Ensure that the **UI** layer is still unlocked and that it is the active layer.

2. Select the **Text** tool from the tools panel and look at the **Tool** tab of the **Properties** panel.

   So far, we have used **Static Text** as we haven't needed to change the character values within our text fields at runtime. Now that we need to update things such as the player's health and their overall score, we'll need to change these values while the game is being played.

3. To accomplish this, set the text type to **Dynamic Text** in the **Properties** panel.

4. To effectively use **Dynamic Text** in HTML5 Canvas documents, we will need to use a **Web Font** for the text fields we create. To choose a web font, click the little globe icon near the font selection dropdown:

Figure 11.13 – Invoking Google Fonts

This brings up a small overlay that allows us to select a **Web Font** service from a choice of **Adobe Fonts** or **Google Fonts**. The workflows for each are identical, so I am going to choose **Google Fonts**.

5. Once a service has been selected, a dialog will appear that allows you to filter through and search for the font library you've chosen:

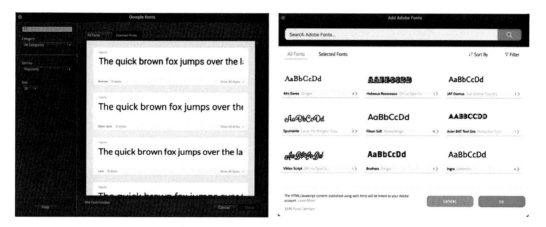

Figure 11.14 – Adding a web font using Google Fonts or Adobe Fonts

6. Locate a font to use within the game, select it, and choose **Done** for **Google Fonts** or **OK** for **Adobe Fonts**. The dialog will close, and the selected font will be added to Animate for use in your project. The **Output** panel will also appear, letting you know the font was added successfully. This is only informational, and you can switch directly back to the timeline.

I'm using a popular Google font called Roboto Mono.

7. Even though the font has been added, it isn't active in the **Text** tool yet. From the **Tool** tab of the **Properties** panel, locate the font selection dropdown and select the web font you just added:

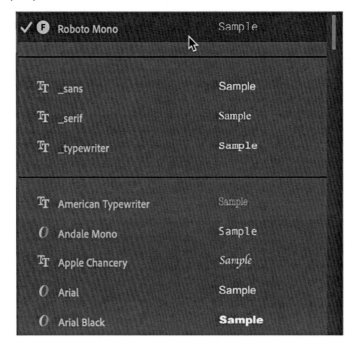

Figure 11.15 – Font selection dropdown

Web fonts are placed at the very top of the selection drop-down list, so they should be very easy to locate.

8. With the font selection process complete, we need to set the remainder of our text properties. I've chosen white (#FFFFFF) for my fill color and have set the size value to 14 pt:

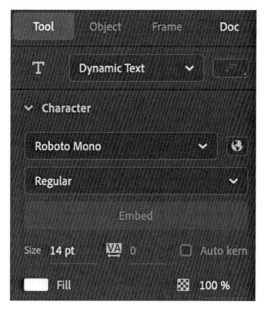

Figure 11.16 – Text Tool properties

9. Click and drag across the top-left corner of the stage (release the mouse around the midpoint of the stage) to add **Paragraph Text** with a set width. It should be about as wide as half the stage.

10. Type Health within the text object as this will display the player's current health. Within the **Paragraph** section of the **Properties** panel, be sure to set the text to align to the left.

11. To make the text stand out better against the background, you can add a **Drop Shadow** filter. With the text object selected, go to the **Object** tab of the **Properties** panel, click the **Add Filter** button, and choose a **Drop Shadow** filter with the default settings:

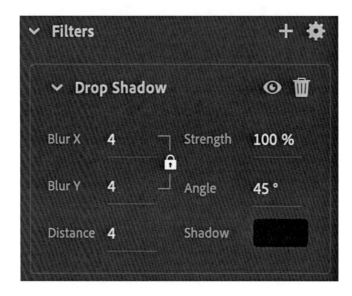

Figure 11.17 – The Drop Shadow filter

12. With one text field complete, let's copy it to create the second. Duplicate the text field by holding the *Alt* key and click and drag a copy onto the opposite side of the stage.

13. Change the text within the new text object to Blasted. Then, in the **Paragraph** section of the **Properties** panel, set the text so that it aligns to the right.

14. The final task in preparing our **Dynamic Text** objects is to provide a unique instance name for each one. Select the text that reads Health and in the **Object** tab of the **Properties** panel, input an instance name of healthdisplay. This will be used to let the user keep track of the player's health:

Figure 11.18 – Instance name provided

An instance name allows us to manipulate the **Dynamic Text** object through code. Be sure to add another instance name to the second text object that reads scoredisplay. This will eventually reflect the current score.

We'll next complete the interactive setup for this game by adding a clickable replay option to the **End Screen** area:

1. Select frame 4 of the **UI** layer. It is a good idea to ensure any other layer is locked.

2. We'll use another instance of the **pseudo** symbol, just like we did for the **Start Screen** area. Drag it from the **Library** panel onto the stage, over the **PLAY AGAIN?** message.

3. Use the **Free Transform** tool to adjust the size and rotation of this instance so that it covers the visual elements of the message:

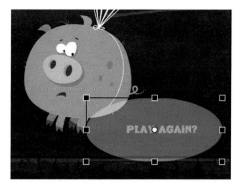

Figure 11.19 – Transform overlay across the prompt

4. With the instance selected, look at the **Object** tab of the **Properties** panel and locate the **Color Effects** section. Take the **Alpha** property down to 1%, making it almost invisible.

5. We will now provide an instance name to be able to address this object through JavaScript code. Give the object an instance name of reduxbutton.

That should take care of the user interface elements across all three states of our game:

Figure 11.20 – The completed timeline

The **Start Screen** and **End Screen** areas both have what will eventually be clickable elements, and the **Game Screen** area is ready to program.

The next thing we need to do is supply similar linkages through the **Library** panel.

Adding Linkage IDs within the Library

When we're building our game, we'll need to create dynamic instances of different objects such as enemies and projectiles on the fly, at runtime. To instantiate symbols in the library on the stage as the game is being played, we must provide **Linkage IDs** to each item we want to address via JavaScript.

> **Note**
>
> Linkage IDs work very similarly to instance names, which you provide to symbol instances on the stage. The big difference is that Linkage IDs are provided to the symbols and other library assets themselves so that we can generate new instances of them by using code.

The **Linkage** column will be, by default, displayed to the right of the **Name** column within the **Library** panel:

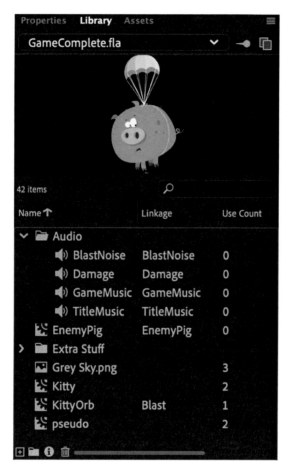

Figure 11.21 – Linkage IDs are assigned

Inputting a Linkage ID is simple. Just double-click within the **Linkage** column beside each item you want to provide a Linkage ID for. You can assign these IDs to both symbols and audio files for programmatic playback.

Set the following Linkage IDs within the game project:

- **BlastNoise**: Assign a Linkage ID of `BlastNoise`. This will be used when the kitty shoots a projectile into the sky.

- **Damage**: Assign a Linkage ID of `Damage`. This will be used when a pig enemy breaches the stage.

- **GameMusic**: Assign a Linkage ID of `GameMusic`. This will be used for the general gameplay music.

- **TitleMusic**: Assign a Linkage ID of `TitleMusic`. This will be used as the music for both the start screen and end screen.

- **EnemyPig**: Assign a Linkage ID of `EnemyPig`. Enemies will be generated randomly and move toward the ground.

- **KittyOrb**: Assign a Linkage ID of `Blast`. This is the projectile that's fired by the kitty to stop the enemies from reaching the ground. Note that the Linkage ID can be the same as or different from the symbol name.

You might have noticed the actual **Kitty** movie clip symbol does not receive a Linkage ID, even though this serves as the player. Instead of providing a Linkage ID to the symbol, since there is only one player object, we will give the **Kitty** symbol instance already on the stage an instance name to control it through code.

Unlock the **Assets** layer to select and manipulate the content within. Select the **Kitty** instance on the stage at frame 4 and provide an instance name of `player`.

In this section, we completed all the game preparation for the stage, timeline, and library so that we can address our content through code via frame labels, Linkage IDs, and instance names. Next, we'll write all the JavaScript code that's necessary for our game to function.

Programming the Game with JavaScript

As we mentioned in the previous section, *Preparing the game's timeline, stage, and library*, since we are targeting the native web with an HTML5 Canvas document, we'll be programming our game with JavaScript. Most code in Animate is bound directly to specific keyframes and is executed when the playhead reaches that frame.

The code we will write is composed of **variables** and **functions**. When we want to hold data or change data, we use variables. The first time a variable is declared, we use the `var` keyword. When we need to group a set of instructions to perform a task, we group them all within a function and then invoke that function when we want to execute the code.

As we start building the code for our game, recall that certain objects exist on the stage already and have been given instance names to allow us to manipulate them. In addition to this, there is a set of objects that only exist within the library and have been given Linkage IDs, which will allow us to create instances of these symbols and sound files at runtime.

The first step in our programming journey is to establish a set of global variables in our game. We'll do this next since many other bits of code will rely on these variables.

Creating Global Variables

Document types that support JavaScript, including HTML5 Canvas, can use **Global Scripts**. Any code placed within the **Global | Script** section of the **Actions** panel is unique, in that the code there is not bound to any specific frame on the timeline. The reason this is so important is that when variables and functions are defined as **Global**, they can be accessed from any nested timeline or varied scope within a project.

To add code to the global scripts area, open the **Actions** panel (**Window | Actions**) and twirl down the **Global** category in the left-hand column:

Figure 11.22 – Actions panel – Global: Script

Selecting **Script** and writing your code in the code editor will establish the variables and functions you create as **Global** in the scope.

We will declare a set of variables within this area so that they can be accessed throughout our game. Enter these declarations into the script editor:

```
var _this;
var stagew;
var stageh;
var health;
var score;
```

These five variables are simply declared here and will be populated with data values from within the frames-based code of our game. We will explore what the data values and other references are intended for once we declare them as part of the **Start Screen** area.

It is often helpful to keep small utility functions global as well. We'll declare a function called `randomize` that can be accessed across our game. Enter the following code into the same **Global** scripts area, along with the previously defined variables:

```
function randomize(min, max) {
    return Math.round(Math.random() * max) + min;
}
```

The `randomize` function accepts a minimum and maximum number value and returns a random number between them. This is great for randomizing the values of position, scale, opacity, and so on.

> **Note**
>
> You have probably noticed the other option within **Global** called **Include**. The **Include** option allows you to link external JavaScript files to your project for use within a game or application. For instance, you could import a JavaScript-based game engine or some sort of effects library here for use within your game!

With our global variables and a global function established, let's move our attention to programming the **Start Screen** area and the game's initialization functionality.

Programming the Start Screen

The **Start Screen** area is pretty simple in terms of user-facing functionality but there is a bit more we need to do here than account for a single button press to start the game. We'll also look at the one-time establishment of core game data structures and make it possible to reinitialize the game parameters for this screen.

The first piece of code we will write in frame 1 of the **Actions** layer mostly defines the values for our **Global** variables:

Figure 11.23 – The Actions panel should display "Current frame" and "Actions:1"

Type the following code into the script editor:

```
if (_this == undefined) {
    _this = this;
    _this.stop();
    stagew = stage.canvas.width / window.devicePixelRatio;
    stageh = stage.canvas.height /
window.devicePixelRatio;
    createjs.Sound.play("TitleMusic");
}
```

There are a set of important variables we need to set right from the start as these will be used on every screen of our game and, for the most part, correspond with the **Global** variables that have already been declared.

We only need to execute these assignments when the game first loads, though. There is no need to declare the game's width and height or preserve reference variables at any other time – these stay the same no matter what and do not change value. To ensure we only perform these assignments once, never to be repeated, we can check whether we've assigned a reference to _this yet by checking if (_this == undefined) {}. If we haven't, it will return undefined and we can safely assign the references and data.

In the code block that follows, we set _this to refer to this, which preserves a reference to the main timeline since that is where we currently are, in the global scope. Now, we can make use of _this to invoke stop(), which immediately stops the playhead at frame 1. Then, we can preserve the width and height of the game stage to perform various calculations in our code against player, enemy, and projectile positions.

> **Note**
>
> Notice that we divide the actual canvas width and height by the device pixel ratio. The devicePixelRatio property will normally return either 1 or 2. The reason this is necessary is to target both retina and non-retina screens as browsers will increase the <canvas> pixel density when necessary. This ensures our calculations will be correct.

The last thing we must do is play the **Start Screen** music. Our sound object has been given a Linkage ID of TitleMusic in the library, so we can easily reference it and begin playback here. We can do so by invoking the play() method within createjs.Sound, which taps directly into the audio management capabilities of CreateJS and SoundJS.

When a user clicks the **PLAY!** button, we need to switch to the **Game Screen** area, but we'll also use this opportunity to set up additional items within the game. Type the following code below the existing code:

```
_this.startbutton.on('click', function () {
    init();
});
function init() {
    health = 3;
    score = 0;
    createjs.Sound.stop("TitleMusic");
    createjs.Sound.play("GameMusic");
    _this.gotoAndStop("gamescreen");
}
```

As you may recall, we gave our PLAY! object an instance name of startbutton so that it could be addressed with code. The first thing we must do is create an event listener on this object and have it run a function called init(), which will initialize and start the gameplay.

The init() function itself sets the initial values for the player's health and the game's score. The useful thing about setting values for things such as health and score in this way is that it can effectively reset the game whenever it is clicked, restoring the player's health and resetting the score.

We must also stop TitleMusic, which is already playing, and then immediately play GameMusic right before moving the playhead to the **Game Screen** area at the frame 4 keyframe, which includes a frame label of gamescreen.

Our programming for the **Start Screen** area is now complete. Next, we'll look at the gameplay and begin by focusing on player movement.

Programming Player Actions

In the game, we want the player instance to be able to move back and forth across the bottom of the stage based on directional arrow key presses. We also need the player to fire projectiles up to the sky to eliminate enemies.

Select the keyframe at frame 4 of the **Actions** layer and type the following:

```
window.addEventListener("keydown", handleKeys);
function handleKeys(e) {
    var newPosition;
    if (e.keyCode == 37) {
        newPosition = _this.player.x - 30;
        if (newPosition <= 0) {
            newPosition = 0;
        }
        createjs.Tween.get(_this.player, {override:
        true}).to({x: newPosition}, 300,
        createjs.Ease.quintOut);
        _this.player.play();
        _this.player.scaleX = -1
    } else if (e.keyCode == 38) {
        fireWeapon();
    } else if (e.keyCode == 39) {
        newPosition = _this.player.x + 30;
        if (newPosition >= stagew) {
            newPosition = stagew;
        }
```

```
            createjs.Tween.get(_this.player, {override:
            true}).to({x: newPosition}, 300,
            createjs.Ease.quintOut);
            _this.player.play();
            _this.player.scaleX = 1
        }
    }
```

We add an event listener to `window` so that any part of the browser viewport can listen for key presses. We have it listen for a `keydown` event and when that occurs, invoke a function named `handleKeys`.

Within the `handleKeys` function, we detect which key was pressed by tapping into the event data that is captured by the keypress and reading the `keyCode` property within. This is numeric code that tells us exactly which key was pressed. The left arrow key is 37, the up arrow key is 38, and the right arrow key is 39. Depending on which of these three keys is detected, our code responds differently.

If a left or right arrow press is detected, we set a variable called `newPosition`, which is calculated based on the direction and represents where the character should end up on the stage. The new position will be 30px to the left or 30px to the right. Here, we compare the new position to the previously calculated stage width (alternatively, the left of the stage at 0px) to ensure that the player does not move off the screen. Additionally, if an up arrow press is detected, a function called `fireWeapon()` is invoked. We will create that function in a bit.

To animate the character's movement, we can invoke the `play()` method on the player instance and also adjust the `scaleX` property to force the instance to face the correct direction when walking. To move the player to a new position, we can use the `Tween` command in `CreateJS`. This command accepts a reference to an instance on the stage and tweens it along to a different position. We can set the length of time this will take, in milliseconds, and even apply `Ease` presets from `CreateJS` as part of the command.

If you were to test the game right now, the `player` instance's internal animation would be constantly looping since it is a **Movie Clip** symbol. We only want this to play when the user interacts with the arrow keys, so we need to stop the internal animation.

Double-click the **Kitty** symbol in the **Library** panel and type the following code into the **Actions** layer at frame 1:

```
this.stop();
```

This will effectively stop the walk cycle until we give the command for it to `play()` through the movement code. Once it hits frame 1 after playing, it will stop once again. This provides full control of the symbol's internal timeline.

As part of our keypress listener, we must invoke a function called `fireWeapon()` when an up arrow keypress is detected. We need to instantiate projectiles when this occurs and have some way of managing them as well.

Add a few line breaks below the `handleKeys()` function and enter the following lines of code below it:

```
var blasts = new createjs.Container();
stage.addChild(blasts);
function fireWeapon() {
    var blast = new lib.Blast();
    blast.x = _this.player.x;
    blast.y = _this.player.y;
    blasts.addChild(blast);
    createjs.Sound.play("BlastNoise");
}
```

The first thing we do is create a `CreateJS Container` for our projectile `Blast` instances. By adding the instances to a `Container` in this way, we can keep track of and check the properties of each `Blast` instance in a loop later. `Container` is added to the stage.

The `fireWeapon()` function creates a new `Blast` instance from the library by using the given Linkage ID. Then, we set the position just atop the player instance and add the new `Blast` instance to our `Container`.

Lastly, we generate sound playback from the library so that firing projectiles makes an audible sound.

Projectiles are to be fired against an invading set of enemies. Next, we'll write some code to generate the enemies for our game.

Programming Enemy Behavior

The enemies in this game are pigs that parachute down from the sky. Their goal is to reach the ground, beyond the height of the stage, while the player's goal is to shoot them out of the sky before that happens.

To generate our enemies, we'll create an `addEnemy()` function that can be called from within our eventual game loop, as enemies are needed. Type the following below the previous code block:

```
var enemies = new createjs.Container();
stage.addChild(enemies);
function addEnemy() {
    var enemy = new lib.EnemyPig();
    enemy.x = randomize(50, stagew - 50);
    enemy.y = randomize(100, 2000) * -1;
    enemy.speed = randomize(0.5, 3);
    var direction = randomize(-1, 2);
    if (direction == 0) {
        direction = -1;
    }
    enemy.scaleX = direction;
    enemy.gotoAndPlay(randomize(1, 120));
    enemies.addChild(enemy);
}
```

Enemies are added to a `Container`, much like the `Blast` projectiles are, and for the same reasons. When we write the game's heartbeat function, or game loop, we can constantly monitor both enemies and projectiles and respond to collisions, movements, and boundary extremes.

Within the `addEnemy()` function, we instantiate `EnemyPig` from the library and then make heavy use of the global `randomize()` function to add some variability to the enemy's position, fall speed, facing direction, and internal animation starting frame. Lastly, we add the new `EnemyPig` instance to our `Container` with these given properties.

At this point, our player character is set up with a full move set, projectiles can be generated, and enemies can be spawned. The game loop ties all of this together, and that is what we will write next.

Programming the Game Loop

The game loop (or heartbeat) is a function that runs continually and monitors the game environment for changes. When changes are discovered, a set of additional instructions are executed as the program requires. The game loop brings everything together in a meaningful way and controls all the reactions between the elements within the game's structure.

To begin writing our game loop, we will make use of `CreateJS Ticker` (which, in Animate, is bound to our document's FPS value) and a function that executes at every `tick`.

Write the following JavaScript below any previous code:

```javascript
var heartbeat = createjs.Ticker.on("tick", gameLoop, _this);
function gameLoop(e) {
    _this.healthdisplay.text = "Health: " + health;
    _this.scoredisplay.text = "Blasted: " + score;
    /* BLAST MANAGEMENT PLACEHOLDER */
    /* ENEMY MANAGEMENT PLACEHOLDER */
}
```

It is important to give your `Ticker` listener an identifier so that you can manage it later. We set the listener to a new variable called `heartbeat` here, which will allow us to easily turn off the game loop once a game over occurs.

The game loop can also be made to constantly monitor and update things such as player `health` and overall `score`. Recall that we created dynamic text fields on the stage for each and gave them both instance names. This allows us to output `health` and `score` data within related text objects to let the player know how the game is going.

Following this are two placeholder `comment` blocks. Comments in JavaScript are not executed but can serve as developer notes or placeholders like this. Single-line comments in JavaScript are written as `// COMMENT`, whereas multiline comments are written as `/* COMMENT */`. Of course, you can use multiline comments for a single line as well.

The first of these comments has to do with projectile monitoring and management. Delete that comment and type the following code in its place:

```javascript
for (var i = blasts.numChildren - 1; i >= 0; i--) {
    var b = blasts.getChildAt(i);
    b.y -= 10;
    if (b.y < -50) {
        blasts.removeChild(b);
    }
```

```
        var blastTarget = enemies.getObjectUnderPoint(b.x,
        b.y, 0);
        if (blastTarget) {
            enemies.removeChild(blastTarget.parent.parent);
            blasts.removeChild(b);
            score++;
        }
    }
```

We begin this code block with a `for` loop. The `for` loop is constructed as follows:

```
for(index; condition; adjustment){ body }
```

- For our `index`, we set the `i` variable, which is assigned the number of projectiles within their `Container`, minus 1. We remove one because we want the `index` value of the projectile and not the total number of projectiles. If there are no projectiles present within `Container`, the index value will be `-1`.

- `condition` checks to see if our index value is greater than or equal to `0`. Indexes in JavaScript begin with `0` and count upwards, so an index of `1` is the second spot and not the first, which would be `0`.

- Finally, we make an `adjustment` to the index value for the next iteration of our loop. In this case, we decrement the index value by `1` each time the loop runs. When all the projectiles have had their turn, the loop terminates.

- Within the curly braces is the `body` area of our loop, which runs once for each loop iteration.

Within each loop iteration, we begin by creating a reference to a specific projectile with `getChildAt()`. Passing in the current index, we target a specific projectile instance within the `blasts` container.

Once we have established the reference, we can manage the blast projectile. We set a new position for the projectile that is `10px` closer to the top of the stage than it currently is. Then, we check the position to see whether it has gotten so high as to have left the stage. At that point, we remove the instance entirely.

The last block of code is all about collision detection. We use the
getObjectUnderPoint() function of CreateJS to check whether the position of the
projectile overlaps any of our enemy instances. If it does, we remove the enemy it collided
with, the projectile itself, and increment our score by a value of 1.

The second comment placeholder in our game loop has to do with enemy monitoring and
management. Delete that comment and replace it with the following:

```
for (var i = enemies.numChildren - 1; i >= 0; i--) {
    var e = enemies.getChildAt(i);
    e.y += speed;
    if (e.y > stageh + 50) {
        enemies.removeChild(e);
        health--;
        /* GAME OVER DETECTION PLACEHOLDER */
    }
}
if (enemies.numChildren < 10) {
    addEnemy();
}
```

Very similar in construction to our projectile management loop, we manage enemies in a
for() loop as well. The logic is the same, except we are performing the loop against the
enemies container.

Here, we move each enemy down the stage toward the bottom by a number based on
the random speed value that was assigned upon generation. If the enemy's position is
more than 50px below the stage bottom, we remove the enemy instance and decrease the
player's health by 1 point. It is at this time that we can also detect whether the health is
low enough for a game over, but that is a placeholder comment for now.

Following the for() loop, we do a simple check to see whether the number of enemies
we currently have at play is less than 10. If it is, we invoke addEnemy() to add another,
ensuring there is a constant stream of enemies in play. Since this is part of the game loop,
enemies will be constantly generated as the need arises.

The last bit we need to write is the game over detection and cleanup script. Replace the
game over detection comment with the following code block:

```
if (health <= 0) {
    createjs.Ticker.off("tick", heartbeat);
    window.removeEventListener("keydown", handleKeys);
```

```
        stage.removeChild(enemies);
        stage.removeChild(blasts);
        createjs.Sound.stop("GameMusic");
        createjs.Sound.play("TitleMusic");
        _this.gotoAndStop("endscreen");
    }
```

The only condition for a game over is if the player's `health` drops to `0`. When that happens, we disable `Ticker` so that the game loop no longer runs, remove the `keydown` listener, remove all instances of enemies and projectiles by removing their associated `Containers`, stop the `GameMusic` playback, play `TitleMusic` again, and send the playhead to the **End Screen** area. This effectively ends the game.

With the **Game Screen** code in place, all we need to do is program the **End Screen** events and the entire game is complete!

Programming the End Screen

The **End Screen** area contains the least amount of code out of all our game screens. This is because all we have to do is add an event listener to detect whether the player wants to go another round.

Select the keyframe at frame 7 of the **Actions** layer and write the following within the script editor:

```
_this.reduxbutton.on('click', function(){
    _this.gotoAndStop("startscreen");
});
```

This should be easy for you to interpret by now. The **Movie Clip** instance called `reduxbutton` is given an event listener of the `click` type. Once a click is detected, we go back to the **Start Screen** area.

Once on the **Start Screen** area, the initial setup is ignored since those references already exist. When the player clicks `startbutton` again, `health` and `score` are reset to their default values and the game begins again.

In this section, we programmed an entire game using JavaScript for the native web. We examined how to write code to control existing elements on each screen, how to generate new elements from the document library, and how to write a game loop and associated logic to monitor and respond to all sorts of game events. Coming up, we'll consider a few things we can do to finish the project in Animate through **Publish Settings**.

Finishing the Game Project

Now that the code has been written and the game is functionally complete, it makes sense to look at everything we've done and reflect on how it is all organized within Animate.

Have a look at the **Actions** panel now that the game has been written:

Figure 11.24 – Code bound to specific locations

Notice that in the left-hand column of the **Actions** panel, specific chunks of code are listed and organized according to the specific objects, layers, and frames they have been bound to. We have global script code, code segmented across the main timeline, and a bit of code within a symbol. It all works together to create a cohesive gameplay experience!

To finish the project, there are a few considerations you may want to look over to add some extra polish to how the game is published.

Open the **Publish Settings** dialog by choosing **File | Publish Settings...** or by going to the **Doc** tab of the **Properties** panel under **More Settings...**:

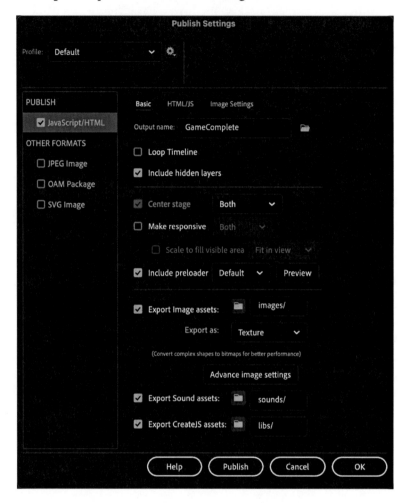

Figure 11.25 – HTML5 Canvas – Publish Settings

There are a lot of options here, as we discovered in *Chapter 4, Publishing and Exporting Creative Content*. For our game project, let's choose **Center stage** and **Include preloader** for our options. This will center the game on the HTML page that is generated and add a little preloader animation to let the user know the game is loading.

In this section, we finished our game project by organizing the code we've written and tweaking our **Publish Settings** to provide the user with a more refined game experience.

Summary

We've accomplished so much in this chapter! We began by examining the starter document, which already had several assets in place on the stage and within the project library, all derived from the **Assets** panel. Then, we went through each screen and library item to organize our timeline with frame labels and to provide instance names and Linkage IDs where needed. The bulk of our time in this chapter was spent in the **Actions** panel, writing all the JavaScript code that controls the player character, enemy and projectiles, internal variables and references, and how all of these elements interact with one another to produce a full game experience for the web. Closing out, we looked at **Publish Settings** and adjusted some of the attributes for our published game content.

In the next chapter, we'll explore a somewhat related web-based project in the form of **virtual reality** experiences using **WebGL glTF** document types.

12
Producing Virtual Reality Content for WebGL

In the previous chapter, we explored the concept of game development for the native web and programmed an entire game using JavaScript and the HTML5 Canvas document type.

This chapter will focus on the **Virtual Reality** (**VR**) and **WebGL glTF** document types within Animate. Virtual reality is cutting-edge technology and Animate has its own take on this space using both panoramic and 360-degree VR concepts. We'll get an overview of the VR document type within the software and then move directly on to assembling our Virtual Reality environments with scenes and textures. Once these environments are established, we'll add in additional assets as part of each scene, animate them using the **Asset Warp** tool, which we first encountered in *Chapter 9, Manipulating Warped Objects through Advanced Rigging*, and write code to allow interaction with the user. Finally, we'll explore a panel in Animate specifically for testing and adjusting VR content.

After reading this chapter, you'll be able to perform the following functions in Animate:

- Discover a variety of VR and WebGL document types in Animate and know how to create content specifically for each format.

- Understand specific workflows for creating, managing, and testing VR environments.

- Import equirectangular and panoramic photographs to be used as textures, along with drawings and rendered 3D images that can be made interactive.

- Use the **Asset Warp** tool and warped object workflows to produce subtle animations on imported drawings.

- Write code that allows the user to move between scenes and interact with objects.

Technical Requirements

You will need the following to complete this chapter:

- Adobe Animate 2022 (version 22.0 or above).

- Please refer to the *Animate System Requirements* page for hardware specifications: `https://helpx.adobe.com/animate/system-requirements.html`.

The code in action video for this chapter can be found here:
`https://bit.ly/3CB9tnX`

Overview of Virtual Reality Documents

In this section, we are going to get an overall idea of the VR document types within Animate and how they relate to one another. Following this, we'll learn how to configure scenes in our project and apply photographic background textures to those scenes.

Though separated into two distinct classifications, both the VR and WebGL document types are based on the WebGL glTF standard at their core. When using VR document types, we get a few extra workflow choices within Animate as opposed to the more general WebGL glTF document types.

> **Tip**
> To learn more about the WebGL glTF specification, visit `https://www.khronos.org/gltf/`.

All of the VR and WebGL document types can be found under the **Advanced** category of the **New Document** dialog:

Figure 12.1 – Both the VR and WebGL document types are considered BETA

While we will be focusing on VR projects in this chapter, it is important to understand that these document types are built on a standard WebGL glTF foundation. The WebGL glTF specification is a platform-agnostic asset delivery format specifically geared toward **3D** and **GPU**-accelerated content.

Here are the differences between these four choices, in order of complexity:

- **WebGL glTF Standard**: This conforms to the standard specification and can be played back in any environment that supports standard WebGL such as the Babylon.js sandbox: `https://sandbox.babylonjs.com/`.

- **WebGL glTF Extended**: Builds upon the standard specification by extending it for fuller usage within the Animate environment to include things such as interactivity.

- **VR Panorama**: Adds extra tools to Animate to define layers as cylindrical VR textures and makes use of the **VR View** panel to position symbol instances in 3D space and test projects.

- **VR 360**: A variant of the **VR Panorama** document that applies the VR textures to a sphere in place of a cylinder.

There are also a set of limitations to consider for each of these platforms. For instance, **WebGL glTF Extended** allows you to use **Button** symbols, but both VR formats do not! When it comes to sound, the VR formats can only make use of **Event Sync** when it comes to sounds. An additional limitation is that all four document types only allow **Static Text**. Remember that all four of these formats are in beta and limitations are to be expected.

> **Note**
>
> Depending on the type of project you'd like to work on, you can create either a **VR Panorama** or **VR 360** document. Aside from a few small differences, they function the same. I've included assets for both formats in the files for this chapter, which can all be downloaded from `https://github.com/PacktPublishing/Adobe-Animate-2022-for-Creative-Professionals-Second-Edition`.

Let's create a new Virtual Reality document in Animate to work with in this chapter:

1. Create a new document by choosing **File | New** and clicking the **Advanced** category of the **New Document** dialog.

2. Choose either **VR Panorama** or **VR 360**, noting that both are considered beta. The beta label indicates that Adobe is still working on these document formats and that certain aspects may change in future releases of Animate.

3. Check that the document's properties have been set to `550px` in width and `400px` in height, with a framerate of `24fps`. We will need to adjust these settings later but the defaults are fine for now.

4. Click **Create** and save your new document via **File | Save** once it appears in Animate.

The new document is pretty plain right now and looks just about identical to any other freshly created document in Animate.

Now that we have created our document, we can start preparing it for use in our project concept.

Managing Scenes for Virtual Reality

The use of **scenes** in VR projects is not required but they allow for some pretty interesting user experiences. For instance, you can allow the user to explore the experience and, by interacting with different objects in the world, they can travel to additional rooms and environments. In our project, the user will be able to move from a park to a pond and back again.

Traditionally, scenes within an Animate document break the main timeline into manageable chunks. So, an animator might create one scene as an establishing shot and then have the second scene serve as a tighter shot focused on some action or character.

> **Note**
>
> HTML5 Canvas and WebGL glTF Standard documents cannot make use of the scenes feature within Animate, but just about every other document type can! Scenes effectively break the main timeline into segments and were originally used to construct scenes within a running animation.

As we mentioned previously, we will include two scenes within this project, so let's create those now:

1. Open the **Scene** panel by choosing **Window | Scene** from the application menu:

Figure 12.2 – Scene panel

The **Scene** panel will appear. This panel allows you to create, duplicate, and delete scenes. You can also reorder and rename scenes from here.

You should only have a single scene named **Scene 1** when you first start. This is your main timeline.

2. Double-click on **Scene 1** and type in Park as its name. This will contain all the assets related to the park-based environment we will create.

3. Click the **Add Scene** button that appears as a small plus (+) icon at the bottom left to create a new scene.

4.   Rename your new scene Pond:

Figure 12.3 – Scene management

Similar to layers, library items, frame labels, and more, it is always a good idea to name your items in a way that provides organization and helps with recollection.

Clicking on either scene name within the **Scene** panel will switch to that particular scene. You can also switch scenes by using the **Edit Scene** selector above the stage:

Figure 12.4 – Scene switcher

Of course, you can include as many scenes as you like within a project. We are going to stick with two here and keep things fairly simple.

Now, before we start importing image content into our project, it is good to become familiar with how to acquire or generate photography for tasks like this.

Capturing Photographs for Virtual Reality

While you can acquire 360 **equirectangular** and **panoramic** photographs from various stock photo services, it is always good to know how to generate your own – especially for projects like this.

With VR documents in Animate, you need to use something for your environmental texture. If targeting VR 360, the texture is wrapped across the inside of a sphere with the user viewing from the center outward. For VR Panorama, we wrap our texture across the inside of a cylinder instead.

> **Note**
>
> You can also simply draw out your content for VR textures using software such as Adobe Photoshop, Illustrator, or even within Animate itself! It all depends on whether you want your environment to be photorealistic or not.

In the exercise files for this chapter, you will find examples of the same environment captured in both equirectangular and panoramic formats.

The easiest way to understand each format is to just open them and have a look:

Figure 12.5 – Panoramic versus 360 photograph

The panoramic image is very wide, without much height, and includes a bit of distortion to the perspective when viewed as a flat photograph. The 360 equirectangular photo will always present itself in a 2:1 ratio regarding width to height and is massively distorted when viewed as a flattened photograph.

With modern mobile devices, it is very easy to capture these types of photographs. It is a bit of a tedious process with Android or iOS as you must use camera software that can guide you to generate these photos, based on capturing and integrating multiple shots to compose the image.

> **Tip**
>
> Mobile device camera software normally does a fine job, but for even greater precision and ease, you can use hardware that is made specifically to take photos using these modes. Generally, I'd suggest using what you have first and upgrading if needed.

I captured the sample photographs for this project using a Google Pixel 3 XL running Android 11 and using the native camera application:

Figure 12.6 – Google Android advanced camera modes

The preceding screenshots should provide a good idea of what is available for this sort of image capture on Android devices today. As shown in the first screenshot, the camera app has several modes to choose from. I can access both **Panorama** and **Photo Sphere** from the **Modes** option on this screen.

With **Panorama** selected, you simply press record, and the software guides your movements to capture a full panoramic image. You stand on one spot and rotate slowly in one direction until you've captured the entire view.

For **Photo Sphere**, you may need to check your options, as displayed in the preceding screenshot, to ensure that you are creating a **360** photograph and not some other format. Once you press record, the software will prompt you to turn your camera toward different spots to capture a full set of photographs to stitch into an equirectangular image.

When using an Apple iPhone, you only have access to the panorama camera mode within the native camera software. To achieve a 360-degree image, you can use third-party software such as Google Street View or a variety of other camera apps:

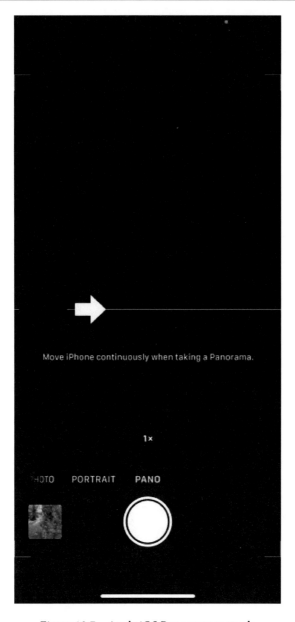

Figure 12.7 – Apple iOS Pano camera mode

The preceding screenshot is of an iPhone 12 using the **Pano** camera mode. It works very similarly to the same photographic mode on Android – however, is a bit more straightforward to access and activate.

With our panoramic and equirectangular images at hand, we are ready to return to Animate and integrate them into the scenes we have created.

Adding Textures to Virtual Reality Scenes

Probably the most important step in creating a VR environment with Animate is to implement the photographic content we've gathered as textures. These textures define the background of the world we create within each scene.

To define a photograph as a texture, perform the following steps:

1. Make sure you are currently in the **Park** scene. If not, switch to it using the scene switcher above the stage.

2. Locate the appropriate park photograph in your filesystem. I'm using the `PXL_20201223_195419259.PHOTOSPHERE.jpg` file since I am using a **VR 360** document type.

3. Drag your image file from the filesystem and onto the Animate stage.

4. Select the new bitmap object on the stage and look at the **Object** tab of the **Properties** panel. Set the **x** position to 0 and the **y** position to 0. You could also use the **Align** panel to align it to the top left.

    Looking at the stage at this point, you will notice that the photograph is much, much larger than our tiny stage. If you're using the equirectangular photograph, for instance, the stage width is 550 but the bitmap object width is 4000! We need to adjust our stage size so that it matches the bitmap object's size.

5. Select the **Doc** tab of the **Properties** panel to view the document's properties and locate the **Document Settings** section.

6. Click the **Match contents** button to resize the stage, as per its contents:

Figure 12.8 – Adjusting the stage's size to Match contents

The stage's width and height are automatically set to match the width and height of the bitmap object.

7. Now, let's mark the layer to be used as a texture when published. Click the **Mark for Texture Wrapping** option within the **Layer_1** layer:

Figure 12.9 – Mark for Texture Wrapping

This marks the layer for texture wrapping. The contents of the layer – in this case, an equirectangular photograph – will be used across the inside of a sphere. The distorted, flat photograph will appear with normal proportions when wrapped as a texture, but you will not see these effects until you test it.

8. You will want to rename the **Layer_1** layer `Texture` for clarity before moving on.

With that, the **Park** scene has been set up with a photographic texture. You will need to switch over to the **Pond** scene and perform the same set of steps there.

> **Note**
> You can mark as many layers as you want in this way but once a layer is marked as a texture, any animation or interactivity that was present in the layer will be disabled.

Once you've completed both scenes, they should each contain a single layer named **Texture**, which is marked as a texture. Each scene includes either a photograph of the pond or a photograph of the park, as per the scene's name.

Again, you can use either the panoramic or equirectangular versions of these photographs for your content:

Figure 12.10 – Panorama versus 360 differences

If you choose **Fit in Window** from the **Zoom** dropdown in the top-right area above the stage, you will see the full scene. Aside from the perspective differences between the VR Panorama and VR 360 document types, everything else should be the same, regardless of what document type you have chosen.

> **Note**
>
> For the remainder of this chapter, I'm going to focus on the VR 360 version of our document, but any of the steps that follow can be used across either document type.

You can perform a **Test Movie** right now and your VR experience will be fully functional, just through this initial setup of importing photographs and marking them as texture layers. When viewing it in the web browser, simply click and drag across the scene to change your view within the environment.

In this section, we provided an introduction to using VR within Animate and how it relates to WebGL glTF file types. We also learned how to manage scenes within a VR document. We then explored how to use mobile device cameras to gather photographs that are suitable for VR use, such as textures, and imported those photographs into our VR documents to be used as textures within each scene. Next, we'll add some additional visual content to our VR scenes by using imported 3D renders and then create some animated content using the **Asset Warp** tool.

Adding Additional Content

As we saw in the previous sections, the simple act of importing properly generated photographs as textures within a VR document goes quite far in establishing our VR environment. This is Adobe Animate, though, and we can add additional objects to our scene to be used for interactivity and animation!

First, we'll set up some additional objects to eventually be used to move between the **Park** and **Pond** scenes in the form of 3D rendered signage. Then, we'll get playful and add a small character drawing that can be animated using one of the most powerful creative motion tools in Animate – the **Asset Warp** tool.

Importing Transparent 3D Renders

Recall that we have established two scenes for our VR experience: **Park** and **Pond**. Ultimately, we want the user to be able to locate a sign within each scene that directs them to the other scene. Clicking a sign will transport the user to the other scene.

To create the signage assets, I used **Adobe Dimension** to configure and generate 3D models, which were then rendered as transparent PNG files. Dimension comes packed with a set of models, materials, and more to be used to create 3D scenic renders. In 2021, Adobe also released a new set of 3D applications as the **Adobe Substance 3D** collection. This includes **Adobe Substance 3D Stager** – an updated, more powerful version of Dimension. You can use either piece of software to create similar rendered objects for your Animate projects, but Adobe seems to be more committed to Stager moving forward and Dimension may disappear in the future.

> **Tip**
>
> To learn more about Dimension, visit the following URL: `https://www.adobe.com/products/dimension.html`.
>
> Information about Stager can be acquired from `https://www.adobe.com/products/substance3d-stager.html`.

These renders have been made available alongside the photographs in the exercise files for you to download and are named `ParkSign.png` and `PondSign.png`.

Let's set up our signage for each scene:

1. Insert a new layer above the **Texture** layer by clicking the **New Layer** button.

2. Name the new layer `Sign` as this will contain our interactive signage:

Figure 12.11 – The Sign layer added across scenes

3. Locate the `ParkSign.png` and `PondSign.png` image files within your file system and drag each into the appropriate scene. `ParkSign.png` should be placed in the **Pond** scene, while `PondSign.png` should be placed in the **Park** scene.

4. Once the sign images have been placed on the stage, within the **Sign** layer of each scene, you'll want to reposition them to areas that make the most sense:

Figure 12.12 – Positioning the signs properly in each scene

I placed my `ParkSign.png` at an **x** of `460` and a **y** of `930`. My `PondSign.png` is placed at an **x** of `3450` and a **y** of `958`. You may also choose to resize the signs, but I left them at their native sizes in my examples.

The signs are now placed within each scene but are only decorative at this point. We will make them interactive later in this chapter.

> **Note**
>
> Since we are dealing with WebGL glTF as the basis of our VR experience, we can also import **GLB** and **GLTF** models for use directly within Animate! However, they are a bit buggy when used within VR documents and sometimes, they will not render properly. This is why we are using PNG-based renders from our Adobe Dimension (or Substance 3D Stager) models.

With our signage placed at the appropriate spots within each scene, we'll move our attention to animating content with **Warped Objects** and the **Asset Warp** tool.

Animating with the Asset Warp Tool

We'll now use the **Asset Warp** tool to create a smoothly animated character dwelling within the **Park** scene. As we saw in *Chapter 9, Manipulating Warped Objects through Advanced Rigging*, you can use the **Asset Warp** tool on both shapes and bitmaps. As you add pins using the tool to various locations across the object, a distortion mesh is created. Moving these pins will adjust the mesh and transform the underlying content. Pin positions can be changed across keyframes and classic tweens can be used to animate the content.

I have drawn a figure and painted it with **Adobe Fresco**, a digital drawing and painting application, that will work great for this:

Figure 12.13 – Spectre PNG file

You can find `spectre.png` in the exercise files for this chapter, alongside the others we've already worked with.

> **Tip**
>
> To learn more about Adobe Fresco, visit the following URL: `https://www.adobe.com/products/fresco.html`.

Let's add the image to our scene and prepare it for animation:

1. Add a new layer within the **Park** scene and rename it `Spectre`.

2. Import the `spectre.png` file into the stage either by dragging it from the filesystem or by choosing **File | Import | Import to Stage...** from the application menu.

3. Select the image on the stage and look at the **Object** tab of the **Properties** panel. Set the **x** value to `1380` and the **y** value to `1015`. **height** should have a value of `160`. This places the figure beneath the large tree.

4. With the object still selected, click the **Convert to Symbol** button:

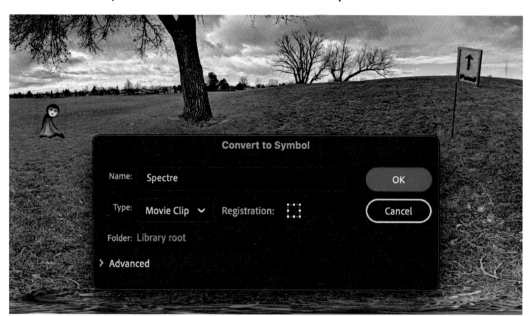

Figure 12.14 – Convert image to a Movie Clip Symbol

5. In the dialog that appears, set **Name** to Spectre and be sure to select **Movie Clip** from the **Type** selection menu. We are using **Movie Clip** to loop its internal animation since the main timeline only consists of a single frame, and for interactivity purposes later. **Movie Clip** allows both of these features. Click **OK** when you're finished.

6. Double-click on the **Spectre** symbol instance in the **Park** scene to enter the symbol timeline.

7. Select the **Asset Warp** tool from the toolbar:

Figure 12.15 – The Asset Warp tool

8. Now, click on various points across the bitmap image to create warp pins and a unified mesh:

Figure 12.16 – Setting the warp pins

It's up to you how many warp pins to use and where to place them, but I suggest referring to the previous figure as a general guide.

With our warped object established, we'll now have a look at animating between mesh states, as established through regular keyframes.

Animating the Spectre Warped Object

We are now going to establish keyframes across the layer containing our warped object and will make use of classic tweens to animate between these keyframes. Any variation in the mesh between keyframes will cause a distortion effect, similar to moving cloth or morphing shapes.

> **Note**
>
> Again, I cannot stress enough how important it is to establish the warp points that are needed before creating additional keyframes or attempting any animation.

Let's start animating our little **Spectre** image:

1. The first thing we must do is establish a set of keyframes across the timeline. The animation will be very subtle, so we only need a few. Insert keyframes at frames 16, 43, and 65:

Figure 12.17 – Adding keyframes across the timeline

2. Now, let's modify the pins that have already been placed across the **Warped Object** mesh to provide small distortions across the timeline. Using the **Asset Warp** tool, shift the various pin locations slightly at frames 16 and 43:

Figure 12.18 – Adjusting the mesh pins across keyframes

Do not modify anything at frames 1 and 65 as we want these to be identical to create a smooth animation loop.

As you shift the pin's locations, the mesh will become distorted and the image will bend and warp to reflect this:

Figure 12.19 – Moving the pin's locations modifies the mesh

Move the pins to adjust the mesh. However, you don't want to shift things too much, as the distortion effect may become too severe and buckle the underlying artwork in undesirable ways.

3. Once your modifications have been made within the necessary keyframes, add a **Classic Tween** to each of the frame spans:

Figure 12.20 – Classic Tween applied to Spectre

Now, you can preview the animation and ensure everything loops correctly by enabling the **Loop** option above the timeline. It should create a seamless loop of the subtle, smooth animation.

Once you're satisfied with your motion, I suggest that you convert the tweens into frame-by-frame animations. With the VR projects in Animate, your animation will likely be much smoother when this step has been taken! The downside of this is that you will not be able to render it as a warped object anymore.

To do this, select all the tweens, right-click, choose **Convert to Frame-by-Frame Animation** from the menu that appears, and choose the desired keyframe density.

Tip

Before converting frame by frame, you can also make a copy of the symbol from the **Library** panel. That way, you can always tweak things, even after conversion.

In this section, we imported a set of external image files to be used as interactive and animated objects within our VR experience. We also explored the **Asset Warp** tool and used it to create and animate warped objects within the VR space. Of course, you can use these tools and techniques in other document types as well! Next, we'll tie both scenes together and complete our VR experience by writing a little code.

Writing Code for Virtual Reality Interactions

As we've seen in previous chapters, there are several different approaches to writing code in Animate. When we programmed our small game in *Chapter 11, Developing Web-Based Games*, we did so by writing our JavaScript directly into the script editor of the **Actions** panel. For other projects, such as the clickable advertisement in *Chapter 6, Interactive Motion Graphics for the Web*, we used the **Actions Wizard** area to guide us.

Unlike coding within HTML5 Canvas documents, we cannot leverage CreateJS for our VR project. Even though all web-based document types in Animate use JavaScript as the programming language, the WebGL glTF and VR document types within Animate use a completely different library from what we've seen previously. This is a WebGL-based runtime library that Adobe has created specifically for these document types. Thankfully, though, the **Actions Wizard** area supports this runtime, so it is fairly easy to work with when you're programming simple interactions.

Moving from Scene to Scene

Our first task will be to program the signs we've already placed within each scene to allow the user to click on each to load a different scene. If the user is in the **Park** scene and clicks the pond sign, they will be taken to the **Pond** scene. Once at the **Pond** scene, if they click the park sign, they will be taken back to the **Park** scene.

Before writing any code, we need to prepare our document and the various objects within it for interactivity. This won't be anything new as we've performed these tasks a few times already in earlier chapters:

1. Our signs within each scene are bitmap images right now. To make them interactive, they must be converted into movie clip symbols. Convert both `ParkSign.png` and `PondSign.png` into movie clip symbols by selecting each and using **Modify | Convert to Symbol** from the application menu.

2. Each of the symbol instances will need to be given instance names to make them available for interactivity. Give them instance names of `ParkSign` and `PondSign` within the **Object** tab of the **Properties** panel.

3. Additionally, we will provide the movie clip instance containing our **Warped Object** animation in the **Park** scene with an instance name. Select the movie clip symbol instance and give it an instance name of `Spectre`.

4. The timeline for each scene will also need a layer without any visuals that we can bind our code to. Create a new layer at the top of the layer stack in each scene and name it `Actions`.

With that, each scene has been configured to make the animated figure and the set of sign instances interactive. Now, it's time to write some JavaScript code for each sign that will listen for mouse clicks from the user and respond by loading the alternate scene.

Let's program both of our sign instances using the **Actions** panel and **Actions Wizard**:

1. Switch to the **Park** scene and ensure that you have selected frame 1 of the **Actions** layer.

2. Open the **Actions** panel by choosing **Window | Actions** from the application menu.

3. Click the **Add Using Wizard** button at the top of the panel to enable **Actions Wizard**. The script editor will be replaced with a step-by-step interface.

4. In **Step 1** of the interface, we are prompted to select an action. Locate **Go to Next Scene** and select it:

Figure 12.21 – Choosing an action in Step 1

5. Click **Next** at the bottom of the panel interface to move on to the next step.

6. **Step 2** prompts you to select a triggering event. Choose **On Click** so that a mouse click will trigger the action you previously chose in **Step 1**.

7. The final task is to select the object that will listen for our triggering event. Since we have provided instance names for two instances within the **Park** scene, they appear here. Choose **PondSign** and click **Finish and add**:

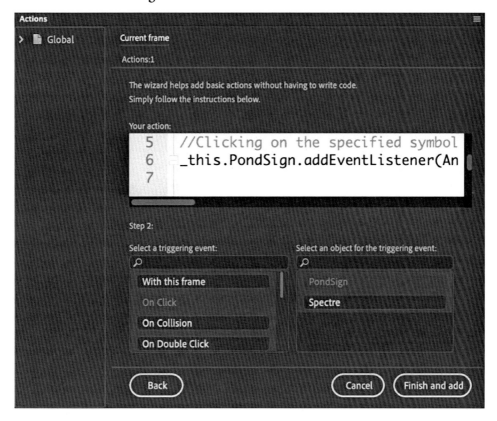

Figure 12.22 – Choosing a triggering event and object

The **Actions Wizard** interface will go away and be replaced with the script editor, with our completed code within it.

The code for moving from the **Park** scene to the **Pond** scene when a user clicks the sign that reads "Pond" is as follows:

```
{
    var _this = this;
    _this.PondSign.addEventListener(AnEvent.CLICK,
    function() {
    anWebgl.nextScene();
    });
}
```

The preceding code establishes a reference variable of `_this` for scope retention, and then adds an `AnEvent.CLICK` event listener to the `PondSign` instance. When a click is detected, the next scene in the order of scenes is loaded via the `nextScene()` method.

> **Note**
>
> Be sure that your **Park** scene is listed first and that your **Pond** scene is listed last within the **Scene** panel. Otherwise, this code will not work as written!

You could always switch to the **Pond** scene now and run through all those steps again, choosing instead to go to the previous scene when the **ParkSign** instance is clicked, but there is a faster way to do this.

Since we've already done most of the work, we can simply duplicate the existing code and adjust it to our needs:

1. Copy the entire code block from frame 1 of the **Actions** layer by selecting it and using the keyboard shortcut *Command/Ctrl + C*.
2. Switch to the **Pond** scene and select frame 1 of the **Actions** layer within that scene.
3. Open the **Actions** panel again and paste the copied code into the script editor using the *Command/Ctrl + V*.
4. In the code, change `_this.PondSign.addEventListener` to `_this.ParkSign.addEventListener` and change `anWebgl.nextScene();` to `anWebgl.prevScene();`.

   That's all that needs to change!

The code for moving from the **Pond** scene back to the **Park** scene when a user clicks the sign that reads `Park` functions the same way as the previous code:

```
{
    var _this = this;
    _this.ParkSign.addEventListener(AnEvent.CLICK,
    function() {
    anWebgl.prevScene();
    });
}
```

With our signs in each scene properly programmed, we can run a **Test Movie** and more fully experience the VR project.

> **Tip**
>
> You could also choose to use the `anWebgl.gotoScene("scene_name");` function, along with the specific scene name, instead of `anWebgl.prevScene();` or `anWebgl.prevScene();` – it all depends on the project and how you want to handle any branching scene navigation.

Next, we'll make our little **Spectre** instance interactive as well by using **Actions Wizard**.

Interacting with Animated Objects

Making our signs interactive is necessary within this VR project because we need a mechanism for the user to be able to switch from one scene to another. We can also make other objects interactive just to be playful, and add some other things for the user to do while exploring the environment we've created.

Let's add some interactivity to the `Spectre` symbol instance and make it respond visually to various mouse movements:

1. Since we are programming interactions for the `Spectre` symbol instance, be sure to switch to the **Park** scene and select frame 1 of the **Actions** layer.

2. Open the **Actions** panel and click the **Add Using Wizard** button at the top of the panel to enable **Actions Wizard**.

3. We will scale the instance up whenever a mouseover action is detected. For **Step 1**, choose the **Set Scale Along X-Axis** action and change the value of the highlighted code that appears from 1 to 3. This scales the visual object by a factor of three.

4. Click **Next** at the bottom of the panel to proceed to the next step.

5. To code the mouseover event in **Step2**, choose **On Mouse Over** from the triggering event list.

6. Now, choose **Spectre** from the set of objects and click **Finish and add**.

The following JavaScript code will be added to the script editor:

```
{
    var _this = this;
    _this.Spectre.addEventListener(AnEvent.MOUSE_OVER,
    function () {
        _this.Spectre.scaleX = 3;
    });
}
```

This code tells the Spectre instance to listen for a mouseover event and then react to that by scaling its width by a factor of 3.

We want to scale the height of our Spectre instance, along with its width, and need to have the scale reset when the mouse cursor moves off the Spectre instance.

Perform the following adjustments to the code using the script editor:

1. Add a line of code beneath _this.Spectre.scaleX = 3; that reads _this.Spectre.scaleY = 3; for the instance to scale in both width and height simultaneously.

2. Copy the entire code block using the *Command/Ctrl + C* keyboard shortcut, add a few line breaks beneath it, and paste a copy there using *Command/Ctrl + V*.

3. In the secondary code block that we just created, change AnEvent.MOUSE_OVER to AnEvent.MOUSE_OUT to detect when the cursor leaves the object.

4. Change the existing scale values from 3 to 1 to reset the scale when the mouse leaves.

The completed mouseout event code should look like this:

```
{
    var _this = this;
    _this.Spectre.addEventListener(AnEvent.MOUSE_OUT,
    function () {
        _this.Spectre.scaleX = 1;
        _this.Spectre.scaleY = 1;
    });
}
```

Click the **Test Movie** button in the top-right corner of the Animate interface to run the completed VR experience in your web browser. Click the signs to move from one scene to the other and interact with the **Spectre** animation to have it scale as per our programming.

The project is now complete, but there are some additional features to know about. We'll conclude this chapter by exploring the **VR View** panel, which we can use to refine the placement of the various objects within each scene.

Refining Perspective within the VR View Panel

You may have noticed when interacting with your VR project in the web browser that some of your interactive objects perhaps looked a bit odd in their initial placement within the VR environment. Recall that the content of the **Texture** layers in each scene looks completely distorted within the authoring environment; it only appears without distortion when rendered in a running project. The various other visual objects we added to the environment appear without distortion inside of Animate, but here is the tricky bit: when viewed within the VR environment, they may not visually map the perspective of the environment, based on the user's perspective. We are trying to fit a round peg into a square hole, no matter what we do. A tool to assist us in refining both placement and perspective is the **VR View** panel.

You can open the **VR View** panel by choosing **Window | VR View** from the application menu:

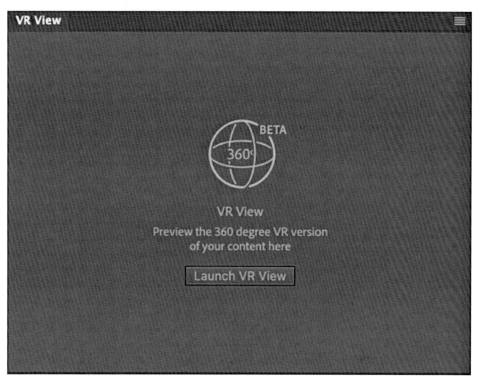

Figure 12.23 – The VR View panel

It appears as a floating panel initially, but you can always dock it to the interface, as with any panel in Animate. To render your VR project within the panel, click the **Launch VR View** button in the panel's center.

> **Note**
>
> The **VR View** panel only allows you to change the view and adjust components within the rendered view so that they appear better-suited to the VR environment. It will not allow you to execute any code in your interactions. For that, you need to run the project.

The currently active scene will render in a similar way to how you would view the project in a web browser:

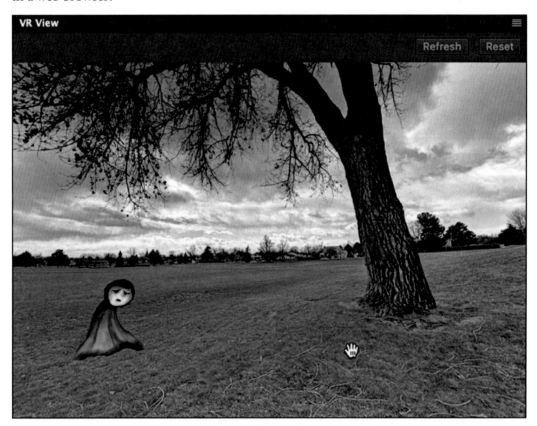

Figure 12.24 – VR View launched

This is a great way to quickly test how your VR project will appear without having to leave Animate to view your content in a web browser. If you change scenes in Animate, the **VR View** panel will then adapt to display the selected scene. You can even click and drag to scroll around the environment, although any interactive elements will not function in this view.

The reason for this is that the various **Movie Clip** symbol instances you've established can be moved around and even transformed using your mouse cursor once selected:

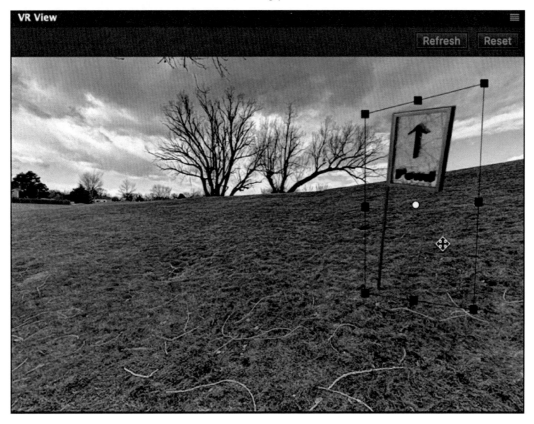

Figure 12.25 – Adjusting Movie Clip instances in VR View

It is much easier to place objects against a distortion-free perspective than the flat Animate stage with distorted environmental textures. While using **VR View** may not be necessary for your project if you've placed everything correctly on your first try, it's a good tool to be aware of for those times you may need it.

In this section, we prepared our visual objects for interactivity and then added the ability to move from one scene to another using JavaScript and the **Actions** panel. We then wrote additional code to make the animated figure react to mouse movements to add additional options for the user to explore. Finally, we looked at the **VR View** panel and how it can be useful in refining object placement and perspective against a properly rendered environmental texture.

Summary

In this chapter, we examined the different aspects of VR documents within Animate, alongside their relationship with WebGL glTF documents and the wider glTF specification. We gained an understanding of how VR 360 and VR Panorama documents differ from one another and explored how to generate photographic textures in formats appropriate to each document type. Expanding on this, we implemented our photographic imagery as textures across different scenes and imported renders of 3D models and a small drawing into our scenes. With everything positioned within each scene and subtle animations added to our drawing with the **Asset Warp** tool, we wrote JavaScript code to enable the user to interact with the various imported visual objects and animations in different ways.

In the next chapter, we will explore how to enable the Adobe AIR runtime and build a small application with this amazing cross-platform technology.

13
Building Apps for Desktop and Mobile

In the previous chapter, we designed an interactive **virtual reality** (**VR**) experience using beta document types in Animate based on WebGL standards.

For this chapter, we'll focus on the **Adobe Integrated Runtime** (**AIR**) platform and build a small utility application for browsing photographs. To develop this application, we'll need to download and install an AIR **software development kit** (**SDK**) and make use of **ActionScript 3** (**AS3**) as a programming language. We'll populate our application with the help of both components and button symbols, two features of Animate that we haven't explored until now. To close, we'll examine how to convert the application for use on iOS and Android.

After reading this chapter, you'll be able to perform the following functions in Animate:

- Learn how to download and install an **AIR SDK** from HARMAN.
- Lay out an application interface using text, **Button** symbols, and **Components**.
- Write ActionScript code within an **ActionScript 3** (**AS3**) Class to develop a simple desktop experience.
- Navigate AIR publish settings and target both desktop and mobile platforms using the same code base.

Technical Requirements

You will need the following software and hardware to complete this chapter:

- Adobe Animate 2022 (version 22.0 or above).

- Refer to the Animate system requirements page for hardware specifications
  `https://helpx.adobe.com/animate/system-requirements.html`

The code in action video for this chapter can be found here:
`https://bit.ly/3Dln3ga`

Working with the Adobe Integrated Runtime

In this section, we will download and install an **AIR Software Development Kit (SDK)** within Animate and configure a new **AIR for Desktop** document using the chosen SDK version.

AIR is simply one of the most amazingly flexible development platforms available. We went over the general history and usage of AIR in *Chapter 2, Exploring Platform-Specific Considerations*, but will really dive into building with the platform now. Since it's been a while, I suggest perhaps going back to that chapter to refresh your memory.

We are going to use AIR to build an image file browser application in this chapter. The user will be able to select a folder from their local filesystem, and any image files from that folder will display within a data grid. We'll write a bit of logic so that only image file types will be displayed in the grid. When the user chooses a file from the grid, the image will be rendered within the application.

The first step in all of this is to install an AIR SDK in order to work with AIR documents.

Installing an AIR SDK in Animate

Before 2020, Animate would include the most recent version of the AIR SDK packaged along with it, so it was easy to get started with the platform. Following the June release of that year, users would be greeted with a notice when attempting to create a new AIR-based document for the first time.

The notice appears when choosing **AIR for Desktop**, **AIR for iOS**, or **AIR for Android** from the **New Document** dialog:

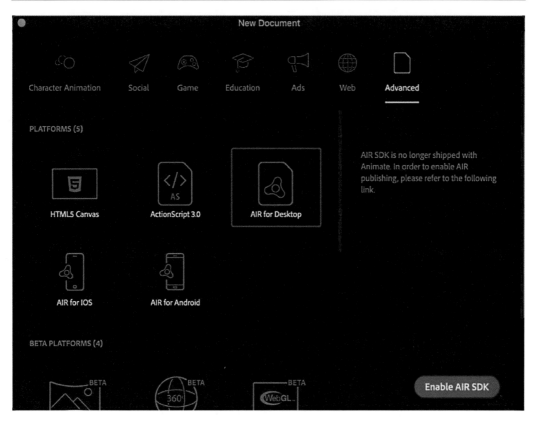

Figure 13.1 – Animate prompts users to install the AIR SDK

The notice reads: **AIR SDK is no longer shipped with Animate. In order to enable AIR publishing, please refer to the following link**.

Clicking the **Enable AIR SDK** button at the bottom of the panel brings the user to a page hosted by Adobe (`https://helpx.adobe.com/animate/kb/get-started-with-latest-airsdk.html`) that explains how to acquire and install the HARMAN version of Adobe AIR.

- To locate and download current versions of the AIR SDK as maintained by HARMAN (version 33+), you'll visit the HARMAN website: `https://airsdk.harman.com/download`.

If you want to use the older version of AIR that was maintained by Adobe, the final version of the AIR SDK maintained by Adobe (version 32) is now found only through the AIR SDK archives at `https://helpx.adobe.com/air/kb/archived-air-sdk-version.html`. This is not recommended but may be useful in some scenarios.

> **Note**
>
> While Adobe gave the AIR SDK freely, as its development and maintenance were supported by their tooling, HARMAN does charge a licensing fee for use of the SDK. Thankfully, most users who are not using the SDK for commercial purposes can make use of it for free, with the inclusion of a quick splash screen to help market the technology.

In order to locate and download an AIR SDK on your computer, perform the following steps:

1. From the **New Document** dialog, choose **AIR for Desktop** from the **Advanced** category.

2. Click the **Enable AIR SDK** button, and you will be taken to a website with links to various SDK versions.

   I suggest visiting the HARMAN site at `https://airsdk.harman.com/download` as the most recent version of AIR can be found there.

3. Once at a download location, agree to the terms of usage and choose which version of the AIR SDK you'd like to download for use in Adobe Animate.

   You can choose between macOS and Windows versions and select either the main builds of the SDK or those to be used alongside **Apache Flex**. When dealing with Animate, you'll seek out the non-Flex builds.

   Choose a version of the **Full AIR SDK with new ActionScript Compiler** to download.

4. The AIR SDK downloads to your computer as a `.zip` archive.

5. Open the `.zip` file and examine the contents. There are a large number of files and folders included, and they are all necessary for a working SDK installation:

Figure 13.2 – AIR SDK contents

6. Developers will often have a specific directory created specifically to house various SDKs and related tools. I suggest naming the folder something such as AIR SDK 33 and placing it in the Documents or User directories since these are both easily located. Place the contents of the .zip file in a new folder with an easily identifiable name.

> **Note**
>
> **Apache Flex** (formerly **Adobe Flex**) is a development platform that makes use of **Flash Platform** technologies, including **ActionScript 3.0** and the **Macromedia FleX Markup Language** (**MXML**) markup language, for cross-platform application development. You can learn more at http://flex. apache.org/.

Once you have completed copying the .zip archive's full contents into the folder you've created, you'll want to make note of that location when we go to install the SDK in Animate. You can install many different versions of the AIR SDK—just be sure to keep each one in its own unique directory with an identifiable name.

We'll now turn our attention back to Animate to install the AIR SDK so that we can develop applications and games using the technology. Proceed as follows:

1. To install a new AIR SDK for use in Adobe Animate, open the software and look at the application menu.

2. From the **Help** menu, choose the option labeled **Manage Adobe AIR SDK…**:

Figure 13.3 – Opening the AIR SDK management dialog

3. The **Manage Adobe AIR SDK** dialog will appear:

Figure 13.4 – There are no AIR SDK versions installed

If you haven't installed any AIR SDK versions in the past, this will be empty, but if you have other versions of the SDK installed, they will appear here.

4. Click **Add New SDK** (the small plus (+) button) to open a browser dialog and use it to locate the folder where you previously unzipped the AIR SDK archive contents.

5. Click the **Choose** button in the file browser dialog with the SDK folder selected to install it as a usable AIR SDK within Animate:

Figure 13.5 – Our new AIR SDK version is installed

6. The SDK version and path will appear for the chosen SDK. Click **OK** to close the dialog.

The AIR SDK is now integrated within Adobe Animate, but we will likely need to provide additional permissions to run and test any documents we create.

Before we do that, we'll need to create a new AIR document and perform some basic configuration to set up our project.

Configuring an AIR for Desktop Project

With at least one version of the AIR SDK installed, we can now create and manage **AIR for Desktop**, **AIR for iOS**, and **AIR for Android** documents. While you might think you have to make platform decisions at this point, these three choices can always be modified even when your application development is complete by switching the target platform. We'll see how to do this at the end of the chapter.

Let's create a new **AIR for Desktop** document to work with in this chapter:

1. Open the **New Document** dialog once again by choosing **Create New** or **More Presets...** from the **Home** screen in Animate.

2. Select the **Advanced** category and choose **AIR for Desktop** from the document types listed within:

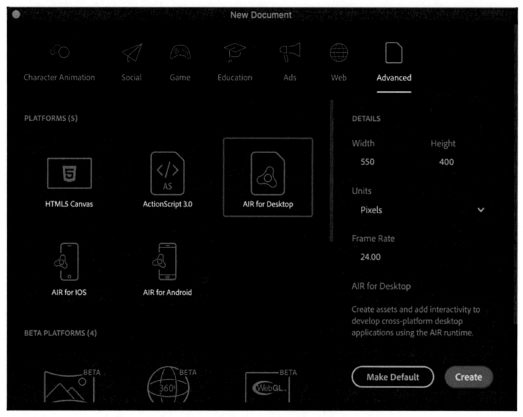

Figure 13.6 – AIR documents can now be created

Because we have at least one version of the AIR SDK installed and ready to go, Animate now displays the document details along with a **Create** button.

3. Click the **Create** button to have Animate generate a new **AIR for Desktop** document.

4. In the **Properties** panel, change the width to 500 **pixels** (**px**) and the height to 700 px. Change the background color to black (#000000):

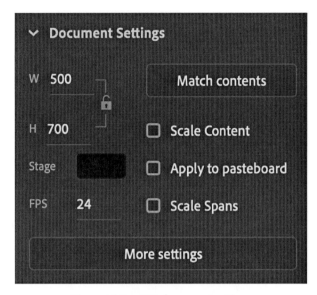

Figure 13.7 – AIR document settings

5. Save your document by choosing **File** | **Save** from the application menu and provide a meaningful name. I suggest something such as PhotoBrowser.fla for a filename.

Aside from these basic document settings, we'll also add a text-based header to the application to provide it with more of a visual identity before laying out all the interactive components in the next section.

To create a text header for the application, perform the following steps:

1. Select the **Text** tool from the toolbar.

2. In the **Tool** tab of the **Properties** panel, configure the tool by choosing a font, size, and color:

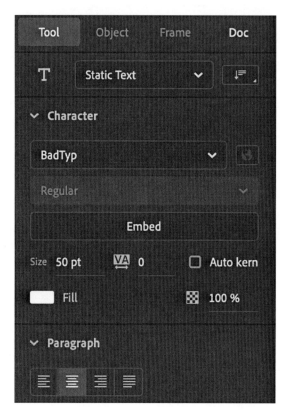

Figure 13.8 – Text tool settings

The text object is non-interactive, so should be set to **Static Text**. I've chosen an Adobe font called **BadTyp** (`https://fonts.adobe.com/fonts/badtyp`) for the text header, made its size `50 pt`, and have set the fill color to white (`#FFFFFF`). In the **Paragraph** section, I've chosen to Center Align my text.

3. Click and drag a new text object across the stage and type **PHOTO BROWSER**:

Figure 13.9 – The application header

The text object is nearly the size of our stage and the text remains centered.

4. Check the **Object** tab of the **Properties** panel with the text object selected to verify its **Position and Size** properties:

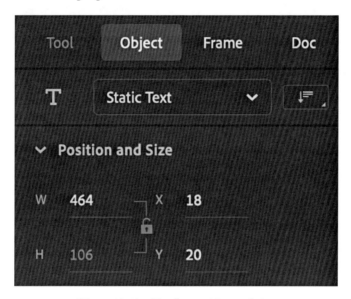

Figure 13.10 – Header position and size

The width should be 464 px with an **X** value of 18 and a **Y** value of 20. This will position the header down the stage a little bit while also centering it within the application.

Our AIR project is now configured with the appropriate **Document Settings** and a nice title header for the application.

Testing Your AIR Project

Before we conclude this section, we should ensure that we are able to run the AIR project effectively in order to test features as they are built.

To test an AIR document, the process is very similar to any other document type we've seen. Click the **Test Movie** button in the upper-right corner of the Animate interface, or you can have finer control over how you test by selecting **Control | Test Movie** and choosing an option from the menu that appears, as illustrated in the following screenshot:

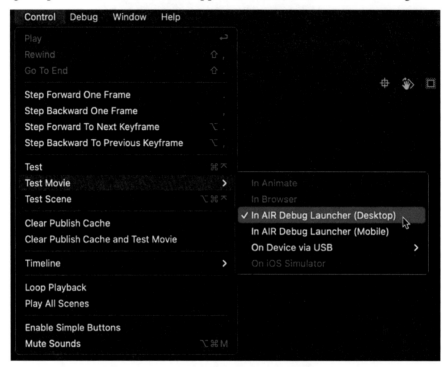

Figure 13.11 – Test Movie menu options

Here is a quick overview of the options presented by this menu:

- **In AIR Debug Launcher (Desktop)** is the default for AIR for Desktop applications and launches in a very similar way to an ActionScript 3.0 document.

- **In AIR Debug Launcher (Mobile)** is the default with AIR for iOS or AIR for Android applications and includes a mobile device simulator.

- **On Device via USB** is an additional option with AIR for iOS or AIR for Android and allows you to test mobile applications directly on device hardware connected by a **Universal Serial Bus** (**USB**) cable.

If you are using Adobe Animate on Apple macOS and have downloaded and added the AIR SDK from the internet, you will likely be presented with a number of security warning dialogs when attempting to run an AIR document with the **Test Movie** option for the first time, such as the following one:

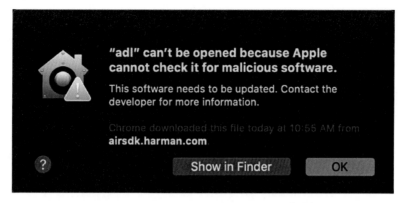

Figure 13.12 – macOS security warning dialog

If this occurs, simply open your Apple macOS **System Preferences** and locate the **Security & Privacy** option. From here, choose the **General** tab and look at the section with the text **Allow apps downloaded from**, and you should see an alert about either the **AIR Debug Launcher** (**ADL**) or the AIR framework processes:

Figure 13.13 – Choosing the Allow Anyway option in Security & Privacy

Choosing **Allow Anyway** will grant permission for these processes to run without problem from Animate. Depending upon how many dialog warnings you receive, you may need to allow multiple processes before macOS stops alerting you of these processes.

When using Windows, simply provide permission to these processes if prompted by the system dialogs. It is normal for everything to just work without any additional procedures when developing AIR projects on Windows.

In accordance with the documentation from HARMAN, you may want to make one additional change to your application before testing. Choose **File | AIR for Desktop Settings** to open the **AIR Settings** dialog. Be sure to choose **Application with runtime embedded** as the **Output as** option, as illustrated in the following screenshot:

Figure 13.14 – Setting the application to compile using embedded runtime

This will ensure that your application will compile and run properly in the current and future versions of AIR provided by HARMAN.

In this section, we downloaded and installed an AIR SDK within Animate, allowing us to create AIR documents. We also created and configured a new **AIR for Desktop** project, added an application title header, and explored the AIR testing options. Coming up, we will focus on the elements required in our application interface to allow a user to interact with the application.

Building a User Interface

In this section, we'll focus on all the interactive parts of the interface we'll build for our AIR application, starting out with a look at how to construct **Button** symbols, followed by the use of precompiled **UI Components**, and wrapping up with a more in-depth look at advanced Movie Clip symbol properties.

Let's start off by building a **Button** symbol that a user will click to choose a folder of photographs within the application.

Working with Button Symbols

Button symbols are not supported in every document type in Animate and are pretty unique as their internal timeline is constrained to four isolated states. Nonetheless, **Button** symbols are very useful for applications such as the one we are building in this chapter.

The easiest way to start building a **Button** symbol in Animate is by creating a simple shape:

1. Choose the **Rectangle Primitive** tool from the toolbar:

Figure 13.15 – The Rectangle Primitive tool

2. Look at the **Tool** tab of the **Properties** panel and set the **Rectangle Options** value to 4 to enable slightly rounded corners. Set the fill color to a dark gray (#595959) color.

3. Draw a Rectangle Primitive across the stage slightly less than its width:

Figure 13.16 – A Rectangle Primitive object

4. The object should measure 480 x 60 and have an **X** position of 10 and a **Y** position of 150. Verify this through the **Properties** panel.

5. Select the object and choose **Modify | Convert to Symbol** to summon the **Convert to Symbol** dialog, as follows:

Figure 13.17 – The Convert to Symbol dialog with Button chosen as the type

In the dialog, name the new symbol ChooseFolderBtn, since this is the button a user will click to choose a folder of files. We are creating a **Button** symbol, so be sure the **Type** selection is set to Button.

6. When finished with the dialog, click **OK** to create a new **Button** symbol. The **Rectangle Primitive** object on the stage becomes a **Button** symbol instance.

7. With the instance still selected, in the **Object** tab of the **Properties** panel, enter an instance name of `ChooseFolder`:

Figure 13.18 – Button with a provided instance name

Recall that providing a movie clip or **Button** symbol instance with an instance name will allow us to address this object with code.

With our **Button** symbol created, we can now enter into its internal timeline and complete setting up our button to provide it with a set of interactive states and a text label so that the user knows what the button's function is.

8. Double-click the button instance on the stage to enter the symbol and look at the timeline.

9. Rename the existing layer **Skin** as this will hold our button skin variants. Notice that the **Button** symbol timeline includes four distinct frames with names above each one: **Up**, **Over**, **Down**, and **Hit**.

10. Duplicate the initial keyframe at frame 1 across all four frames by clicking the **Insert Keyframe** button with frame 1 selected. All four keyframes are identical.

11. With each keyframe, we are going to change the color of the shape fill on that keyframe to distinguish between button states, as follows:

a) **Up**—Leave the color at #595959. This is our resting state.

b) **Over**—Change the color to a lighter gray color at #999999. This is the hover state.

c) **Down**—This is the state of the button when pressed. It will be a darker gray fill color at #333333.

d) **Hit**—You can leave this be, but I like to change any non-visible elements to a vivid green (#00FF00). The **Hit** state is not rendered visually and determines which pixels count toward interaction with a mouse cursor. You can make the **Hit** state a completely different shape from the visual elements, but in this case, we want it to be identical.

12. Create a new layer above the **Skin** layer and rename it **Text**.

13. Within the **Text** layer, use the **Text** tool to create a simple button label that reads **Choose Photograph Folder**, as illustrated in the following screenshot:

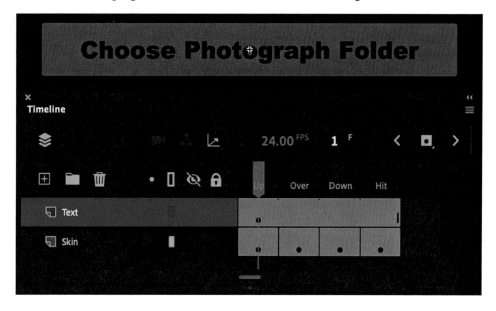

Figure 13.19 – The completed Button timeline

Use whichever text settings look good. I used a 27 pt, **Arial Black** font with a completely black fill. Notice that this text spans all four states, though you could create keyframe variants with this layer as well, if desired.

When your internal button timeline is complete, click the **Scene 1** label in **Edit Bar** above the stage to return to the main timeline.

One of our three user interface elements is now complete. For the remaining two elements, we will use prebuilt Components.

Using Components within an AIR Project

Components are a feature of HTML5 Canvas, ActionScript 3.0, and AIR documents. They are prebuilt, modular packages that generally serve a single function. Some function as video playback or a progress bar, or even a data grid or media display mechanism, as we'll see for this project.

> **Note**
>
> The set of available components will differ drastically between **HTML5 Canvas** documents and all other document types that support the use of components.

We will make use of two different components in this project: the DataGrid component and the UILoader component. Proceed as follows:

1. To access any components in an AIR document, we must first open the **Components** panel. To do so, choose **Window | Components** from the application menu. You should then see a screen like this:

Figure 13.20 – The Components panel

The **Components** panel lists a number of different component types. We will be using components from the User Interface folder.

2. The first component to locate is the DataGrid component. This component is useful for displaying data in columns and rows. Drag an instance of the DataGrid component onto the stage. A placeholder is now visible on the stage.

3. Select the component instance on the stage and set its properties in the **Properties** panel. The **width** should be 480, with a height 160, and the position should have an **X** of 10 and a **Y** position of 220. This places it nicely below the **Button** instance. Give it an instance name of PhotoGrid.

4. The second component to locate is the UILoader component. This component is useful for displaying images and other media. Drag an instance of the UILoader component onto the stage, as follows:

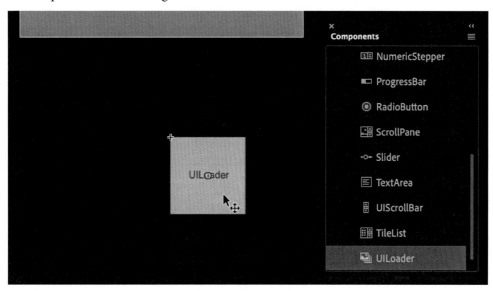

Figure 13.21 – A UILoader instance placed on the stage

A placeholder for this component instance will be visible on the stage.

5. Select the component instance on the stage and set its properties in the **Properties** panel. The width should be 480, the height 300, and it should have an **X** position of 10 and a **Y** position of 390. Give it an instance name of PhotoViewer. This places it directly below DataGrid.

6. While we can adjust general settings for components within the **Properties** panel, we need to adjust component-specific settings for our DataGrid component. In order to do this, we will need to invoke the **Component Parameters** panel. With the DataGrid instance selected on the stage, you will find the **Component Parameters** button in the **Properties** panel. It's the one that looks like this:

Figure 13.22 – The Component Parameters button

This opens the **Component Parameters** panel and displays all parameters for the selected `DataGrid` component.

7. We only need to tweak two of these parameters. Set `rowHeight` to `40` and `horizontalScrollPosition` to `off`. Some of the component parameters can be seen in the following screenshot:

Figure 13.23 – Component parameters

These settings will make each piece of data more clickable, especially if we were to publish this app to a mobile device. `UILoader` does not require any parameter adjustments. You may need to scroll down in the **Component Parameters** panel to locate both parameters.

The UI elements of our AIR application are now in place and the project is ready for programming with ActionScript. Here's what it looks like now:

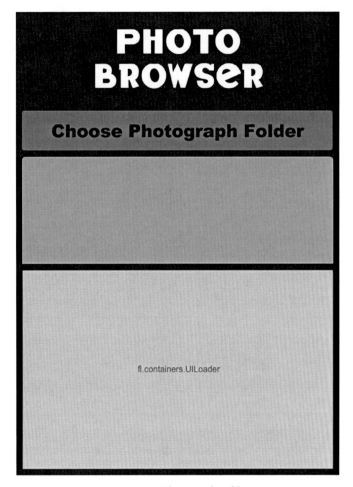

Figure 13.24 – The completed layout

Our UI elements have now been established within the project layout. Before moving on to the next section though, we should explore some additional properties of movie clip symbols, as they are also incredibly useful in building application interfaces.

Exploring Advanced Movie Clip Symbol Settings

We've now established our application interface through the use of **Button** symbols and components. If you look in the **Properties** panel with a component selected, you'll discover that these components are actually Movie Clip symbols! Additionally, in place of any of the objects we've used for the layout, Movie Clip symbols are always a great choice for custom interactive controls in AIR applications.

While we aren't going to be using these advanced settings for Movie Clip symbols in this project, it is good to know about them—especially with the relationships that exist between Movie Clip symbols and components.

With the more common Movie Clip settings covered in *Chapter 5, Creating and Manipulating Media Content*, let's expand on that overview and have a look at the **Advanced** settings of Movie Clip symbols available to us. To access these advanced properties, select a Movie Clip symbol in the **Library** panel, right-click to open the contextual menu, and choose **Properties…**. Once the dialog appears, expand the **Advanced** settings section.

The first section of the **Advanced** settings is the most important and appears at the top of the expanded portion of the dialog, as illustrated here:

Figure 13.25 – Movie Clip Advanced settings

The first option you see here is actually more of a design setting than anything to do with development. When enabled, the **Enable guides for 9-slice scaling** option will allow you to enter into a symbol from the **Library** panel and modify a set of guides to specify which visual areas of your symbol should scale and which should stay their original size if an instance of the symbol is scaled. This allows a good amount of control for properly resizing UI elements that you create so that different sized instances can easily be created upon the stage from the same exact symbol. This is only available with ActionScript 3.0-based documents.

Below this are the **ActionScript Linkage** settings:

- **Export for ActionScript**—This generates a `LinkageID` property in the **Library** panel that allows symbol instantiation through code, just as we did with JavaScript in *Chapter 11, Developing Web-Based Games*.

- **Export in frame 1**—This makes a symbol marked for export available for instantiation at the beginning of the timeline. Notice that our app exists on a single frame; this is very important for single-frame projects, especially in conjunction with the use of `LinkageID`.

- **Class**—You can specify a custom ActionScript 3.0 **class** for your symbol, otherwise Animate will generate a default one for you.

- **Base Class**—This is the class that your custom class extends through ActionScript code. It appears in the form of a **package**, and the default for a Movie Clip symbol is `flash.display.MovieClip`.

Again, most of these options have to do with ActionScript development. While very convenient, unless you are creating applications or games using AIR, as we are in this chapter, they likely will not matter much.

Following the **ActionScript Linkage** settings are two additional groups of settings:

- **Runtime Shared Library**—This option will package up your symbol into a **Shockwave Flash** (**SWF**) file, which you can then make available as an online resource only for the intention of sharing linked symbol assets at **runtime**. This was heavily used while Flash Player was popular but is no longer very useful.

- **Authortime Sharing**—Somewhat similar to sharing assets at runtime, this option allows the creation of a symbol package that you can share among Animate users to access various shared symbols during **authortime**, within Animate itself. This fact alone makes this a much more valuable feature and can even be used in other document types, such as **HTML5 Canvas**.

Most Animate users will have no need for either of these settings, but it is good to be aware of what each is for.

> Note
> Again, while we won't be using Movie Clip symbols in our project, apart from the existing components, it is good to have an understanding of their advanced properties and settings.

In this section, we built out our entire user interface using custom **Button** symbols and prebuilt components. We also had a look at advanced symbol properties that tie directly into ActionScript programming. Coming up, we'll start writing all the ActionScript code to drive the functional aspects of the application.

Programming an AIR Application

In this section, we'll use **ActionScript** to tie all of our interface components together into a unified application. ActionScript is similar to JavaScript in some ways (they are both based on **ECMAScript**), but very different in other ways, since both are derived from different branches of the specification.

While we could write all of our ActionScript code using frame scripts, it is better to leverage the **Object-Oriented Programming** (**OOP**) features that are so prominent in the language and create a **Document Class**.

Establishing a Document Class

We'll now create a document class and bind it to our `.fla` document. The document class will exist as a `.as` file separate from the `.fla` file. When you use a document class for your project, it must extend either the `MovieClip` or `Sprite` classes, depending upon whether you require animation or not in your main document timeline. Extending one class with another will give you access to all the functionality you write, plus all the functionality that is within the base class. It's a powerful way of programming!

Let's go ahead and instruct Animate to create a new Document Class for us:

1. Open the **Publish Settings** dialog from the **More Settings** button in the **Doc** tab of the **Properties** panel.

2. Within the **Publish Settings** dialog, locate the **Script** selection dropdown and click the small wrench icon to the right of it:

Figure 13.26 – AIR Publish Settings dialog

3. This opens the **Advanced ActionScript 3.0 Settings** dialog:

Figure 13.27 – Advanced ActionScript 3.0 settings

This dialog contains imported ActionScript settings for your project. You'll want to check and be sure that **Export classes in frame** is set to 1 and that **Automatically declare stage instances** is selected. They should be selected by default, but it never hurts to check.

4. In the **Document Class** input, type in Main for a class name and click the small pencil icon next to it to edit the class definition.

    You will likely receive a warning from Animate informing you that it cannot find the specified class file. This is expected, as we have yet to save it! Dismiss the warning dialog if it appears.

    A new ActionScript class appears within Animate.

5. Click **OK** to commit your choices, and you'll be left looking at the actual starter code for your class fully displayed with Animate. Notice this is very different from writing code in the **Actions** panel as your new class opens as a full **ActionScript** document within the interface.

6. Save the class using **File | Save** and name the file Main.as since a class filename in ActionScript must be identical to the internal class name reference. The filename and class name are both Main.

The newly created document class will look like this:

```
package {
    import flash.display.MovieClip;
    public class Main extends MovieClip {
        public function Main() {
            // constructor code
        }
    }
}
```

This is boilerplate code that defines a Document Class named `Main`, which `extends` `flash.display.MovieClip`. Note that we also have to import `flash.display.MovieClip` in order to use it. Within the class is a single function called a constructor function. Any code within this function runs immediately upon initialization.

> **Note**
>
> Any additional functions we create later will go below the constructor function, one after the other. These functions and any variables created must all exist within the class definition.

Be sure that the **class Target** dropdown is set to bind to your Animate document named `PhotoBrowser.fla`:

Figure 13.28 – The target of Main.as is PhotoBrowser.fla

Once everything looks to be set, we can move on to write the rest of our application code within the `Main` class.

Writing ActionScript Code

The first task we have is to import a set of additional classes to be used within the application. Type the following `import` statements directly beneath the existing `import`:

```
import flash.filesystem.File;
import fl.controls.DataGrid;
import fl.data.DataProvider;
import fl.containers.UILoader;
import flash.events.MouseEvent;
import flash.events.Event;
import flash.events.FileListEvent;
```

We'll touch upon each of these classes as we get to them in the various functions we'll define further on.

Directly following `public class Main extends MovieClip {`, enter a set of variable declarations, as follows:

```
var photoDirectory:File;
var photos:Array;
var photoGridProvider:DataProvider;
```

These are class-level variables that are accessible from any function within the class. `photoDirectory:File` will be used to reference a selected folder, `photos:Array` will hold references to each image file we find, and `photoGridProvider:DataProvider` will be used to display these files within our `DataGrid` component.

> **Note**
>
> Variables and other references in ActionScript must be assigned a type through the use of a colon after the name is declared—as AS3 is a strongly typed programming language.

The next lines of code will go directly within our constructor function beneath the line that reads `public function Main() {`:

```
ChooseFolder.addEventListener(MouseEvent.CLICK,
chooseDirectory);
PhotoGrid.addEventListener(Event.CHANGE, photoSelected);
PhotoGrid.columns = ["Name", "Type", "Size"];
```

```
photos = new Array();
photoGridProvider = new DataProvider();
PhotoGrid.dataProvider = photoGridProvider;
```

The first line adds a `MouseEvent.CLICK` event listener to the `ChooseFolder` button symbol instance. When a click is detected, we will invoke a function named `chooseDirectory`. We also add an `Event.CHANGE` listener to the `PhotoGrid` `DataGrid` component instance. When the selection is changed by the user, the function named `photoSelected` will fire off. We also set the column names within `PhotoGrid` directly afterward to *Name*, *Type*, and *Size*.

The remaining lines of code instantiate the class-level variables declared previously.

All that is left is to write the various functions referenced in our listeners and any additional functions they will need to invoke. Add a few line breaks following the closing curly braces below the constructor function to make room, as illustrated here:

```
public function Main() {
    ChooseFolder.addEventListener(MouseEvent.CLICK, chooseDirectory);
    PhotoGrid.addEventListener(Event.CHANGE, photoSelected);
    PhotoGrid.columns = ["Name", "Type", "Size"];
    photos = new Array();
    photoGridProvider = new DataProvider();
    PhotoGrid.dataProvider = photoGridProvider;
}
```

Figure 13.29 – Insert the next function here

We'll begin with the `chooseDirectory` function and will place it directly after the closing curly brace of the constructor function, as follows:

```
private function chooseDirectory(e:MouseEvent):void {
    photoDirectory = new File();
    photoDirectory.addEventListener(Event.SELECT,
    directorySelected);
    photoDirectory.browseForDirectory("Select Photo
    Folder...");
}
```

Here is where the `photoDirectory` file variable is instantiated. This will clear out any existing references from a previous folder selection. We then add a listener to this file of the `Event.SELECT` type, which will trigger when a new folder is selected and will invoke a function called `directorySelected`. We have to open a system-level file explorer in order for the user to browse the filesystem and make a folder selection, so use the `browseForDirectory()` method of the `File` class to do so.

We'll next write a `directorySelected` function in response to the folder selection. Place the following code directly beneath the previous function:

```
private function directorySelected(e:Event):void {
    photoDirectory.getDirectoryListingAsync();
    photoDirectory.addEventListener(FileListEvent.DIRECTORY_
    LISTING, directoryListed);
}
```

In this function, we first invoke the `getDirectoryListingAsync()` method to get a list of all the files within the selected directory. We need to listen for an event to tell us when this process has been completed so that we can perform further manipulation on the file references, so listen for the `FileListEvent.DIRECTORY_LISTING` event, and this will invoke the `directoryListed` function once it is safe to do so.

The `directoryListed` function will do most of the work in this application. We'll write it directly beneath the previous function, as follows:

```
private function directoryListed(e:FileListEvent):void {
    photos = new Array();
    for(var p:uint = 0; p<e.files.length; p++){
        if(e.files[p].extension == "jpg" || e.files[p].
        extension == "png" || e.files[p].extension == "gif")
        {
            photos.push(e.files[p]);
        }
    }
    photoGridProvider.removeAll();
    for(var i:uint = 0; i<photos.length; i++){
        photoGridProvider.addItem({"Name":photos[i].name,
        "Type":photos[i].extension, "Size":photos[i].size});
    }
}
```

In this function, we start by clearing out the `photos` array to prepare it for holding the valid image file references from our `FileListEvent`, which was triggered from the initial folder selection.

We then set up a `for` loop to iterate over all the files that were detected within this folder. `for` loops in ActionScript work exactly like they do in JavaScript, if you recall their usage from *Chapter 11, Developing Web-Based Games*. For each iteration, we check the file extension to determine whether or not it is an image file using the *or* operator, a double pipe: `||`. If it is, we then add the file reference to our `photos` array.

Once the array is built, containing only image files from the chosen folder, we can populate our `DataGrid` component with data. First, we will remove any existing data from `photoGridProvider` so that it is empty. We then run another `for` loop, but this time it simply adds information about each image file to `photoGridProvider`, which is then reflected within the visible `DataGrid` component for the user to select.

The final function to write is the one that is invoked when the user selects an image reference from the `DataGrid` component. Place the following function directly beneath the last one:

```
private function photoSelected(e:Event):void {
    var selectedPhoto:File = photos[e.target.selectedIndex];
    PhotoViewer.source = selectedPhoto.url;
}
```

This function simply creates a new `File` variable reference called `selectedPhoto` and populates it with data from a certain position of the `photos` array, which matches the row selected by the user as part of the visible `DataGrid` component on the stage. The `source` property of our `PhotoViewer UILoader` component on the stage is then set to the `url` property of that `File` reference, thereby rendering the visible image within the `UILoader` component for the user to view.

For reference, here is the full, completed code for the `Main.as` class:

```
package {
import flash.display.MovieClip;
import flash.filesystem.File;
import fl.controls.DataGrid;
import fl.data.DataProvider;
import fl.containers.UILoader;
import flash.events.MouseEvent;
import flash.events.Event;
import flash.events.FileListEvent;

public class Main extends MovieClip {
var photoDirectory: File;
var photos: Array;
var photoGridProvider: DataProvider;

public function Main() {
ChooseFolder.addEventListener(MouseEvent.CLICK,
chooseDirectory);
PhotoGrid.addEventListener(Event.CHANGE, photoSelected);
PhotoGrid.columns = ["Name", "Type", "Size"];
photos = new Array();
photoGridProvider = new DataProvider();
PhotoGrid.dataProvider = photoGridProvider;
}

private function chooseDirectory(e: MouseEvent): void {
photoDirectory = new File();
photoDirectory.addEventListener(Event.SELECT,
directorySelected);
photoDirectory.browseForDirectory("Select Photo Folder...");
}

private function directorySelected(e: Event): void {
photoDirectory.getDirectoryListingAsync();
photoDirectory.addEventListener(FileListEvent.DIRECTORY_
```

```
LISTING, directoryListed);
}


private function directoryListed(e: FileListEvent): void {
photos = new Array();
for (var p: uint = 0; p < e.files.length; p++) {
    if (e.files[p].extension == "jpg" || e.files[p].extension
    == "png" || e.files[p].extension == "gif") {
        photos.push(e.files[p]);
    }
}
photoGridProvider.removeAll();
for (var i: uint = 0; i < photos.length; i++) {
    photoGridProvider.addItem({
        "Name": photos[i].name,
        "Type": photos[i].extension,
        "Size": photos[i].size
    });
}
}


private function photoSelected(e: Event): void {
var selectedPhoto: File = photos[e.target.selectedIndex];
PhotoViewer.source = selectedPhoto.url;
}


}
}
```

Once all of your code is written, perform a **Test Movie** and locate a folder of image files on your system to see the application in action:

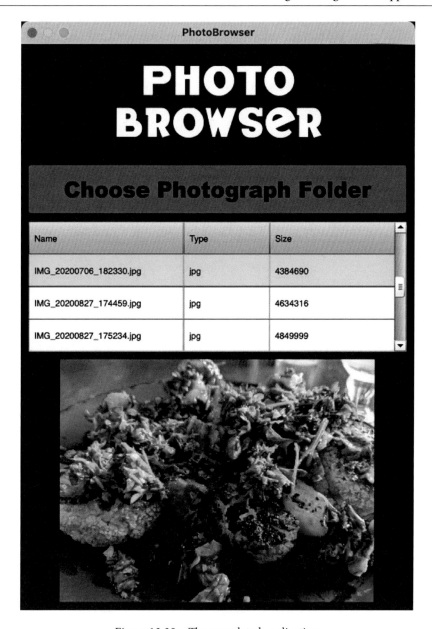

Figure 13.30 – The completed application

In this section, we created our **Document Class** in ActionScript, bound it to our project, and then wrote all of the code necessary for our application to function. Coming up, we will finish off this chapter with a look at how to convert our **AIR for Desktop** project to be used on mobile devices.

Converting an AIR Application for Mobile Devices

We developed our application using **AIR for Desktop**, but it is possible to create versions of the application using **AIR for iOS** and **AIR for Android** so as to target mobile devices as well. Since the underlying code is all ActionScript, and AIR includes the capabilities of publishing ActionScript to mobile platform packages, we can often convert our documents without much hassle.

> **Note**
>
> For a refresher regarding the various platforms that AIR can target, you may want to refer to *Chapter 2, Exploring Platform-Specific Considerations*, and locate the sections on Adobe AIR. To further explore the publish settings available across different AIR targets, refer to *Chapter 4, Publishing and Exporting Creative Content*.

In order to convert a document from one AIR target to another, perform the following steps:

1. With the existing project open, choose **File | Save As...** from the application menu and save a copy of your `.fla` file with a meaningful name.

    Note that this `.fla` file will still make use of the `Main.as` file for all functionality, so you will likely want to re-engineer your class file to be more modular or simply have a unique **Document Class** for each version of the app.

2. Open the **Publish Settings** dialog from the **More Settings** button in the **Doc** tab of the **Properties** panel.

3. Within the **Publish Settings** dialog, locate the **Target** selection dropdown and select it to locate alternative AIR runtimes, such as **AIR for Android** or **AIR for iOS**, as illustrated in the following screenshot:

Figure 13.31 – Changing the target in Publish Settings

4. Click **OK** and the dialog disappears. Your document will now publish to the platform you've chosen.

> **Note**
>
> Publishing to mobile platforms is complicated, and you will need to register as a developer with Apple or Google to do so. This also involves paying a fee and installing a code-signing certificate. These steps are beyond the scope of this book.

You will likely want to consider some of the mobile-specific classes in ActionScript when looking through your code and testing against mobile hardware. You will also need to take screen size and dynamic interface scaling and positioning into consideration. There is a lot to think about!

Of course, there is a lot more to know about design and development for mobile devices. While such topics are beyond the scope of this book, there are many other resources dedicated to such development.

> **Tip**
>
> I cover a number of mobile-specific design and development considerations and functionalities in my book, *Flash Development for Android Cookbook*, which is focused on AIR for mobile devices: `https://www.packtpub.com/product/flash-development-for-android-cookbook/9781849691420`.

In this section, we converted our **AIR for Desktop** project to target mobile devices through **AIR for iOS** and **AIR for Android**.

Summary

In this chapter, we wrote an entire application from scratch using Adobe AIR! We first downloaded and installed an AIR SDK within Animate and then created a new document with that SDK and configured it for desktop usage. Following this, we built the application interface with the use of button symbols and special premade Movie Clip packages called components. Next, we created a new ActionScript class and wrote all of our application code to develop a fully functioning application. Finally, we had a look at how to convert our desktop project for use on mobile devices using the same AIR technologies.

The final chapter of this book is next, in which we'll explore a number of neat ways of extending Adobe Animate yourself or through the work of others.

14

Extending Adobe Animate

In the previous chapter, we built a working application in **ActionScript** that interacts with native filesystems through the use of **Adobe AIR** on desktop and mobile.

This chapter concludes our book with an exploration of a set of options available to extend **Adobe Animate**. We can extend Animate through the creation and execution of custom in-app tutorials and will walk through how to accomplish this screen by screen. We can also use a **JavaScript** API, **JavaScript for Flash** (JSFL), to automate actions in the **user interface** (UI) or make use of the **Custom Platform Support Development Kit** (CPSDK) to extend the power of Animate to new platforms.

After reading this chapter, you'll be able to perform the following functions:

- Build custom in-app tutorials that can be executed and navigated within Animate itself.

- Extend Animate processes and actions through the use of the internal JSFL scripting language.

- Gain an understanding of the role of the CPSDK for adding additional platform targets to Animate.

- Work with additional platforms such as **LottieFiles** by extending Animate through the **Adobe Creative Cloud** Marketplace and with dedicated extension managers.

Technical Requirements

You will need the following to complete this chapter:

- **Adobe Animate 2022** (version 22.0 or above).

- Refer to the *Animate system requirements* page for hardware specifications:

  `https://helpx.adobe.com/animate/system-requirements.html`

Creating Custom In-App Tutorials

In this section, we'll explore how to build in-app tutorials within Animate. These tutorials run within the application, highlighting tools and panels as the user works through them one step at a time.

Beginning with Animate 2020, Adobe began to ship a number of in-app tutorials within the software. While this began with a set of two introductory tutorials, the selection has now grown considerably larger and includes around 15 tutorials of varying complexity.

Adobe-supplied tutorials can be activated under the **Help** menu by selecting a specific tutorial from the **Hands-on Tutorial** submenu:

Figure 14.1 – In-app tutorial selection

These tutorials are meant to showcase certain techniques within the application in a way that is visual, engaging, and reliant upon the willful action of the user. They appear within the application directly, in the form of little card overlays on the application UI.

Card overlays can include text instructions, motion previews of the step in action, and the ability to navigate across the various steps of a tutorial:

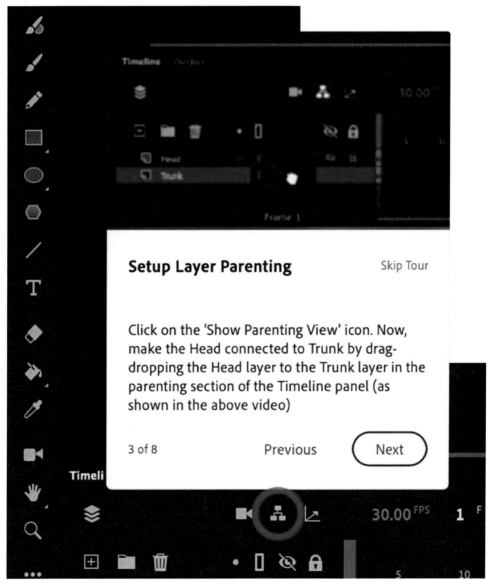

Figure 14.2 – Steps appear as contextual cards within Animate

Each tutorial will contain a curated set of steps prompting the user to perform certain actions in order to provide a step-by-step walk-through directly within the application.

The tools to build these same types of tutorials are now available to any Animate user through a built-in extension. All you need to do to get started is open **Window | Extension | Hands-on Tutorial Creator** to access this feature. With the panel open and ready, you'll then proceed step by step through the process, building out various cards that contain explanatory steps, preview images or animations, and contextual prompts anchored to the application UI.

The first screen you see in the **Hands-on Tutorial Creator** panel allows you to either create a new tutorial or edit one that has already been created and saved as a .zip archive:

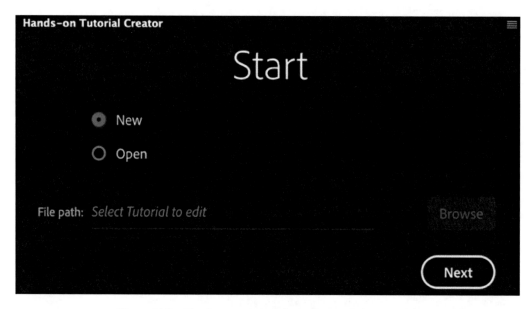

Figure 14.3 – Create a new tutorial or edit an existing tutorial

To edit an existing tutorial, choose the **Open** radio button and then select **Browse** to find the tutorial bundle you want to modify.

Whether you are creating a new tutorial or editing an existing one, you'll next be taken to the **Hands-on tutorial details** screen:

Hands-on Tutorial Creator

Hands-on tutorial details

(Path:/Users/joseph/Downloads/Vectorize a Photograph.zip)

Name: *   Vectorize a Photograph

Tutorial ID: c76d8ec0-0a66-11eb-8014-d3fa1282f8d7

Version: *   1

Document: * vectorize.fla   Browse

Preference File: * AllSettings.anp   Browse

Pre-Script: Enter JSFL Script

Post-Script: Enter JSFL Script

Additional Options...

Previous   Next

Figure 14.4 – The Hands-on tutorial details screen

Here, you are able to modify general properties in the **Name** and **Version** input fields, alongside an autogenerated tutorial ID.

You must have an existing Animate authoring **document** (.fla) file prepared to start with, in addition to an Animate **preferences** (.anp) file. The document file can be empty or may contain content across the timeline, stage, and library. An Animate preferences file can be exported from **Preferences | Export Preferences…**, and it is useful for arranging the workspace and other preferences exactly as you want for the tutorial you are creating.

Optionally, you can also include JSFL scripts to run alongside the tutorial. JSFL scripts allow you to automate certain processes within the Animate software while it is open. You can read more about JSFL in the next section.

There is a set of additional options that allow the inclusion of an overview video to welcome and inform the user, as well as a full description of the tutorial. If you choose to access these properties, you can include a preview image or even an animated **SWF** to give the user an overall idea of the tutorial contents and the expected results.

Clicking **Next** will take you to the **Card list** screen of the **Hands-on Tutorial Creator** panel:

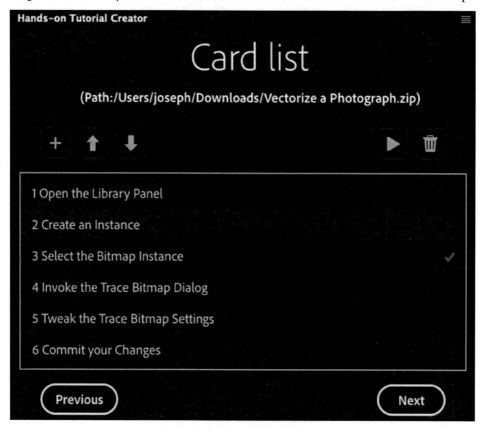

Figure 14.5 – The Card list screen

This section is where most of the work takes place, and it is where tutorial cards are created. Each step in your tutorial is a card, and this screen is where you manage the order and details of each step.

Initially, no cards will be present in a new tutorial, so the first step would be to click the **Add Card** (+) button to add a new card. The **Move the Card Up** and **Move the Card Down** arrow buttons allow you to change the order of a selected card within the card list, and the preview selected card button (the play symbol) provides an in-app preview of the selected card. The delete button will, of course, remove the selected card.

Whether you are editing an existing card or creating a new one, next, you will be taken to the **Card details** screen:

Figure 14.6 – The Card details screen

Each card you create must have a title and a description. Similar to the overall tutorial details, a card video can also be provided, and this will appear as part of the visual card along with the title and description text.

Cards can be anchored to specific portions of the Animate UI so that they are in close proximity to their content. You accomplish this when you choose an anchor node by clicking on the Animate user interface once the **Choose** button is activated. The card can be anchored to the top, bottom, left, or right of the selected anchor node with the **Anchor Side** drop-down selector. Choosing the **Highlight** checkbox will place a blue circular indicator overlay at the chosen anchor node.

Labels for the card's **Previous** and **Next** buttons can also be customized to read whatever you like. A card can also be excluded from the list of steps by choosing the **Do not count as step** checkbox. This is good to provide a card with additional or expanded information but isn't itself an actual step in the overall tutorial.

You can preview individual cards while you edit them and see exactly how they will appear in the UI. Clicking **Ok** will bring you back to the card list.

From the overall card list, you can choose **Next** in order to publish your tutorial:

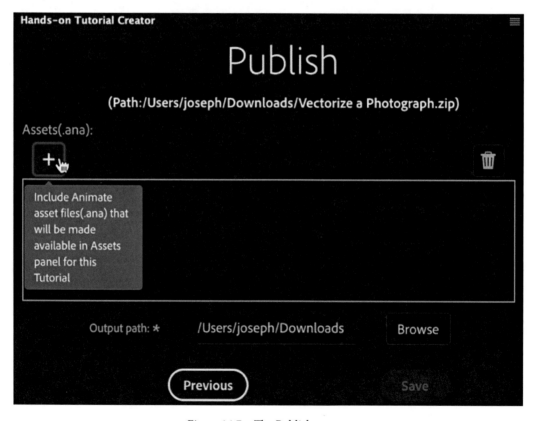

Figure 14.7 – The Publish screen

When publishing your tutorial, you can include additional assets in the form of Animate **asset** (.ana) files for the user to access during their interaction with your tutorial. When the tutorial is activated, any Animate asset files that are included here will be populated within the **Custom** area of the **Assets** panel.

When the tutorial is complete, choose a folder on your filesystem and click **Save** to generate a distributable .zip file. This file contains all the settings, images, videos, assets, data, and anything else your tutorial comprises. Because it takes the form of a ubiquitous .zip archive, it can easily be distributed to other Animate users. The archive also acts as a backup in case you'd like to edit your tutorial further.

To use a tutorial, it must be imported to the **Help | Hands-on Tutorial** menu by choosing **Import Tutorial…** and locating the .zip archive. Once a tutorial is imported, it becomes part of the menu of hands-on tutorials under **Help** and can be launched from there.

> **Tip**
>
> If you ever want to remove your custom tutorial from the list of tutorials, it can be removed by choosing **Remove Tutorial** from the **Hands-on Tutorial** menu. The default tutorials that ship with Animate cannot be removed.

In this section, we examined the workflow for creating hands-on tutorials which can be generating using Animate, and distributed to other Animate users to be installed with their version of Animate in order to learn in a hands-on manner within the program. Coming up, we'll have a look at another mechanism you can use to extend Animate functionality through JSFL scripts.

Writing JSFL Scripts

In this section, we explore the use of JSFL scripts in Animate. Using JSFL scripts will allow the automation of certain tasks that can be run with a menu-based command within an Animate document. These scripts can generate objects, or they can manipulate objects that already exist within a document. In our example for this chapter, we'll create a randomly generated splatter pattern across a document using JSFL.

This is one of those features that users will often hear about but never actually explore. JSFL scripts can not only improve workflows when dealing with repetitive tasks but can also be used to encapsulate specific procedures to share with others.

All of the JSFL commands can be executed and managed by selecting **Commands** from the application menu:

Figure 14.8 – The Commands menu

You have a number of different options here, but any installed JSFL scripts will appear in the lower portion of the **Commands** menu. By default, you will have four commands, but you can always add your own JSFL scripts as part of this menu. Choosing **Run Command…** from this menu lets you browse for a .jsfl file anywhere on your local system to run as a command.

The two main ways of writing JSFL scripts are to either write the code manually or to use the **History** panel. Either way, you'll first need to create a new .jsfl file in order to write any scripts.

Let's create a new .jsfl file now:

1. From the **Home** screen in Animate, click on either **Create New** or **More Presets** and the **New Document** dialog will appear.

2. Click the **Advanced** category along the top of the dialog in order to choose a new document by a specific document type.

3. Scroll down past the **PLATFORMS** and **BETA PLATFORMS** groupings and you will find a new header for **SCRIPTS** at the very bottom. A set of code-based file types can be created here, including ActionScript 3.0 class files and JSFL script files.

4. Choose **JSFL Script File** and then click the **Create** button to generate a new JSFL file that you can edit directly within Animate:

Figure 14.9 – JSFL Script File

The JSFL file opens in Animate in a similar way to how ActionScript files do, as discussed in *Chapter 13, Building Apps for Desktop and Mobile*.

5. You'll want to save the file right away. Choose **File | Save** from the application menu and a save dialog will appear:

Figure 14.10 – Saving the JSFL file

The save dialog lets you define a name and location for your new file. There is only a single file format to choose from.

6. Type in a name for the file. We'll be writing JavaScript code to generate a splatter pattern across the screen in this example, so I've named mine Splatter.jsfl and saved it to a location that is easy to remember.

7. Click **Save** to save your new .jsfl file.

While we could just start writing code, there is a useful mechanism within Animate that makes it very easy to preserve certain actions for the purpose of automation. This is accessible through the **History** panel.

The **History** panel records a step-by-step record of every action taken within an Animate document. This could be the creation of a shape, a selection change, color assignment, or much more.

Let's now go ahead and make use of the **History** panel to assist us in writing our scripts:

1. Create a new **HTML5 Canvas** or **ActionScript 3.0** document by selecting **File | New** from the application menu.

2. Open the **History** panel by choosing **Window | History** from the application menu.

3. Perform a number of actions within the document. Create shapes, change selections, and add layers until a handful of steps appear within the **History** panel.

4. Highlight the steps you want to copy within the **History** panel. Certain steps are not able to be copied – they are marked with a red **X** symbol over the step icon.

5. With at least one valid step selected, open the panel options menu and choose **Copy Steps**:

Figure 14.11 – Copying steps from the History panel

6. With the selected steps copied, switch to the JSFL document we created previously and paste in the steps using *Ctrl/Command + V*:

Figure 14.12 – The pasted code

The code to enact the step or steps is placed into the .jsfl file. In the previous figure, the code to create a new oval shape is added, along with the required location and size information, through an object defining the shape bounds across the left, top, right, and bottom values.

If you click the Run Script button at the top right of the script editor, the script will execute and your code will execute, performing the same steps that were copied within the .fla document.

We will want to make this more useful, of course. In my example, I'll automate and randomize the generation of many ovals in order to produce a cool splatter effect across the document.

> **Tip**
>
> Learn more about JSFL files and their capabilities by reading the Animate JavaScript API documentation at https://www.adobe.io/apis/creativecloud/animate/docs.html.

Let's walk through the creation of a splatter command by modifying the JSFL scripts to produce something much more useful. Follow these steps:

1. Return to the .jsfl file and remove the initially pasted code to create the oval so that the file is completely empty. We'll add similar code later that does the same thing but in a smarter way.

2. Insert the following code at line 1 of the script editor:

```
function randomize(min, max) {
    return Math.round(Math.random() * max) + min;
}
```

Look familiar? This is the same randomization function we used when building the game in *Chapter 11, Developing Web-Based Games*. It accepts two numbers and returns a random one in between them.

3. We'll next define a set of variables to be used within the script. Add a few empty lines following the `randomize()` function and write the following beneath it:

```
var x;
var y;
var r;
var c;
var h = an.getDocumentDOM().height;
var w = an.getDocumentDOM().width;
var fill = an.getDocumentDOM().getCustomFill();
fill.style = "solid";
```

Here, we set variables to determine the x and y positions, the radius, and the color alpha percentage. These will all have elements that are somewhat random and are simply declared at this point with no values.

Then, we set variables to retain the width and height of the Animate document with the JSFL JavaScript API. Finally, we create a new variable named `fill` to act as a custom color, and we set its `style` attribute to `"solid"`.

The remainder of our script resides within a `for` loop, which is similar to the loops created within our JavaScript game and AIR application development experiences in previous chapters.

4. Do you recall the initially pasted code to create the oval, that we removed? It will make a re-appearance now! Add the following code block below the existing lines of code:

```
for (var i = 0; i < 500; i++) {
    x = randomize(-50, w);
    y = randomize(-50, h);
    r = randomize(10, 60);
    switch(randomize(0,2)){
        case 0:
            c = "E6" //90%
            break;
        case 1:
```

```
                c = "BF" //75%
            break;
        case 2:
                c = "FF" //100%
            break;
        default:
                c = "FF" //100%
        };
    fill.color = "#440000"+c;
    an.getDocumentDOM().setCustomFill(fill);
    an.getDocumentDOM().addNewOval({left:x, top:y,
    right:x+r, bottom:y+r}, false, true);
}
```

Let's examine this loop, as there is a lot going on here. The `for` loop itself runs 500 times to create 500 oval shapes in our document. Within the loop, we invoke `randomize()` to set the x and y position properties that were previously declared. When we request random position values, we make use of the stage width and height references through the w and h variables to ensure we cover the document stage with ovals. We also set a random radius size between `10` and `60` and set this to the r variable.

Following this is a `switch` statement, which determines the alpha transparency of the fill color, which is set directly following the `switch` block. To do this, we grab a random number between `0` and `2` and set the value of our c variable to a hexadecimal fragment alpha percentage based on the number returned. This is appended to the `color` attribute of our `fill` variable in order to create a color with varying opacity values, from 100% to 75%.

The last few lines of code set the custom fill color and then draw a new oval based on everything determined within the loop previous to this point. Note that the `addNewOval()` method is really the only remnant of our initial pasted code from the **History** panel.

5. Be sure to save your .jsfl file.

In order to make this available as a command in the **Commands** menu, there is a special folder that the .jsfl file must be moved to. The location of this folder will vary depending on your operating system. The locations for both **Windows** and **macOS** are as follows:

- The Commands folder on Windows:

```
C:\Users\<USER>\AppData\Local\Adobe\Animate
<VERSION>\<LOCALE>\Configuration\Commands\
```

- The Commands folder on macOS:

```
/Users/<User>/Library/Application Support/Adobe/Animate
<VERSION>/<LOCALE>/Configuration/Commands
```

> **Tip**
>
> The Library folder is hidden by default on macOS. In **Finder**, click the **Go** menu at the very top of your screen and hold down the *Option* key. **Library** will appear as a menu option. Alternatively, select the **Go to Folder…** option from the **Go** menu and use ~/Library as your location.

In order to run the newly created command in Animate, perform the following steps:

1. Move or copy Splatter.jsfl into the Commands folder alongside the JSFL commands that are installed with Animate:

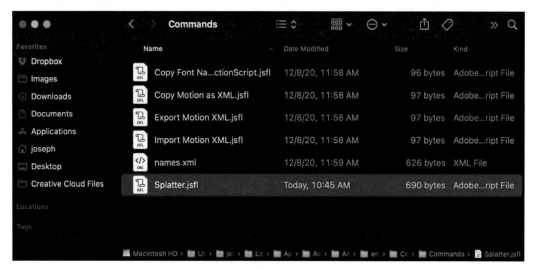

Figure 14.13 – Adding jsfl to the Commands folder

2. With the file in place within the Animate Commands folder, close the file explorer and launch Animate once more.

3. Create a new HTML5 Canvas or ActionScript 3.0 document by selecting **Create New** or **More Presets** and generating a fresh document.

4. Once the new document is created, choose **Commands** from the application menu. At the bottom of the **Commands** menu is our new **Splatter** command option:

Figure 14.14 – The Commands menu and the Splatter command option

5. Click **Splatter** and the command runs the associated JSFL script, generating a cool splatter pattern across the stage:

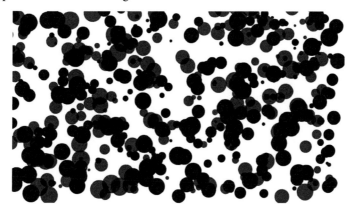

Figure 14.15 – The Splatter command run results

As you can see, using JSFL scripts and the Animate JavaScript API is a highly versatile way of extending Animate for all sorts of different purposes.

Once you have a number of custom commands installed, you can choose to manage, rename, or delete them by choosing **Manage Saved Commands...** in the **Commands** menu:

Figure 14.16 – Managing commands

Custom commands appear alongside the default commands in this dialog, so be sure to only modify the ones you really want to!

To download additional JSFL scripts, a browser-based search for `download jsfl scripts` or `download jsfl commands` will yield many results. Some of these collections can be found at the following locations:

- `https://github.com/markknol/flash-jsfl-tools`
- `https://megacharlie.com/plug-ins.html`
- `https://ajarproductions.com/blog/flash-extensions/`
- `https://github.com/Simtey/Animate`

In this section, we explored the use of JSFL scripts to create and execute commands within Animate. Next, we'll see how it is possible to extend Animate through the use of the CPSDK and add new publish targets to the software through the installation of plugins developed with this SDK.

Understanding the Animate Custom Platform SDK

In this section, we'll look at the Animate CPSDK and see how to install extensions from **Adobe Exchange** through the **Creative Cloud** desktop application.

Back before Adobe decided to re-brand *Flash Professional* to *Animate*, they were working under the hood to establish the software as a completely platform-agnostic solution for motion and interactivity. One team cannot target all platforms that exist in the world, so they came up with the solution to allow anyone to add target platforms to Animate through the use of the CPSDK.

Visit the **adobe.io** website and go to the Animate section (`https://www.adobe.io/apis/creativecloud/animate.html`), and you'll be able to view all of the ways to extend Animate:

Extend Adobe Animate using JavaScript and C++

Write scripts in JavaScript to automate Animate functions or add capabilities. Create C++ libraries that you can call from your JavaScript scripts.

Build plug-ins with powerful tools

Use the Eclipse IDE and your favorite C++ dev environment to create code libraries for your scripts to access.

Work with multiple output formats

Build automations that export Animate projects to HTML5 Canvas, WebGL, SVG, Flash, and more.

Support custom platforms

The Custom Platform Development Kit and sample app show you how to build plug-ins to define your own document types and enable support for them within Animate.

Figure 14.17 – The adobe.io resources for Animate

You can find full documentation along with the actual CPSDK, which can be downloaded and put to use to implement a custom document type and publish workflow.

> **Note**
>
> Creating a new document type for Animate using the CPSDK is not trivial. If you ever decide to undertake such an effort, you should be intimately familiar with the platform you are targeting.

To make use of an extension that leverages the CPSDK, you will need to browse the plugins available for Animate within the Creative Cloud Desktop application:

1. The first step in this process is to close Animate completely and open the Creative Cloud Desktop application.

2. With the application open, locate the **Stock & Marketplace** tab along the top and choose the **All plugins** category.

3. We can filter the plugins displayed by selecting the Creative Cloud application we want to find plugins for. Choose **Animate** and only plugins compatible with Animate will be visible:

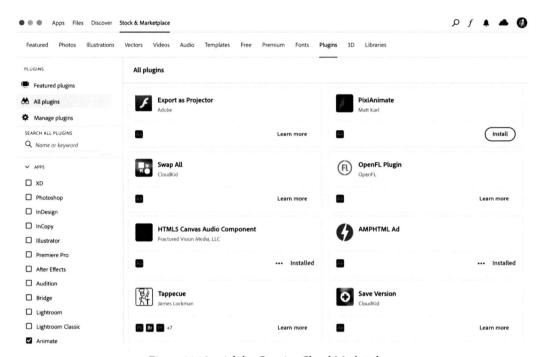

Figure 14.18 – Adobe Creative Cloud Marketplace

Not all plugins that you find here use the CPSDK. Some create new panels using JSFL, and others may be components or other workflow tools.

4. Once you locate a plugin, all you need to do is click **Install** and the plugin will be installed onto your computer:

Figure 14.19 – Installing a plugin for Animate

You can also uninstall plugins that were previously installed using this same mechanism. Adobe is moving more and more functionality into the Creative Cloud desktop application from other sources.

You might be wondering what all of these available extensions for Animate can be used for. Here is a short list of some interesting extensions and what they do:

- **HTML5 Canvas Audio Component**: Adds an audio playback component to the **Components** panel in HTML5 Canvas documents.

- **PixiAnimate**: Adds a custom publish workflow targetting **PixiJS** – a 2D rendering engine for web browsers.

- **AMPHTML Ads**: Adds the ability to create documents targeting the **Google AMP** platform.

Once you've installed a plugin, you'll want to use it. One of the reasons we closed Animate before installing a plugin is that Animate will only detect newly installed plugins on startup. If a plugin using the CPSDK is installed, we can now fire Animate back up and create a new document with it.

5. From the **Home** screen in Animate, click on **Create New** or **More Presets** and the **New Document** dialog will appear.

6. Click the **Advanced** category along the top of the dialog in order to choose a new document by document type.

7. Scroll down past the **PLATFORMS** and **BETA PLATFORMS** groupings and you will find a new header for **CUSTOM PLATFORMS**. The new document type using the CPSDK can be located there:

Figure 14.20 – Creating a Custom Platform document

8. Select the custom document type and click **Create** to generate a new document that targets the new platform.

Depending upon the platform, certain tools and features may not be supported. This is to be expected and is similar to what we've seen when comparing the native document types in Animate.

When it is time to publish your project, the CPSDK also includes the ability for developers to include their own platform-specific publish settings:

Figure 14.21 – Custom document Publish Settings

> **Note**
>
> Certain custom platform publish workflows may rely on additional processes to be installed and running to function correctly. Keep an eye on the **Output** panel when using a custom platform document type in case you are prompted to take additional action.

You can also install certain extensions by making use of an extension manager. This is useful when you want to install an extension that isn't available through the Creative Cloud Marketplace – especially in the case of beta extensions such as the **LottieFiles for Adobe Animate** plugin.

Lottie is an open source, JSON-based, platform-independent, animation-focused file format that can be played back on the web, **iOS**, **Android**, Windows, macOS, and more! The LottieFiles extension converts Animate content into a Lottie file and provides a number of additional tools around this process, such as a render graph and the ability to manage your creations.

You can locate and download a beta of the LottieFiles plugin from `https://lottiefiles.com/plugins/animate`:

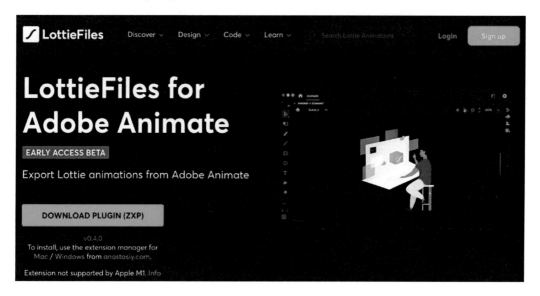

Figure 14.22 – LottieFiles for Adobe Animate plugin

The extension will download as a `.zxp` file that must be installed through an extension manager. There are a handful of extension managers available for use, but I would recommend the **Anastasiy's Extension Manager**, which can be acquired from `https://install.anastasiy.com/`.

Once you install the extension manager, you can use it to install your .zxp file into Animate:

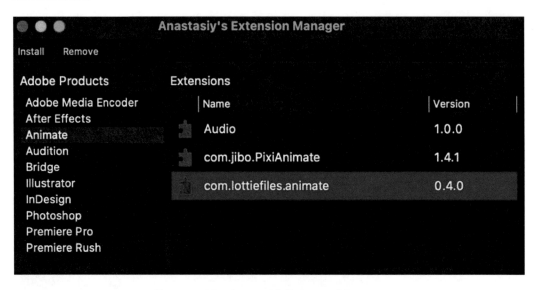

Figure 14.23 – Anastasiy's Extension Manager

With the extension installed, you'll want to be sure to restart Animate if it was open during the installation process. You will find that instead of installing as a custom platform, the extension is accessible as a panel in Animate and works seamlessly with existing Animate content.

To open the LottieFiles panel, choose **Window | Extensions | LottieFiles** from the application menu:

Figure 14.24 – The Animate Extensions menu

With the panel opened, you will need to authenticate with your LottieFiles account. If you do not have an account, it is free to set one up, and the extension will guide you through this simple process.

> **Tip**
>
> You can set up a LottieFiles account at `https://lottiefiles.com/` by clicking **Sign up** in the upper right.

Once authenticated, the LottieFiles panel offers a number of useful tools to preview and generate your LottieFiles content directly from your animated content within Animate:

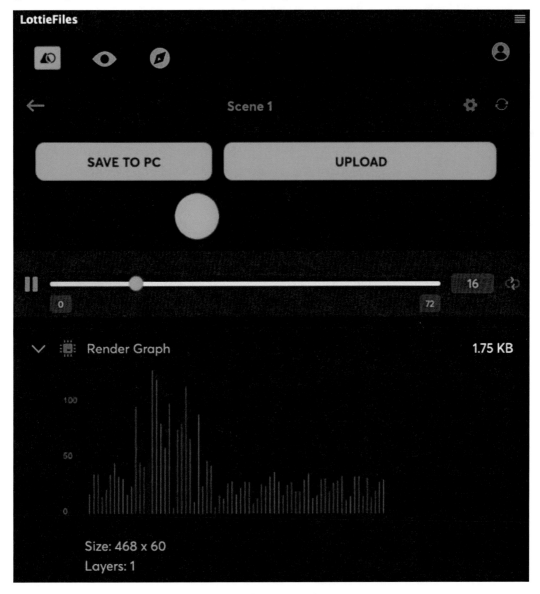

Figure 14.25 – Making use of the LottieFiles extension in Animate

One of the nice things about this extension is that it does not rely on any custom document type. This means it can be used on a wide variety of content within the application.

> **Note**
>
> Remember that the LottieFiles extension is in *beta* right now – so, the extension's functionality is somewhat limited within Animate. However, they have a great history of building extensions for **After Effects**, so things should only improve as work continues.

In this section, we had a look at the CPSDK for Animate and explored how to locate, install, and make use of custom platform plugins and additional third-party extensions by using the Adobe Creative Cloud Marketplace and a separate extension manager. We also had a look at how to make use of LottieFiles – an exciting new extension for Animate!

Summary

In this chapter, we looked at three ways to extend Adobe Animate beyond its default state through the creation of in-app tutorials, the writing of JSFL scripts and the configuring of their associated commands, and the installation and management of plugins, making use of the CPSDK to add new document types, export formats, and other functionality to Animate.

This concludes our journey for now. You should feel confident in using Adobe Animate to design an assortment of creative projects, and I hope you continue to master all aspects of the software as your familiarity with its workflows and platforms continues to grow.

Index

Symbols

3D Transform tool 50

A

ActionScript 390
ActionScript 1.0 31
ActionScript 2.0 31
ActionScript 3.0
  about 31, 74
  files, exporting 74
ActionScript 3.0 documents
  about 28-37
  ActionScript Language 31, 32
  Adobe Flash Player 29
  publishing 79, 81
  SWF file format 30, 31
ActionScript code
  writing 393-399
ActionScript Language 31, 32
ActionScript programming language 4
Actions panel
  code, writing with 173-176
Adobe After Effects 31

Adobe AIR
  about 36-38
  exploring 36
  for Android 40
  for Apple iOS 39, 40
  for desktop 38, 39
  reference link 38
Adobe Animate
  about 4
  history 4-7
  updating 19
  usage 8
Adobe Animate, advanced rigging
  rig mapping 236, 237
Adobe Animate, features
  active layer, filling with Paint
    Bucket Tool 16, 17
  Asset panel update 18, 19
  Auto KeyFrame option 113
  Canvas Blend Modes 133, 134
  color effect, for HTML5 Canvas
    Documents 17, 18
  exploring 9
  Hands-on Tutorial Creator 404, 406

Last Frame Options, for Graphic
   Symbol Looping 13-15
 Layer Parenting Enhancements 13
 Paint Fills Only Option 15, 16
 with Warped Objects 9-12
Adobe Animate, timeline and symbols
 layers, converting to symbols 127, 128
 symbols, converting to layers 128
Adobe Audition 196
Adobe Creative Cloud Desktop 19-21
Adobe Flash Player
 about 25, 29
 reference link 30
Adobe Font 156
Adobe Fresco
 about 109, 352
 reference link 352
Adobe Illustrator 109
Adobe Integrated Runtime (AIR)
 about 5, 26
 configuring, for Desktop
   project 373-377
 working with 368
adobe.io
 reference link 421
Adobe MAX
 about 21
 URL 21
Adobe Media Encoder 89
Adobe Photoshop
 using 149
Adobe Substance 3D Stager 350
Adobe Systems 5
Advanced Layers mode
 about 179
 benefits, assessing 178
 features, in Animate documents 180
 working with 178

Advanced Movie Clip Symbol settings
 exploring 387-389
AIR application
 ActionScript code, writing 393-399
 converting, for mobile devices 400, 401
 Document Class, establishing 390-392
 programming 390
AIR Debug Launcher (ADL) 379
AIR document types
 publishing 86, 87
AIR for Android
 about 36
 selecting 40, 41
AIR for Desktop 36, 368
AIR for iOS 36
AIR for mobile devices
 reference link 401
AIR project
 testing 377-380
AIR Software Development Kit (SDK)
 about 368
 download link 369
 installing, in Animate 368-373
Anastasiy's Extension Manager
 reference link 425
Animate Asset packages
 content, sharing as 96-100
Animate Beta Platforms
 experimenting 41
 VR 360 42
 VR Panorama 42
 WebGL glTF (Extended) 42
 WebGL glTF (Standard) 42
Animate Custom Platform SDK
 overview 420-428
animated gifs
 exporting 91-94
 preview example 93

animated objects
  interacting with 361
  interacting with   362
Animate document, types
  custom platforms, opening 27, 28
  exploring 24, 25
  Flash platform runtimes 25, 26
  Native Web, branching out 26, 27
Animate interface
  exploring 46
  start settings, modifying 54-56
  start settings, selecting 53, 54
  user elements 46
Animate preferences
  customizing 66, 68
  exporting 70
  importing 71
  keyboard shortcuts 68, 69
  managing 66, 70
Apache Flex
  about 370
  reference link 371
Apache Royale
  URL 32
Apple iOS
  Adobe AIR for 39, 40
Armatures
  about 208, 210
  building, with Inverse Kinematics 208
  creating, with Warped Object 255-262
  used, for animating Warped
    Object 253, 254
assets
  preparing, for Layer Parenting 183-187
Asset Warp tool
  about 240, 349
  animating with 351-354

Audio for Stream Sync
  importing 196, 197
authortime 389
Auto KeyFrame option 113

B

BadType
  reference link 376
Basic Layers mode 178
beta document types
  publishing 88, 89
Bind Tool
  used, for refining shapes 223, 224
Bones 240
Bone tool
  about 208
  using, to rig shapes 222, 223
  using, to rig symbol instances 211-215
Button symbol
  working with 381-383

C

camera
  about 270
  activating 273-276
  animating 284
  common uses 270
  filters, adding to layer 295, 296
  keyframes, setting 284-289
  Layer Depth, using without 282, 283
  layer effects, applying 294
  layer filters, applying 293
  layers, attaching 292, 293
  manipulating 273-276
  motion and eases, adding 289-291

starter project, examining 271-273
text, creating 291-293
Camera tool
    properties 275
Canvas Blend Modes 133, 134
Canvas element 34, 35
character
    animating, with Layer Parenting 182
character animation features
    Audio for Stream Sync,
        importing 196, 197
    exploring 194
    Graphic symbol frames,
        configuring 198-200
    Graphic symbol, using 194, 195
    lip syncing, automating 200-203
    visemes, assigning 200-204
Classic Motion Guides
    using 139-141
Classic Tween
    about 123, 289
    animating with 135-139
    properties, exploring 141-143
code
    writing, with Actions panel 173-176
code, writing for virtual reality
        (VR) interactions
    about 356
    interacting, with animated
        objects 361, 362
    moving, from scene to scene 357-360
components
    using, within AIR project 384-386
content
    exporting 78
    exporting, options 89
    sharing, as Animate Asset
        packages 96-100

Content Delivery Network (CDN) 34
CreateJS
    about 27
    reference link 302
CreateJS libraries
    about 35
    EaselJS 35
    PreloadJS 35
    SoundJS 35
    TweenJS 35
Creative Cloud for desktop application
    reference link 19
CSS 4
custom in-app tutorials
    creating 404, 407-411
Customize Timeline editor 64
custom platforms
    opening 27, 28
Custom Platform Support
        Development Kit (CPSDK) 28

D

Desktop project
    Adobe Integrated Runtime (AIR),
        configuring 374-377
digital advertising
    document, creating for 146-149
    external content, importing 149-154
    reference link 149
    text objects, creating 155-158, 172
Dimension
    reference link 350
document
    creating, for digital advertising 146-149
    designing, for Native Web 146

Document Class
  about 390
  establishing 390-392
document exporting
  versus document publishing 74-76
document publishing
  versus document exporting 74-76
dynamic text 156

E

ECMAScript 31, 390
ECMAScript 4 31
Europa font
  reference link 292
external content
  importing 149-154

F

Flash platform
  runtimes 25
Flash Professional 6, 97
Flex software development kit (SDK) 68
Forward Kinematics
  versus Inverse Kinematics 208, 209
frames 48
frames per second (FPS) 51, 244
FutureSplash Animator 4, 30
FutureWave 4

G

game
  clickable overlays, creating 310-318
  dynamic text, creating 310-318
  library, preparing 307

Linkage IDs, adding within
    library 318-320
  stage, preparing 307
  timeline, labeling 308, 309
  timeline, preparing 307
game concept
  about 300
  HTML Canvas document,
    overview 300-302
  project library, exploring 306, 307
  stage, exploring 302-305
  timeline, exploring 302-305
game, programming with JavaScript
  about 320
  End Screen, programming 332
  enemy behavior, programming 327, 328
  game loop, programming 329-332
  Global Variables, creating 321, 322
  player actions, programming 325-327
  Start Screen, programming 322-325
game project
  finishing 333-335
Global Scripts 321
GL Transmission Format (glTF) 42
Graphics Interchange Format (GIF) 91
graphic symbol frames
  configuring 198-200
Graphic symbol
  using 194, 195

H

Hands-on Tutorial Creator 404, 406
HARMAN
  about 37, 38
  reference link 38
HTML 4, 33, 34
HTML5 26, 29

HTML5 Canvas 6
HTML5 Canvas document
  about 32, 33
  CreateJS libraries 35
  element 34, 35
  HTML 33, 34
  JavaScript 33, 34
  overview 300-302
  publishing 81-86
HTML canvas element
  reference link 34
HyperText Markup Language
      5 (HTML5) 384

I

IK armature
  additional poses, creating 225-229
  animating 225
  armature poses, managing 230, 231
IK rig
  importing, within Assets Panel 235
  saving, for reuse 232-234
  sharing 232
Illustrator 5
image file sequences
  exporting 94, 95
In-App Tutorial 71
instances 123
interactivity
  adding, with JavaScript 173
Inverse Kinematics
  aspects 210, 211
  used, for building armature layer 208
  versus Forward Kinematics 208, 209

J

JavaScript
  about 4, 33, 34
  interactivity, adding with 173
JavaScript API (JSAPI) 28
JSFL files
  reference link 415
JSFL scripts
  writing 411-420

K

keyboard shortcuts, Animate preferences
  about 68
  managing 69
keyframes 48

L

Layer Depth panel
  about 276
  activating 276, 278
  considerations 278
  manipulating 276
  modifying 279-282
  using, without camera 282, 283
layer hierarchy
  establishing 188-191
layer modes
  switching between 181, 182
Layer Parenting
  about 182
  aspects 210
  assets, preparing for 183-187
  used, for animating character 182
  using, for animation 191-193

library items 165, 166
Library panel
   export options 95
Linkage IDs
   adding, within library 318-320
LottieFiles 28
LottieFiles plugin
   reference link 425

M

macromedia 4
Macromedia FleX Markup
      Language (MXML) 371
mobile devices
   AIR application, converting for 400, 401
Motion Guides
   about 164
   animating with 168, 169
Motion Tween
   about 123, 158, 289
   additional library items,
      including 165, 166
   animating with 158, 159
   properties, exploring 170-172
   symbols, building to use in 159-164
   timeline, adjusting 166-168
Movie Clip symbol 98

N

Native Web
   branching out 26, 27
   document, designing for 146

O

OAM bundles 75

Object Oriented Programming
      (OOP) 390

P

panels
   collapsed panel, expanding 59
   collapsing 59
   docking 59
   grouping 59
   managing 56
Photoshop 5, 109
Pins 240
platform-agnostic 27
plugin 4
projector files 75, 81
Publish Settings dialog
   about 76, 77
   for document types 79

Q

quick publish
   about 101
   selecting 102, 103

R

Rig properties
   refining 215-222
runtime 389

S

scenes
   managing, in virtual reality (VR) 340
   using, in virtual reality (VR) 341

shape properties
   manipulating, across Shape
      Tween 118-123
shapes
   working with 108
shape tools 108-110
Shape Tween
   about 111
   animating with 111-116
   properties, exploring 116-118
   shape properties, manipulating 118-123
Shockwave Component (SWC) 80
Shockwave Flash (SWF) 30, 389
SmartSketch 4
social share
   about 101
   selecting 102
Software Development Kit (SDK) 36
Spectre Warped Object
   animating 354, 356
Stager
   reference link 350
SWF Archive 81
SWF file format 30, 31
symbols
   building, to use in Motion
      Tween 159-164
   creating 123-126
   types, exploring 129-135
   working with 123
symbols, types
   Button symbol 123
   Graphic symbol 123
   Movie Clip symbol 123

T

text objects
   creating 155-158
timeline
   adjusting 166-168
Timeline panel
   customizing 62
   layers 48
   tools, customizing 65, 66
   tools, exploring 64
Tools panel
   customizing 62-64
Tweens 48

U

Universal Serial Bus (USB) cable 378, 379
user elements, Animate interface
   about 46
   Assets panel 52, 53
   Document panel 47
   Library panel 52
   Properties panel 50, 51
   Timeline panel 48
   Tools panel 48, 49
User Interface
   Advanced Movie Clip Symbol
      settings, exploring 387-389
   building 380
   components, using within
      AIR project 384-386
   working, with Button symbols 381-383

V

video files
  exporting 89-91
virtual machine (VM) 31
Virtual Reality (VR)
  about 27, 41
  additional content, adding 349
  animating, with Asset Warp
    tool 352-354
  documents, overview 338-340
  photographs, capturing for 342-345
  scenes, managing of 340-342
  textures, adding to 346-349
  transparent 3D renders,
    importing 349, 351
  warped object, animating 354, 356
VR 360 41, 42
VR Panorama 41, 42
VR View Panel
  perspective, refining within 363-365

W

Wallaby 26
Warped Object
  about 240, 242, 351
  animating, with Armatures 253, 254
  distortion meshes, creating
    with Pins 244-250
  meshes, animating 250, 252
  modern rigging techniques,
    animating with 263-267
  properties 242, 243
  used, for creating Armatures 255-262

WebAssembly 29
web font 312
WebGL 27, 29
WebGL glTF 41
WebGL glTF (Extended) 41, 42
WebGL glTF specification
  reference link 338
WebGL glTF (Standard) 41, 42
workspaces
  customizing 57, 58
  custom workspaces, deleting 61
  custom workspaces, saving 60
  default workspaces, using 57
  managing 56, 60, 61
World Wide Web 4

Z

z-depth 180

Packt.com

Subscribe to our online digital library for full access to over 7,000 books and videos, as well as industry leading tools to help you plan your personal development and advance your career. For more information, please visit our website.

Why subscribe?

- Spend less time learning and more time coding with practical eBooks and Videos from over 4,000 industry professionals

- Improve your learning with Skill Plans built especially for you

- Get a free eBook or video every month

- Fully searchable for easy access to vital information

- Copy and paste, print, and bookmark content

Did you know that Packt offers eBook versions of every book published, with PDF and ePub files available? You can upgrade to the eBook version at packt.com and as a print book customer, you are entitled to a discount on the eBook copy. Get in touch with us at customercare@packtpub.com for more details.

At www.packt.com, you can also read a collection of free technical articles, sign up for a range of free newsletters, and receive exclusive discounts and offers on Packt books and eBooks.

Other Books You May Enjoy

If you enjoyed this book, you may be interested in these other books by Packt:

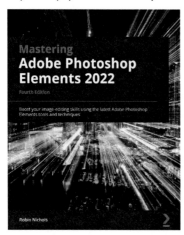

Mastering Adobe Photoshop Elements 2022 - Fourth Edition

Robin Nichols

ISBN: 978-1-80323-824-1

- Identify the five parts of Elements and discover how to set up your computer, camera, and color monitor for best results
- Import, organize, and keep track of your imported media library
- Add impressive visual effects to your work in seconds
- Develop advanced picture retouching skills
- Discover how to add text and graphic elements

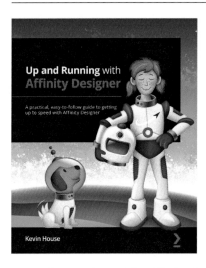

Up and Running with Affinity Designer

Kevin House

ISBN: 978-1-80107-906-8

- Explore the interface and unique UX characteristics of Affinity Designer
- Discover features that allow you to manipulate and transform objects
- Apply color, shading, and effects to create unique compositions
- Employ layers to organize and simplify complex projects
- Use grids, guides, and snapping features as design aids
- Adapt to Affinity Designer's custom workspaces and keyboard shortcuts
- Explore the workflow and design best practices for more predictable and successful outcomes

Packt is searching for authors like you

If you're interested in becoming an author for Packt, please visit authors.packtpub.com and apply today. We have worked with thousands of developers and tech professionals, just like you, to help them share their insight with the global tech community. You can make a general application, apply for a specific hot topic that we are recruiting an author for, or submit your own idea.

Hi!

I am Joseph Labrecque, author of Adobe Animate 2022 for Creative Professionals. I really hope you enjoyed reading this book and found it useful for increasing your productivity and efficiency in Adobe Animate.

It would really help me (and other potential readers!) if you could leave a review on Amazon sharing your thoughts on Adobe Animate 2022 for Creative Professionals.

Your review will help me to understand what's worked well in this book, and what could be improved upon for future editions, so it really is appreciated.

Best Wishes,

Joseph Labrecque

Made in United States
North Haven, CT
11 May 2022

19099185R00259